THE
BEST LAWYER
YOU CAN BE

A Guide to Physical, Mental, Emotional, and Spiritual Wellness

STEWART LEVINE

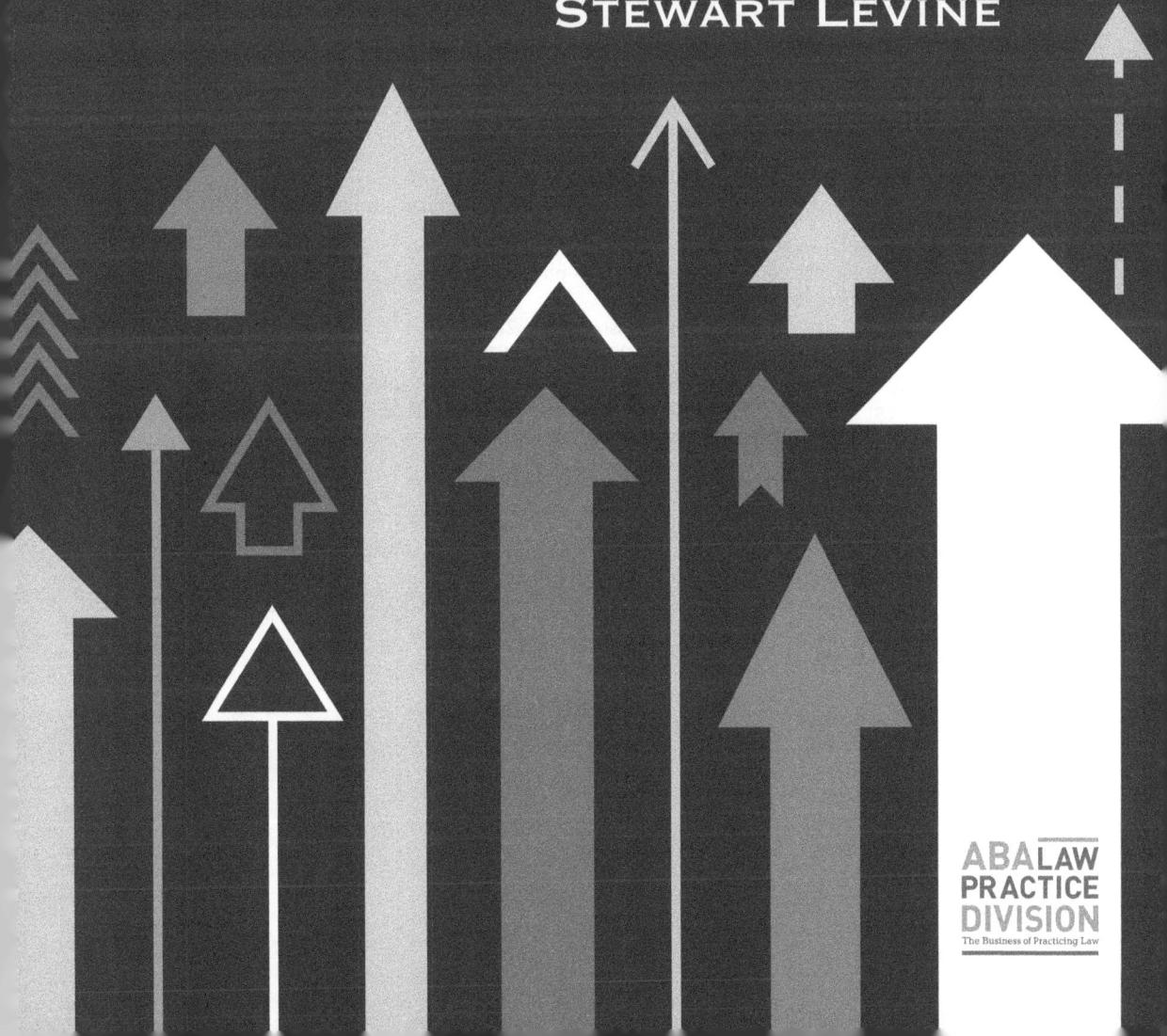

ABA**LAW**
PRACTICE
DIVISION
The Business of Practicing Law

Cover design by Lachina Creative, Inc.

Printed in the United States of America.

22 21 20 19 18   5 4 3 2 1

ISBN: 978-1-64105-217-7
e-ISBN: 978-1-64105-218-4

Library of Congress Cataloging-in-Publication Data

Names: Levine, Stewart, editor.
Title: The best lawyer you can be: A guide to physical, mental, emotional, and spiritual
   wellness / Edited by Stewart Levine.
Description: Chicago : American Bar Association, 2018.
Identifiers: LCCN 2018015143 | ISBN 9781641052177 (print)
Subjects: LCSH: Lawyers—United States. | Practice of law—United States.
Classification: LCC KF297 .B47 2018 | DDC 340.023/73—dc23
LC record available at https://lccn.loc.gov/2018015143

For Martha Fay Africa, with enduring gratitude

Stewart Levine's collection of essays will make lawyers and those who care about the lawyers in their lives stop and think about how to find fulfillment, happiness, and wellness in the practice of law. My hope is that those who read Stewart's collection will then be the new driving force for change in the legal profession that will make a difference in the depth of fulfillment, happiness, and wellness achieved by lawyers and judges for decades to come.

> Judith Perry-Martinez, American Bar Association President-elect Nominee, Chair of the ABA Presidential Commission on the Future of Legal Services, Of Counsel, Simon, Peragine, Smith & Redfearn

At a time when we are hearing too much negative news about our world and our profession, we are fortunate to have Stewart Levine's book. Stewart has brought together excellent authors and their thoughts to help us be the best we can be—mind, body, spirit, and lawyer. Thank you, Stewart, for this timely and useful book.

> Linda Klein, Immediate Past President, American Bar Association 2017–2018; Chair ABA House of Delegates, 2015–2016; Managing Shareholder, Baker Donelson

In *The Best Lawyer You Can Be* Stewart has compiled a selection of writings by experts that collectively reveal a secret about participation in the legal profession that he has known for a long time: Happiness, well-being and satisfaction in life as a lawyer does not come as a result of hourly and financial goals, or wins in the courtroom, but by living a well-rounded life. This important collection helps readers understand the importance of understanding oneself and self-management of personal physical and spiritual resources, to achieving balance and success in one's life and practice. Taken collectively, these writings show that the key to personal and professional fulfillment, and true personal well-being, is exceptional, innovative and sacrificial service for others; taking care of ourselves so that we will have the opportunity to positively influence with a higher purpose. Thanks to Stewart for putting together this important compilation.

> Thomas C. Grella, author of *Lessons in Leadership: Essential Skills for Lawyers*; Chair ABA Law Practice Division 2

Many lawyers are not convinced that they can find material personal and professional benefit by taking care of themselves. Even if they are interested in better self-care, tackling the many elements of leading a more healthy life can be daunting for hard-working professionals. *The Best Lawyer You Can Be* provides accessible and practical insights and tools from which even the most skeptical and overwhelmed can immediately pick and choose in order to start on an individual path to better mental and emotional health and success in their chosen field and beyond.

> Miriam J. Frank, Leader, Talent Management Consulting, Major, Lindsey & Africa

Reading Stewart's book is a deeply rewarding experience. When I started practicing law in 1962, lawyers focused on identifying the problems they faced in that industry, with little understanding of how to find solutions. In *The Best Lawyer You Can Be,* contributors are focused on how to support individual well-being while practicing law. There is a single sound, a common voice, to Stewart's writers. By sharing their individual experiences, they deliver the tools that lawyers can use to be fulfilled within their practice. It is a must read for attorneys who feel trapped in an adversarial system and who are seeking actions they can take that support attorney well-being.

> George Kaufman, author, *The Lawyer's Guide to Balancing Life and Work*; Vice Chair and Director of Development, Omega Institute

At this time when the legal profession is facing a crisis of well-being, Levine's book is a timely must-read for lawyers across the country.

> Bree Buchanan, J.D., Director, Texas State Bar Lawyers Assistance Program, Chair ABA Commission on Lawyer Assistance Programs

Stewart Levine has compiled one of the most important books for lawyers in a generation. An expansive follow-up to Steve Keeva's *Transforming Practices*, *The Best Lawyer You Can Be* will indeed be a crucial ally to lawyers of all stripes seeking to improve their physical, mental, emotional, and spiritual well-being. The essays and references within are primed to guide you on the path forward and upward. They represent some of the best wisdom of the modern day. I hope many lawyers are exposed to this volume early in their careers.

> Doug Chermak, Esq., Mindfulness teacher and speaker for legal professionals; Former Law Program Director, Center for Contemplative Mind in Society

Stewart offers good counsel to all lawyers. This collection offers tools for crafting a rewarding and meaningful career. Each author invites readers to step away from the "in box" and take stock. The common theme: success and satisfaction follow authenticity. I came away thinking of the U.S. Marine Corps slogan—Adapt, Improvise, and Overcome. Practical exercises and advice give readers tools to take charge of their destinies. This book is about growth, resilience, and having the life and career you want.

> Susan Manch, Chief Talent Officer, Winston Strawn LLP

If we truly care about serving the interests of justice, then we must also care about the lawyers, the judges, and the future lawyers (aka law students) whom we rely on to serve and deliver justice. I am so grateful to the editor and authors for their commitment to this national conversation focusing on the health and well-being of the legal profession.

> Michael J. Higer, 2017–2018 President, The Florida Bar Association, Partner, Berger Singerman

As someone who works closely with law students and lawyers, I can't think of another book that I would consider a must-read as this one is for those in and about to enter the legal profession. As recent studies have reported, this is a profession that demands much of its members, and the results are often depression, anxiety, substance abuse, physical ailments, and more. Stewart Levine has brought together some of the best thinkers and practitioners in the world of lawyer wellness. *The Best Lawyer You Can Be* not only provides practical information on wellness practices, such as mindfulness, exercising, taking care of the body, and nourishment, but also how to build resilience, emotional intelligence, and self-empowerment—the self-awareness elements that help one find and sustain satisfaction in life as a practicing lawyer. The book's primary message is, "Put your oxygen mask on first." As flight attendants will tell you, when in need of air, take care of yourself first so that you can take care of others. So few lawyers ever hear this message, let alone understand how to do it. The discussions on Effective Engagement—Client Service, Collaboration, Diversity, Mentoring, Pro Bono, Innovation, and leading democracy—help those in the practice of law (or those considering a life in the law) to create an environment where they can flourish and serve their clients. To anyone who is struggling to find happiness and wellness as a practicing lawyer or to those law students beginning their legal careers, the wisdom in this book has the power to transform your life and career into something meaningful, where you feel the energy and engagement to make an impact on your clients and society around you, and most importantly, enjoy your life! I know this book will be on the reading list for our law students, and if I could require it, I would.

> Marcia Pennington Shannon, Assistant Dean, Office of Career Strategy, Georgetown Law School

I'm not a lawyer, but I have friends who are . . . they need this book! But they're not alone. I've coached corporate executives and their teams for three decades, helping them strengthen crucial competencies and collaboration. As I work with them, I inevitably find they need help dealing with overload, stress, and conflict. They might be brilliant, experienced leaders . . . but they forget to breathe. Many believe they can multitask and others talk more than they listen. I will buy them this book! Congrats Stewart for collecting just the right people to co-create this treasure trove of stories and strategies, dedicated to improving lawyers' lives. I have no doubt it will make a big difference to your intended audience and well beyond.

> Sharon Jordan-Evans, Executive Coach, Speaker, Co-author of the international best seller *Love 'Em or Lose 'Em: Getting Good People to Stay*, Berrett-Koehler Publishers 2014

Stewart Levine, as the editor and compiler of *The Best Lawyer You Can Be*, asks *the* question for lawyers, statistically the most unhappy of professionals: how do I practice law and hold on to my humanity—the inner promptings of my own being that bind me to what makes life worth living? Stewart asks this of his contributors, who not surprisingly answer in a wide variety of useful ways. But he also asks this of each of us. It's all too easy to forget the idealism and vitality and zest with which many of us entered the legal profession but somehow lost touch with amidst the pressures of professional and familial responsibilities. This book reminds us. More than merely a set of prescriptions for optimizing well-being in various domains, *The Best Lawyer You Can Be* reminds us of what really matters and demonstrates that we can be lawyers *and* happy and fulfilled human beings. As the book demonstrates, it's not necessarily easy, and it's certainly not guaranteed. Yet there are many different ways we can find professional and personal fulfillment as lawyers, if we are willing to ask Levine's question and listen to our minds, hearts, and bodies for our own unique set of answers. For those of us who struggle to maintain balance and meaning in a profession that demands so much from us, *The Best Lawyer You Can Be* is essential reading.

Stephen H. Sulmeyer, J.D., Ph.D., lawyer, clinical psychologist, mediator and collaborative coach

Contents

PART I   SELF-AWARENESS

CHAPTER 1
Being the Happiest, Most Effective Lawyer You Can Be

CHAPTER 2
Lawyering as a Spiritual Path

CHAPTER 3
Mindful Lawyering

Professor Nathalie Martin

CHAPTER 4
Transform Lawyer Well-Being into a Team Sport

Anne Brafford, Esq., MAPP

CHAPTER 5
Using Emotional Intelligence to Promote Lawyer Wellness

Dr. Larry Richard, Esq., PhD

PART II   SELF-MANAGEMENT

Introduction

During my second year of law school I had my first "real" lawyer's job. I was an intern at a local legal services clinic. On my first day, I was handed 25 cases "to work on." This would be my job for the semester. Three weeks later I asked the managing attorney for more cases. When he asked about the 25 I had been given, I told him that I had resolved them.

He was surprised, and curious! He asked how I did it. I told him I had reviewed the files, spoken to the clients, thought about a fair outcome and what needed to be done, called the attorney or agency on the other side, and reached a satisfactory resolution.

I knew nothing about being a lawyer. I had no inkling that the cases were difficult, needed to take a long time, or had to be handled in a particular way. With common sense and a "beginner's mind," I found the solution that worked best for all concerned. Simple? It was for me!

I spent the next 12 years becoming a "successful" lawyer—and becoming less effective at resolving matters. Then, feeling frustrated, anxious, fearful, and very stressed, I stopped practicing law. I have been in "recovery" ever since, recovering what I knew about resolution when I started, discovering its many component parts, and learning how to teach and model it for others.

As a young attorney, although I listened politely to more senior lawyers, I was surprised at the coaching I received. Standard practice discouraged communication among parties in conflict, communication that I used in those legal services cases, communication essential for efficient resolution. Many lawyers were playing a very different game from the one my instincts chose.

I was fascinated with how the most effective judges and lawyers paid attention to people's real concerns. They listened and knew what to honor and respect. They knew how to frame situations and condition expectations. They embodied a tradition that knew how to accommodate competing concerns and build consensus.

Winning or losing was not the point of their work. Their game was resolution and getting people back to their lives.

I had a similar orientation. I believed that everyone had a lot to learn about conflict, and I focused on trying to understand conflict, a pervasive aspect of life, and the practice of law. Amid all the business and personal conflict, there was some clarity. We could do a lot better at managing disagreement—and preventing a great deal of it—if we formed professional and personal relationships in a different way.

I had a varied and fulfilling career after leaving the practice of law. I spent time as a corporate executive, divorce and commercial mediator, professional speaker, organizational consultant, personal coach, and "edutainer" in all matters related to what are commonly considered "soft skills," though many now call them the hard skills. Along the way I've written three well-received books.

For reasons that are not always clear to me, I have always kept my hand in the legal game—remaining active in the ABA and being a champion for what I considered to be progressive developments in the law. When the opportunity to curate and edit this book came up it, was a no-brainer. I thought of friends and colleagues who navigated the sometimes-challenging world of "what can you do with a 'law degree'" and along the way learned how to create balance and satisfaction in their personal and professional lives. I also had a sense of the essential elements for staying healthy. I have been fortunate to come across others with contributions to make.

Health, wellness, and self-improvement have become a critical part of the culture we live in. Serving others is a lawyer's job. Being fit yourself is a necessary foundation for taking care of others. This book provides a toolkit for lawyers to be able to do that.

It's a must-have book because in the highly competitive practice of law, it's impossible to compete on substantive knowledge. Where you can excel is as a service provider. This book will help lawyers develop that edge.

If you want to be effective as a lawyer, the fitness this book aspires to is as important as—if not more important than—substantive knowledge of law. This book provides what you need for optimum fitness: physical fitness, mental clarity, emotional stability, and a spiritual foundation that will enable you to take care of clients, colleagues and the communities you serve.

As competition increases in the legal marketplace, differentiation will become increasingly important. Lawyer fitness will be an element of that differentiation. Clients, judges, juries, and other lawyers respond differently to someone who is fit and healthy. A fit person is a confident person.

This book will do its best to provide a comprehensive guide for practicing attorneys on how to stay in the best condition they can to serve clients, communities, friends, and family while enjoying the work, leading balanced lives, and making a good living.

As this book was coming alive, someone on the ABA Publications Board said they thought of the book as an update to the late Steve Keeva's *Transforming Practices* (*ABA Journal Book*, Chicago, 1999), which I had the honor of endorsing. Steve's book reflected his personal mission of sharing inspiring stories of how passionate individuals had innovated and changed the way they thought about their role in society and how they practiced law. In a similar way, curating this book reflects my desire to leave a legacy for a legal profession that has served me well and as a capstone to my legal career. I know that all authors in this collection are writing from a place of personal passion and commitment to making a difference.

The timeliness of this book is beyond question. Consider:

> Between 21 and 36 percent of practicing lawyers are problem drinkers. Twenty-eight percent suffer from depression; 19 percent struggle with anxiety; and 23 percent are impaired by stress. Law students fare little better—17 percent are depressed; 14 percent suffer severe anxiety; 6 percent reported suicidal thoughts in the past year; and

22 percent engaged in binge drinking during the year. Those are the dismal results of the 2016 study of 13,000 lawyers by the American Bar Association Commission on Lawyer Assistance Programs and the Hazelden Betty Ford Foundation and a separate Survey of Law Student Well-Being conducted that same year, which included 3,300 law students from 15 different law schools. The adverse effect such statistics have on the legal profession—including the inability of its members to do their best work, or fully comply with the Rules of Professional Conduct, or even enjoy some semblance of job satisfaction and happiness—is obvious. So with the objective of doing something about that unwanted state of affairs, the ABA, the National Organization of Bar Counsel and the Association of Professional Responsibility Lawyers created the National Task Force on Lawyer Well-Being.[1]

As the book emerged, its chapters fell into three parts that are cornerstones of emotional intelligence: self-awareness, self-management, and effective engagement. Each of the experts relates what they know and how it contributes to personal well-being. Twenty-two of these 26 authors have been practicing attorneys; many are still doing their best to get better with more practice.

I am grateful to the authors who took the time to dig in and share from both their expertise and personal experience. I learned a great deal from each chapter and can honestly say, contrary to what others tried to warn me, that the project was not about herding cats. All it took was some gentle nudging, and it all came together. Thank you for making the contribution—each of you.

Prof. Larry Kreiger begins sharing the results of extensive empirical research on what makes lawyers happy, which in some ways is the ultimate barometer of lawyer well-being and satisfaction in the practice of law. Elizabeth Bader reveals the essential contribution of reflective or spiritual practice to well-being. Prof. Nathalie Martin shares the benefits yoga and mindfulness practice have brought her. Anne Brafford introduces the concept of emotional renewal and resilience, backed up by the critical work of Paula Davis-Laack. Dr. Larry Richard frames the critical development of emotional intelligence. Katy Goshtasbi introduces the importance of personal branding critical for a clear identity that best uses individual innate skills. Diane Costigan then focuses on the importance of self-empowerment and staying mindful because lawyers often sabotage their highest aspirations.

Self-management is the next critical set of skills. Dr. Shelley Canter touches on how critical the right career path is. Steve Meyers shares his experience about the importance of maintaining healthy family and relationships and how the dominance of the billable hour gets in the way. Ed Poll discusses financial success as a critical aspect of well-being while Dr. Eva Selhub shares critical aspects of stress and Dr. Felicia Stoler looks at the importance of proper nutrition. John Mitchell adds his reflections on the value of exercise and fitness. Martha Knudson shares her material on the importance of building what she calls "psychological capital." Finally, Anne Collier talks about the value that a good coach can provide.

Turning to engagement with others, Micah Solomon shares essential tips for providing good client service. Dr. Heidi Gardner shares her research on the value of collaboration. Dean Joan Bullock does an excellent job of unpacking and making accessible the subject of diversity and inclusion and how that awareness is essential for well-being. Similarly, Phyllis Weiss Haserot addresses the increasing importance

---

1. Editorial Board, Dec 18, 2017, *Confronting a Legal Profession in Distress*, Connecticut Law Tribune, available at https://www.law.com/ctlawtribune/sites/ctlawtribune/2017/12/15/confronting-a-profession-in-distress/.

of being able to operate in a multi-generational workforce. Julie LaEace shares her experience of the value of pro-bono service and what it can do for individuals and legal organizations. Bill Gibson writes from experience about the value of giving to the profession. Linda Alvarez shares her story of how following her own heart and mind to creative and innovative solutions has contributed to her personal values.

Two chapters are especially important to me because they reflect values I hold, as exemplified by the story of my own legal services experience before I "learned" how to be an effective lawyer. Kim Wright shares her personal journey and chronicles most of the progressive inroads enabling individuals to practice in a way congruent with their own personal values. Marguerite Picard tells us about her current multi-disciplinary practice. Even more important, she elegantly reveals the degree of unhappiness coming from the inability to adapt to a system that is inherently incongruent with the basic goodness and compassion marking us as human beings.

Finally, Cheryl Connor points out the unique contributions lawyers can make serving our democratic form of government because we are a nation of laws. She reminds us of the oath we took upon being admitted to the bar and how we swore to uphold the Constitution. Given what many perceive as current attacks on the rule of law, it is an especially important reminder.

No doubt you will find some overlap and even a bit of duplication in the book. I have taken license to do that in service of this book's mission – to provide information and the personal experiences of others to help you reflect on your own current practices. For new lawyers, these chapters offer some things to stay mindful of. For experienced practitioners, there are points to reflect on and tools to use that relate to your current reality.

My vision is that legal service providers of all kinds will buy in bulk and that the book will generate the necessary dialogue and progressive changes that will contribute to everyone involved in the administration of justice.

Wouldn't it be great if the legal profession served not only clients but also the lawyers and the system we are a part of? That's a triple bottom-line I can get behind and one I invite you to join me in!

Stewart Levine
Alameda, CA
June 2018

About the Curator and Editor

Stewart Levine is the founder of ResolutionWorks, a consulting and training organization dedicated to providing skills and ways of thinking needed to build strong organizational cultures. He spent ten years practicing law before becoming an award-winning marketing executive serving the legal profession at AT&T, where he was recognized as a pioneer "intrapreneur." He uses his approach to form teams and joint ventures in a variety of situations. Stewart has worked with large and small law firms, legal departments, and government agencies across the country.

Stewart served on the Council of the American Bar Association Law Practice Management Division where he was Chair of the Education Board 2000–2003. He was a founding editorial member of the ABA Law Practice Management Ezine, where he wrote a monthly column, "Management By Agreement," from 2003 to 2008. He was featured in an article about "Trend Setters" in the legal profession in *Law Practice Magazine*. He has served on the ABA Diversity and Inclusion Committee since 2003 and was appointed to the Publications Board in 2015 and the Lawyer Wellness and Leadership and Management Committees in 2016.

His book, *Getting to Resolution: Turning Conflict into Collaboration* (Berrett-Koehler, 1998, 2009), was called a "must read" by *Law Practice Management Magazine*. It was an Executive Book Club Selection; featured by Executive Book Summaries; named one of the 30 Best Business Books of 1998; endorsed by Dr. Stephen Covey, author of *Seven Habits of Highly Effective People*; and featured in *The Futurist* magazine. It was a finalist for the 2009 Center for Public Resources book of the year. *The Book of Agreement* (Berrett-Koehler, 2003) has been called more practical than the classic *Getting to Yes* and named among the best books of 2003 by CEO Refresher. Stewart also co-authored *Collaboration 2.0* (HappyAbout, 2008) and is a frequent contributor to Legal Publications.

Stewart is an Honors graduate of Rutgers Law School, where he was the Student Writing Editor of the *Law Review*. He served as a Deputy Attorney General for the State of New Jersey and was a Law and Humanities Fellow at Temple Law School, where he was a law teacher; he was also a member of the faculty at the University of California Berkeley Law School. In October 2010, Stewart was inducted into the College of Law Practice Management.

Part I
Self-Awareness

CHAPTER 1
Being the Happiest, Most Effective Lawyer You Can Be
New Research

Larry Krieger

Editor's Note: I selected this as the opening chapter because of the extraordinary empirical research done by Professor Larry Krieger with psychologist Dr. Ken Sheldon. Given lawyers' love of empirical data, I thought the chapter would provide a powerful context for all else that follows. It's about connections, people, and treating others well—most importantly, yourself!

This chapter is a practical guide to broadly improved lawyer happiness, satisfaction, and performance. It explains the five critical sources of well-being identified in a landmark psychological study of 6,200 lawyers and judges. It then provides specific, practical suggestions for applying these findings to both work and personal life. You also learn a powerful stress reduction technique and a single organizing principle for understanding the keys to lawyer well-being in order to facilitate ongoing improvements in your life experience and work output.

Larry Krieger is an international authority on lawyer well-being. Since 2004, he has conducted cutting edge research with psychologist Dr. Ken Sheldon, focusing on lawyers and law students. Their studies have appeared in leading psychology and legal journals. Their recent study of 6,200 lawyers, "What Makes Lawyers Happy?" was featured in the *New York Times* national news, and was the most shared article in the *Times* for two days. Larry was a litigator for 11 years and has been a Clinical Professor of Law at Florida State University since 1992. He was selected as one of 25 subjects for the 2013 Harvard Press book, *What the Best Law Teachers Do*, and was the founding Chair of the Section on Balance in Legal Education of the Association of American Law Schools.

GETTING STARTED AND AVOIDING OBSTACLES

Congratulations on picking up this book. We all came to law school to become the best lawyers we could be, and this book will help further your goals and desires. In this chapter, I describe some exciting new research findings that pinpoint what makes lawyers happier and more effective. I then offer some steps to concretely apply the findings to your life and work. I practiced law for 11 years before coming to teaching, so I appreciate many of the demands vying for your time and attention. The ideas I suggest are intended to be focused, practical ways to improve your life and work comfortably with modest inputs of your time and attention.

Let's first address a few common blocks to progress so that you are ready for them if they come up. First, we all feel the tension of competing interests for our precious time. That will probably never change. But we all make time for what we decide is important to us, and let's agree that becoming your best should be very near the top of that list. Maximizing your mental, physical, emotional, and spiritual fitness (or any of them that you choose to focus on) are among the highest, worthiest goals you can imagine, so they deserve your attention. As you find ideas that resonate for you, you may feel the impulse to defer them because of time. Perhaps take a moment each day to set priorities that include your own improvement in whatever time frame works for you. If you decide to defer on yourself, consider setting a specific time to come back to yourself.

A second common obstacle in your quest for greater wellness and fitness is the feeling that you "should" do something for improvement. It is easy for most to put ourselves aside for others or our work, forgetting that our well-being is the basis of anything good we can do. "Should" is a weak motivator. It comes with a feeling of guilt if the action doesn't happen. If you feel "shoulds" about positive ideas, see if you can shift that feeling to more clear desires for improvement so that you *want* to try the activity to benefit your health, happiness, or performance. This more internal motivation will bring you more persistence, enjoyment, and greater results.

We all share the human tendency towards comfort with what we are accustomed to, and hesitation to change. Remind yourself when this comes up that no growth or improvement can happen without change. Everything is constantly changing, so why not go with the reality and follow your present instinct to improve? Appreciate yourself for approaching this book with positive interest and expectations, and if resistance to trying something new comes up, try it anyway. Steps can be small and comfortable, and may very well lead to major improvements. Don't let a bit of discomfort with change hold you back.

THE RESEARCH ON THE BEST, THE HAPPIEST, AND THE MOST PROFESSIONAL LAWYER YOU CAN BE

Let's look at the factors shown in the leading research to be most effective for making us the best and happiest lawyers we can be.[1] For this large study, Dr. Ken Sheldon and I gathered and analyzed information from more than 6,200 practicing lawyers and judges in four diverse states. The results and related research demonstrate a most

---

1. Krieger, Lawrence S. & Sheldon, Kennon M., *What Makes Lawyers Happy?: A Data-Driven Prescription to Redefine Professional Success*, 83 GEORGE WASHINGTON LAW REVIEW 554 (2015); FSU College of Law, Public Law Research Paper No. 667. Available at SSRN: https://ssrn.com/abstract=2398989.

fortunate situation for lawyers—that all of the most desirable and important things run together and tend to support each other in an upward spiral. For example, being the best you can be also means being the happiest you can be and having the most supportive relationships possible. Further, maximizing your satisfaction and well-being also means you are the most professional, competent, and effective you can be. Any improvement you make in any area will likely have added benefits in other areas as well.

Keep in mind the global nature of these benefits for you and those around you in order to maintain your motivation to take some of the practical steps suggested. With the explanation of each of major well-being factor, I will suggest simple ideas for you to reflect upon, write about, and use to identify small, beneficial changes you can make. Please consider buying a notebook or journal for this purpose. You can certainly use a computer or device instead, but first consider a traditional notebook or journal. Research shows that writing notes by hand yields deeper and more useful thought.

Based on the numbers we see in research findings, the factors I discuss appear to be mandatory for a lawyer to experience well-being and satisfaction. The reflective process suggested is very direct and will help you quickly identify areas for improvement so you can make gains in ways you choose.

WHAT DO WE MEAN BY A "HAPPY LAWYER"?

Everyone wants to be happy. That desire underlies every behavioral choice we make. But "happiness" can mean different things to people, ranging from a simple freedom from cares or worries to a state of giddiness or excitement or an unshakeable, deep state of contentment—and there are many other definitions.

Lawyers may find the idea of being free from cares and concerns foreign—even inappropriate—given the seriousness of our work. We might also find the idea of deep inner contentment to be unrealistic given the vexing situations of clients and the complexities of managing problems within the legal system. Nonetheless, I encourage you to know at the start that regardless of your current level of well-being, you can increase your experience of day-to-day happiness and satisfaction with your life and work. It makes sense to be optimistic about improving our experience—people do it all the time, and many lawyers are extremely happy. The research on attorneys shows exactly which attitudes and choices in work and life predict elevated happiness (or depression) in lawyers. It also points the way to improvements that will be simple and attainable.

The meaning of "happiness" as used in this study is validated and well established by decades of research. Like other modern researchers, we measured the "subjective well-being" (SWB) of our lawyers to determine their happiness. This approach to understanding happiness is useful because most people immediately and personally relate to it. It is a reliable approach because it aggregates dozens of different relevant experiences into a single well-being measure.

To determine SWB, we included numerous measures of lawyers' moods, both positive and negative, which we combined with several measures of their level of satisfaction with life. When I discuss factors that increase the "happiness" of thousands of lawyer subjects, I refer to those factors that proved to most strongly predict *increased positive moods*, *decreased negative moods*, and *increased life satisfaction* among lawyers.

Please think about this model of happiness and see if it applies directly to your own desires for your life and work. Would it be welcome to have more positive moods and fewer negative moods each day? To feel more satisfied with your life and work? How to accomplish that depends on understanding what will make it happen—those few factors that best predict lawyer happiness.

THE SURPRISING FINDINGS: WHAT ACTUALLY MAKES LAWYERS HAPPY?

I spent the first 11 years of my legal career as a government litigator in a variety of demanding positions. I enjoyed all of the work. I often noticed that lawyers I encountered did not seem to be as happy as our relative intelligence, power, and income would suggest. It struck me that many highly successful lawyers were not particularly happy as a group. I wondered whether the achievements we typically define as "success" do not bring happiness.

This was a question of importance because at times I received offers to pursue more traditionally successful career tracks that offered greater compensation and more prestige than my government work. When I began teaching law school, I had the opportunity to investigate this question and engaged a respected psychologist to help. The study looked at these questions: Does the achievement of career success as we commonly define it lead most lawyers to happiness? If not, what does? Based on previous research, we expected the first answer to be "no," that "success" would not be very important for happiness. We did not think that gaining rewards and status, including entry into prestigious schools, high law school grades, other honors and credentials, or partnership in a law firm, would reliably identify the happy lawyers. We also hypothesized that more subjective, personal, and relational factors would be the real markers of thriving, happy lawyers.

The resulting study of 6,200 lawyers and judges in four states confirmed all of these hypotheses, so consistently that the conclusions are clear. **The happiness of thousands of lawyers varied strongly only with personal factors such as their attitudes, integrity, relationships, and purposes and goals in life. The usual markers of "success" in our society and profession—those external, competitive factors of grades, money, and prestige—were essentially ineffective for producing happy lawyers.** The results were sufficiently surprising that the *New York Times* report of this study was featured in the national news and was the most shared article in the *Times* for two days.[2]

In a nutshell, much of what has been driving so many of us, what we strive for with most of our energy, worry about at length, and which has been forming our dreams for our children and other loved ones, does not actually produce happiness. This is an important realization to reflect on, though it certainly does *not* mean that we should avoid or renounce success and the comforts and benefits that it can bring. It does mean that there are several more important factors in life that should not be *sacrificed* for success as commonly understood.

Figure 1.1 shows these results in numerical detail, with each factor measured for the strength of its association with the well-being of our thousands of lawyers. Note that the numerical correlations with happiness of the different factors vary from zero (or even negative) to a maximum of 0.66. A theoretically "perfect" relationship would have a correlation of 1.00, meaning that a particular variable and lawyer

---

2. "Public Defenders Are Happier than Prestige Lawyers," May 17–18, 2015.

Lawyer WB: Success vs. Human Factors

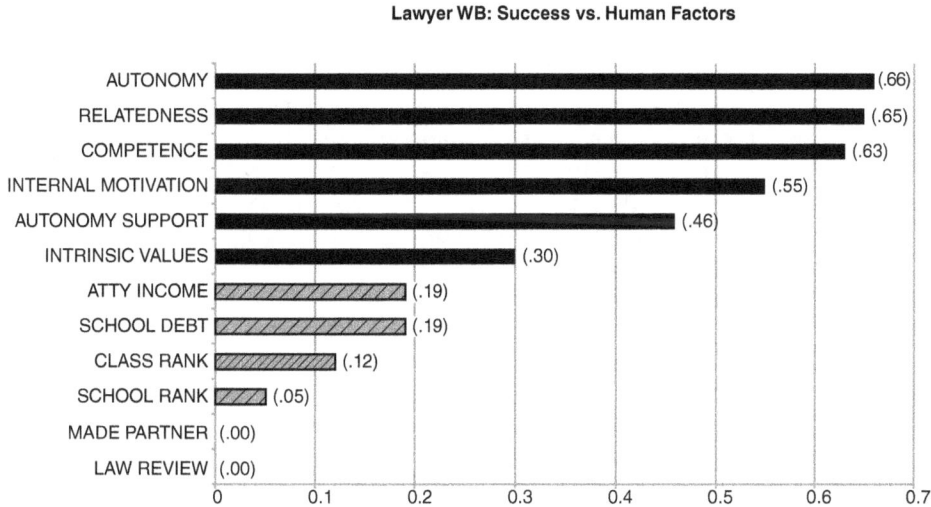

FIGURE 1.1 *Human Factors, Rather Than "Success," Drive Lawyer Happiness*

happiness increase or decrease together in equal amounts. Similarly, a 0.50 correlation means that happiness increases one-half as much as the variable being measured. Correlations that approach or exceed one-half (0.50) are generally considered very strong in this type of research. Correlations greater than about 0.35 could be considered strong; about 0.20 to 0.35, moderate; 0.10 to 0.20, weak; and below 0.10, very weak to meaningless (even if statistically valid).

Figure 1.1 shows you the stark contrast between the two types of factors in this study—traditional success and personal/relational factors—and their apparent effects on lawyer happiness. The common markers of success are shown in grey bars, and the more personal and internal factors are in black. Each factor is followed by the strength of its relationship with well-being. One view of the chart tells the tale starkly: the first finding of this large study is that "success" as normally understood simply does not produce much happiness, while identifiable internal and relational dynamics do. Please also see that the "success" factors are largely competitive and outside any personal sphere of control—someone else might always get the prize. So they are stressful to pursue and inherently produce anxiety and stress for people who overemphasize them.

HOW TO INCREASE LAWYER HAPPINESS FACTORS IN YOUR LIFE RIGHT NOW

1. Integrity/Authenticity

The data shows that integrity (also referred to in this domain of psychology as "authenticity" or "autonomy") is the critical foundation of a good life. It is listed first in Figure 1.1 and is the strongest predictor of lawyer happiness in this study. Its contrast with the success factors in grey could not be clearer.

The term "autonomy," when used in this research, goes well beyond the ordinary meaning of freedom to make one's own choices. It includes the need to have coherence between our self and our behaviors in day-to-day life. This means that choices and actions express our "true self" and "true values" (these are the actual terms we use in the survey to measure autonomy). You can see that in normal parlance it means your *integrity*—the extent to which you say what you mean, do not misstate or bend reality, and otherwise express what is inside you in your words and actions. This is the most important predictor of whether or not a lawyer is happy and satisfied most of the time.

It is helpful to realize that you fully control your own integrity—the extent to which your words and actions genuinely show what you feel, know, want, or believe in. If you cannot state a strong "yes" to the idea of living with integrity or authenticity as your usual behavior, it is very unlikely that you can be happy. However, you have the ability to work on this aspect of your personality to express more truth and consistency with who you really are.

Our first reflection looks at how each of us might increase our authenticity, our integrity, regardless of where we are right now. First, if you don't have an established method of reflection or journaling (I didn't until very recently), I suggest you keep an open mind and try it. It's only for you, so it should be comfortable, and it will definitely be worth the brief time and attention it needs because you will be looking at the very few, most important keys to increasing your happiness and effectiveness. As previously mentioned, have a journal, notebook, or electronic medium set for your use. Pick a regular time you are comfortable with. It can be quite brief, just a few minutes daily, weekly, or whatever you are willing to devote to yourself. Of course, do this as and when you prefer for your own improvement.

To keep content brief and most useful, two keys are helpful: 1) I like to include my stronger as well as weaker points in each area. We will all have both, and this exercise is entirely for our own personal benefit, not to make ourselves feel bad. 2) I always try to look with open eyes, without fear of finding something that isn't the best. How else can I learn and grow? This is like a quick search for a gold mine. Every time I find a weak spot, I have identified fertile ground for improving my life experience directly and without delay.

Exercise One: Authenticity

As mentioned, authenticity (integrity) is the most personal factor in your life and also the most important for your happiness and satisfaction. Its importance is even greater because two other "most important" contributors to your well-being—your relationships and motivation for your work—also require strong authenticity. Your integrity or authenticity is the primary foundation of your entire life experience. Because your authenticity applies in so many areas of your life, this reflection will be broader and may need more attention than for the remaining factors we will discuss. Don't be dissuaded if it takes a bit of focus. It is that important.

For a direct approach to looking at your integrity, your authentic self, I suggest you answer a few questions that are so fundamental most of us rarely think about them. The answers will probably be easy and quick once you focus on the questions. For example: *What are the most important things in your life? What is your purpose in each area of your life? What do you care about, and want, in your work? What do you desire in your personal life? How do you feel you should act and treat others, and yourself? What do you appreciate the most in life, and what might you regret the most toward the end of your life if not achieved? When do you feel you might be violating your conscience or ignoring your beliefs and values?*

It can help to make two columns on a sheet, listing the work and personal life areas separately so you address key questions and points in both these domains of life. This may take just a few minutes or you may need to come back to it once or twice. The factors that follow will be simpler for you to cover. It is worth it to stay with this authenticity consideration until you feel you have expressed on paper in some basic way who you really are and what life is really about for you—this clarity is the foundation of your entire life, including your happiness and satisfaction.

When you think you have a good sense of it, next *think about how often you actually express these core parts of yourself in your daily words and actions.* You could list the places, in both work and personal life again, where you are strong in authenticity with yourself and with others. Where do you both know yourself well and express the truth about who you are, what you want and believe, how you feel, etc.? This always calls for consideration of the situation and the trust you feel for others there, of course.

This sort of subjective personal analysis is quite different from what we are used to as law-trained thinkers. Don't mind that. Just be honest with yourself and include strengths to keep a positive balance, as previously mentioned. Note, of course, any places where your integrity or authenticity could be greater, where you could be more honest with yourself or others or express what is inside you more fully in your work choices or other life activities. Reflect on what you do and what you say when with different people or in different situations. Is there consistent, strong coherence between your insides and your outsides? Are there gaps between what you feel, believe, know, or want, and what you say or do in different situations? If so (and we all will have some gaps), remember that each gap you find is a gold mine. Each inconsistent act or word generates some level of tension, an internal contradiction or lack of integrity. As you become aware of them, you move towards eliminating them and thus eliminating hidden sources of stress that undermine your well-being and health.

Law Practice Can Challenge Your Authenticity

Law practice itself creates endless opportunities to practice integrity (or not), so lawyers need to be particularly vigilant to remain happy. Be fully honest in considering your authenticity in your work. First, are you doing work you care about and enjoy? Are you genuine in billing your time? Do you engage in less than admirable, respectful practices, in discovery, negotiation, or general treatment of clients, staff, court personnel, or adverse parties/counsel? Perhaps most importantly, how often do you feel a twinge of conscience about something you are doing or not doing? Conscience represents a core connection to yourself. If you ignore it, you break your integrity and generate well-being deficits that cannot improve without eliminating the contradictions between your conscience and your actions. Fear not, because if you find such conflicts you have found fertile ground for making different choices that will yield greater happiness. Your health will also improve as these tensions fall away.

With all these considerations in mind, look back to the italicized list of suggested questions and complete your notes and thoughts. Assuming you have found some room for improvement, decide on one or two small things to commit yourself to do to begin to strengthen your authenticity, and do them faithfully for the next two weeks. Be careful about large commitments unless you are sure you can carry them out. It does not matter if these are big, small, even tiny steps. Be sure that you do what you say you will. If you fall short here, you will not trust yourself to go further—this actually constitutes another integrity lapse. Your current commitment to improve your happiness may falter if you can't trust yourself to follow through for your own benefit. So pick modest things and do them as consistently as you can.

Once you have reflected on your authenticity and identified one or more things on which you can realistically follow through, a final useful step is to form a quick habit of checking on these commitments to yourself. Take one minute each day for at least two weeks (and this might generate a good habit for the future as well), to keep your life moving forward and upward. It's easiest to choose a regular time each day or evening to maintain a routine of looking back on the day to verify you are trying to conform with your decisions—whatever change or behavior you decided to institute. If you see you are not following through or you need to amend your plan, give yourself room to amend your commitment. Be clear with yourself and write down the amendment, then track it with integrity as suggested here.

2. Relatedness to Others

In Figure 1.1, the second most critical need for your happiness is relatedness to other people. You experience satisfaction of this need when you feel a meaningful, close connection to important others in your life, at work, home, or elsewhere.

The impact of this factor on our happiness is as great as is our sense of being authentic, perhaps because we must constantly express authenticity to relate well to others. *It is not possible to feel closely connected to others if you are not authentic about who you really are, what you really believe or want, or how you really feel.* This need is not satisfied by just "being with people" in a variety of ways; it is about how often you feel a close, meaningful connection, and that will require feeling and being authentic.

Exercise Two: Your Relatedness to Others

This and the remaining reflective journal entries are simpler than the first because the factors are more concrete and more focused. *For your relatedness need, think about your current life, perhaps the past few weeks or months. Picture the people you have been with in all areas of your life, and consider how often you have felt close and connected to them in a meaningful way.* This sense of connection need not be anything intense or particularly "deep" (although it can be), but it needs to feel genuine. It might be felt in moments when you sense that you are really understanding another person and being well understood. *Note in your journal those relationships that give you such feelings and how often this typically occurs.* Be honest and open with yourself. You have everything to gain.

Now, *consider all interactions in your recent personal and work life, and be sure to include in your notes the relationships where you do feel authentic as well as not so much.* Where do you tend to express yourself most honestly, and where not? In the latter relationships and interactions, once again you have found "pay dirt" where you can make large gains in well-being and life satisfaction. Keep in mind that the relatedness need correlates with lawyer happiness to almost to the same extent as does your integrity—each is about 2/3 of a perfect correlation. Each improvement in your feeling of closeness or connectedness to others should produce a tangible increase in your happiness.

As you identify specific relationships or situations where you could benefit from a greater sense of closeness and connection, think about modest things you can do over the next few weeks to encourage that. Perhaps being more patient, more open, more attentive or responsive, more positive, or more supportive. Would this involve family members, friends, coworkers, or members of other communities and groups you are involved with? *Be very specific. Write down those things you can realistically try in the immediate future and do them for the next 2–3 weeks. Recheck yourself each day—did you do what you committed to try?*

These steps may challenge you to offer more attention, honesty, patience, and understanding in certain relationships so you feel more connected, genuine, or intimate. As with autonomy, the effort you make will be worth it. Just remember to make modest commitments you can stick with, and where you fall short, amend your plan and keep going. It will pay off quickly in a more fulfilling life experience, and not just for you!

Performance and Professionalism Rise with Greater Happiness

I mentioned the tendency of the important aspects of our life and work to all rise or fall together with our level of happiness. It will help you stay motivated to address the remaining factors to know that this reflective process will naturally increase your performance output and your professionalism along with your well-being. Having reflected on the first two factors for attorney well-being, you can probably already see why that is true. When I think about my career, it is obvious that my reputation as an attorney (no different now as a teacher) primarily hinged on whether I was honest, trustworthy, and candid with others and the court and, secondly, on the extent to which I was genuine, respectful, understanding, kind, and sensible with others. Your law practice and professional behavior and reputation improve as you become increasingly authentic and capable of close, meaningful relationships with other people. We have all seen lawyers lacking in integrity and/or the ability (or willingness) to relate in a positive way with other lawyers, clients, and court staff. They are definitely not the lawyers with strong professional reputations, nor the ones you hope to work with or against in your next case.

3. Competence and Motivation, the Third Key to Well-Being

Let's finish our investigation of the critical sources of lawyer well-being. Figure 1.1 shows that the next key factors are primarily related to your work: the need for a sense of competence and doing work for "internally motivated" reasons. These factors also have exceptionally high predictive value for lawyer well-being—both have correlations well above 0.50, and they are closely related to each other. Lawyers who are well motivated perform better and experience a greater sense of competence.

The meaning of "competence" in the research is no different than the common meaning. It's no surprise that as people feel more competent to handle their work and other life demands, they feel much happier. Motivation is a bit more nuanced, as it deals with the reasons we make our daily choices—in this survey, why subjects chose their current work and job. This and similar research shows big differences in whether these motivations are "internal" or "external." Internal reasons for choosing work include doing the work because it is inherently enjoyable or interesting to you or because it supports important personal values. Work done for these reasons generates far more satisfaction than when done for external reasons such as financial gain or other rewards, prestige, guilt, or being required to do it. This makes sense because internal motivations express authenticity, the primary foundation of a happy life. The purpose for the work is proceeding from within you so the powerful positive 0.55 correlation of internal motivation with lawyer well-being is no surprise.

Our study included many specific findings that demonstrated the powerful difference in happiness based on the motivations of lawyers in different work settings. Everything pointed to the inability of external motivators to generate much happiness. Some findings were particularly remarkable. For example, while lawyers in medium to large firms were very well compensated, their motivation was more external (focused on money, in this case) than other lawyer groups, and this appeared to undermine their happiness. As firm size increased, income increased substantially, but so did external (again specifically money) motivation. *As pay dramatically increased with firm size, the well-being of the lawyers steadily decreased.* Most striking was the finding that junior partners in medium to large law firms were no happier than senior associates, despite the quantum leap in security, status, and pay—a 70 percent compensation increase over the associates.

A second contrast further confirms the powerful impact of motivation, especially when compared to income. We found that *lawyers in the most prestigious and typically sought-after positions had very high mean income and had also been the most successful students in law school. However, when compared with the public service/ government lawyers (who did not have equivalent school grades and of course lagged substantially in earnings), the service lawyers were happier and more satisfied with their lives and work than the prestige group.* In this large study, both groups included about 1,000 lawyers, so the statistical validity of and confidence in these results are high.

These contrasts show you how to use the study results to guide you in thinking about career and work choices. A simple approach is to "use the math" in your comparisons and choices—to choose stronger happiness factors over weaker ones when you make choices. For example, the prestige lawyers had much higher income and other benefits that would modestly predict improved happiness (see Figure 1.1—the well-being correlation of income is low at 0.19), but they also had more external motivation for their work (the financial benefits and prestige of the positions). On the other hand, the service lawyers received a greater benefit from their internally motivated purposes for work (see the well-being correlation). They reported feeling better and enjoying greater life satisfaction than the "most successful" lawyers, who were far better paid. As you reflect on your motivations for work, look at ways you can use these numbers to improve your life and work experience without sacrificing income and other desirable benefits.

Exercise Three: Motivation for Work

There are many variations of internal and external motivation, and most people experience all of them. For a different start to this important reflection, you can quickly get a good sense of your own motivational styles for work by responding to the questions below. These are the well-established items we asked in our study survey. Take a few moments to respond with a number for each question, from *1* (you experience this never or very little/not at all) to *7* (you experience this very often and very strongly); *4* is the midpoint and means you experience it modestly and/or occasionally. Just read and mark for each item how much you agree with it with a number between 1 and 7. Do not be concerned if there are other reasons that you do your current job that are not listed here or that many of your responses may be high or low. Be entirely candid. There are no right or wrong answers.

You are in the job you have now (i.e., you currently do this work) because:

1. One or more other people want you to or think you should do this work. _____

2. You want to gain the rewards (income, status, etc.) from it; i.e. you expect to obtain compensation or advantages from the work. _____

3. You feel in some way you "should" do this work, that you would feel some guilt, shame, or anxiety if you did not. _____

4. You genuinely believe this is important work for you to do, that it is an important goal or value to have. _____

5. You believe this work is integral to your value system as a whole, i.e. that it fits well with the rest of your goals and life. _____

6. This work provides enjoyment or stimulation to you by its very nature, so that the experience itself attracts you. _____

It was probably obvious that the first three motivations are more "external," while items 4 through 6 are more internal or autonomous. Remember that stronger motivation of any kind will tend to promote performance, so it is not a bad thing if all of these are relatively high (except that item 3 may deserve some attention if so). You very likely have a mix of external and internal motivations; this is common and also not a problem.

Now total your cumulative external and internal scores, for items 1–3 and then 4–6, and compare the totals. If your internal motivations are clearly stronger or both totals are high, your motivation for work is likely promoting positive performance and your well-being. However, if the internal scores are low, this is an important area for reflection that can lead to major gains in well-being over time. Regardless of actual scores, *any* increase in internal factors will be of real benefit to your work satisfaction and overall happiness. Consider each of items 4 through 6 and reflect on anything you might do to increase the enjoyment, interest, or meaning you find in your work from day to day. Virtually no job is perfect, but you may be able to make positive adjustments if you first identify the less desirable parts of the work and then consider ways to delegate or partition them during the day. Make brief notes of practical things you can do to generate more enjoyment, interest, or meaning in your work, and start doing them to increase your sense of well-being.

More serious thought will be needed if you find that your work is not interesting or does not resonate with your values and life purposes. If you have not been happy with your work, it may take some courage to journal about this honestly, but it's worth it. No matter what you find, you do not need to make changes immediately, and if major changes turn out to be appropriate to remedy a poor fit, you can take your time to develop and execute a plan. There is no hurry, and there is huge potential for becoming happier, so it's worth some focus and patience. You may even decide to consult a lawyer or life coach to sort things out, but first just take an honest look at the ways in which your work is and is not fulfilling. The 6-point motivation survey above is a structured and simple way to start, combined with the reflections above. If you are concerned about lack of fit in your current work, you may gain more clarity when I come back to job satisfaction in the autonomy support section below.

Reality Always Wins

If you hesitated to reflect or write on any aspects of your life and work discussed so far, it may help to consider an important truism that people often ignore to their detriment: Reality Always Wins. Ultimately, it must, because it is reality. So be further encouraged to take those honest looks that you may have skipped over lightly. Whenever you find a place where your life does not fit comfortably with reality, you have uncovered an unavoidable source of tension, and another focus point for immediately increasing your happiness and effectiveness.

Exercise Four: Competence

Anything you do to increase your internal motivation will likely improve your performance and sense of competence. Competence deserves its own focus as one of the three basic human needs, the strongest sources of lawyer well-being. Think about how competent you feel both at work and in your personal life. Though this often is primarily about work, a lack of competence outside of work can also substantially impair your well-being.

It can help to make separate lists for notes about competence in work and personal life in your journal. *Note both your strong and possibly deficient points in both arenas. Then consider ways to improve the latter, whether by yourself or with the help of others. Are you willing to improve in that area? Are you willing, if needed, to get some help with it?*

Alert: people commonly are uncomfortable asking for help and with change generally, and law students and lawyers seem particularly averse to seeking help. This usually results in major negative outcomes, and is counterintuitive, considering that we lawyers depend on others to come to us for help, or we would not have any work! If you feel any such hesitation, notice it but move forward anyway; try to be open to improvement and be willing to be genuine about it. As before, write down one or two things you can realistically do to improve your sense of competence in any such area, then commit to those action steps and follow through. You should notice increasing well-being with such commitments fulfilled—the correlation of competence with well-being is a huge 0.63. When you notice positive shifts here or with any other factor, consider noting them in your journal. This can serve as another motivator to keep you moving forward.

4. One More Critical Contributor: Autonomy Support

The final exceptional predictor of lawyer happiness is autonomy support. Autonomy support is a unique wellness factor because it applies in two important but different ways, to two different fields of your life and work. There is autonomy support that you *receive from* others, and autonomy support you *provide to* others. The effects of autonomy support are broadly positive. They are most pronounced in relationships involving unequal power, with the benefits flowing primarily to the person with less power. The support you receive from those "above" you increases your own well-being and performance, and you always have the same powerful effect on others whom you manage, supervise, or teach. So learning about this factor can benefit you and simultaneously empower you to benefit many others in your personal and work spheres—including your spouse, children, and employees.

Autonomy support is defined as a person's sense that she is *respected for her needs and preferences, rather than controlled* regardless of her needs and preferences. In our studies we used an established measure with three components: (1) Did the lawyers feel that their superiors understood and appreciated their priorities and preferences? (2) How often were the lawyers given choices about what to do and how to do it? (3) How often did the superiors explain their reasons when they controlled the subjects (did not provide them with their preferred choices)?

With a moment of reflection about daily experience, you probably realize that you create more positive feelings and engagement when you give your employees, children, etc. the feeling that you appreciate what they want, and then give them choices that honor their preferences (or explain why when it is not possible to give choices). On the contrary, if you simply control them (i.e., "Do it because I say so . . ." "Forget that and get this done by the end of day (or else . . .)") you will have less happy, less cooperative, and less engaged staff, associates, or children, who complain more and ultimately generate a poorer outcome. In fact, in this large attorney study and our earlier law student studies, when subjects felt increased autonomy support, they felt much better psychologically, were better motivated, and performed better. We were able to definitely measure performance in students, and the results were striking—both grades and bar examination results markedly improved as people felt more supported in this way.

For many practical purposes, then, this is a smart focus area for you. The benefits are broad and powerful, the concept is easily understood and learned, and the benefits accrue to both you and others in measurable ways. Here are my suggestions for approaching this factor.

Exercise Five: Autonomy Support for You and Others

If you do not have a boss or someone you report to at work or in another field of your interest—that is, you run your own law practice or hold the top position in your organization—the following subsection (A) will not apply to you in the usual sense. But it will be important that you read it to understand this factor from the employee's point of view. You will want to know you are supporting your people as much as practicable, and as your employees (or children, etc.) function well, they bring you major benefits in many ways.

A. Receiving Autonomy Support for Yourself

Think about the level of support you feel at work. As you advance and become more senior, there are fewer people in the organization who can control rather than support your autonomy, but the sense of being controlled can come from one boss or many. Consider: *Do you usually feel controlled by the choices of superiors, or more often considered or even included in their decision-making process? Do you generally feel understood for your thinking, and appreciated for your perspectives on what to do and how to do it? Do you commonly feel a sense of autonomy, that you can do your work in the ways you feel best and that suit you? Or is the job mainly about doing what the boss says even though you disagree or were not meaningfully consulted or respected?*

The sense of support or control you feel will powerfully affect your mood, engagement, and performance at work. After thinking about the questions above, if there is no problem with this factor, just move ahead to the next subsection. But if, fairly often, you do feel controlled rather than appreciated, understood, or included in considerations that affect you, take a few moments right now to jot down some thoughts about how you feel about your work and how to improve that situation. Understanding the importance of autonomy support, put some attention on it by writing your ideas for a few things you might try.

I will offer here a few suggestions that have worked for me and for many of my students with difficult supervisors. You may be able to approach your supervisor or other key person and talk to her directly. Many bosses are controlling because they don't know a better way, but are also open-minded and will amend their approach if they understand how you feel. If not, usually nothing is lost by trying, so long as you are positive, factual rather than emotional, and don't make them feel defensive. If you decide to address the situation with your boss, I recommend a "keep it simple" approach. Do not dramatize at all, and of course do not sound critical. You might start with genuine positives, how much you appreciate the position, the work, etc., and then shift to something like, "One thing I wanted to mention. Sometimes I feel that I have good ideas, but they don't get much attention. I know your time is limited, but if it's possible, it would help me if I could understand whether these ideas are useful or not (etc.)." If the boss is not responsive or helpful, accept that. At least you did what you could from your side and now you have that information for consideration going forward. If, given the boss' personality, you decide not to raise the problem directly, that is fine. Trust yourself, but remember reality wins—don't expect improvement unless you or the supervisor move out of your positions.

Is It Time to Start Thinking about a New Job? If you frequently have this kind of discomfort and nothing develops from one or more conversations with your boss (or you decided not to raise it directly), be attentive to whether this is a true well-being problem for you given the other benefits and circumstances related to the work. How much impact is the controlling boss having on you? Do you shrug it off quickly and generally feel good at work, or does the negative feeling stay with you? If you are taking it personally, can you learn to see it as a problem that is about the boss being a poor manager and not about you? Realizing that you have an unskilled boss can mitigate the negative effects but will not eliminate them.

To help with this difficult situation, it would also be useful to revisit what you learned from your survey results and reflections in the motivation section above. Combine that information with your considerations here. For example, if you have high work interest and enjoyment but a sense of being controlled rather than respected by supervisor(s), you are having a mixed work experience that includes some strong positives. This will deserve patience and careful thought before making a serious decision. If motivation, interest, and enjoyment are low and autonomy support is also low, you may do well to start thinking about a change that suits you better. There is no hurry, but do not avoid the realities—they are tremendously important for your life experience.

Even if you decide to look for a better fit, this entire process is helpful because you will better understand what you want next and why this was not working for you. For balance, consider: if your situation lacks autonomy support, bosses may change without warning within an organization you are leaving or joining. Because you do not control supervisory changes at your current or a new work place, making a decision primarily on this one factor can result in disappointment unless the supervisory positions at the new job are clearly set and stable.

Regarding other important factors, if you presently have a good motivation fit—work you enjoy and truly care about—be cautious about changing jobs to find a less controlling boss, unless other factors are also positive (i.e., equally or greater internal motivation for the new job) as well. Ultimately these situations are complex and require deliberation; you might well benefit from consultation with a lawyer coach or other professional. Whatever you decide, have a positive attitude toward your work each day. Make your decision for now and seek to be grateful. Avoid complaining—it has no benefit and creates negative feelings in you and others. Even if things have much room for improvement, you are becoming clear on what needs to happen and, with continued attention, you will find the next and better chapter of your life.

B. Providing Autonomy Support to Others

Most lawyers are simultaneously providing support to employees (or, conversely, primarily controlling them) while also receiving support (or not) from more senior people. When you are able to support the autonomy of your charges, whether staff, attorneys, or others, it powerfully strengthens your relationships with them and improves their morale, motivation, loyalty, retention, and quality of work. The emotional and financial returns are massive, while the cost is usually zero. The very same benefits accrue tor your children, mentees, younger friends and family, etc. in your personal life, if you learn to give others more control. Your own well-being also improves.

Take a few minutes to think about your work and personal relationships and how you conduct yourself. Specifically look at 1) the extent to which you use your position to control people's behavior without clearly explaining why it needs to be that way, 2) how often you offer subordinates choices that show you respect them, and 3) how often you explicitly understand and appreciate what the other person wants, thinks, or does, so the message comes through clearly.

Remember to create separate work and personal life columns to make your reflections simpler and more complete. Then list specific relationships or situations in which, as you think about this, you realize you could convey less control and more respect or support. List the specific people who might benefit from a more supportive attitude, at work, home, or other communities of interest, then start trying some modest things. Consider writing yourself a short sample script of what you could say to your secretary or a junior attorney (or your child or mentee . . .) to express appreciation and understanding of them and their perspectives. With practice, this becomes easy and hugely effective. In addition to expressing understanding and appreciation for the other's position or preference, you want to provide choices when possible and explain why you cannot when you control the situation.

It may sound like this means just letting people do what they want, but you will actually become more authoritative and effective when you need to set boundaries. You are learning to avoid the negative effects of a controlling approach by being flexible with boundaries when possible and, when not, explaining why it needs to be that way. Take modest steps or in less significant situations, at first, until you habituate to the more supportive approach and see the results for yourself.

Practice will quickly overcome discomfort, and this will become natural as you do it. Circle back daily for a minute or so and note for yourself whether you followed through with your intentions. The goal is to increase your happiness in the most effective ways. With the autonomy support factor, this goal now extends to your staff and others as well.

WOULD YOU LIKE TO DROP YOUR LEVEL OF STRESS IMMEDIATELY?

You now have a grasp of the five factors identified by the recent attorney research to be the most powerful positives for your happiness. These factors will be constant allies for you; they go to the very core of what makes your work and personal life satisfying. I hope you will continue to use the journaling and modest change approach (or another you prefer) to keep improving your quality of life in these ways.

Before I close this chapter, let's acknowledge the importance of stress and its impact on well-being, particularly for lawyers. Doing the reflections and action steps suggested previously should eliminate some deep and persistent stresses in the most important areas of your life. Beyond that, I will share a method for decreasing stress that many students and lawyers have reported to be effective. It applies any time you want more peace of mind, and can provide massive benefits for your health and happiness. It involves distinguishing what you control from what you do not control in the situation at hand, and then learning to keep your focus primarily on what you control.

Here is a practical exercise that I use in class or presentations that makes this clear; you can replicate it quickly now. *Take a page in your journal to consider any example of a difficult situation or event that is or has been on your mind. Mark out two columns; in the first <u>list all the things that matter about that situation that you have control over</u>. This is not about things you can do, or things you can try to influence. Write down only things you actually have control over. In the second column, list <u>all the things that matter in the situation that you do not have control over</u>. Get a clear idea of your actual, and very limited, sphere of control, and then resolve to focus 95 percent of your attention only on column one.*

As with any reflection, this is only effective when you consider and come to your own conclusions. For a sense of the kinds of things to consider, I suggest you do not control anything that anyone else does, says, thinks, believes, wants, or chooses. You certainly do not control outcomes that involve anyone else. You can immediately realize this this includes most of the outcomes that you are seeking. Why stress about other people, events, and outcomes? Learn to put most of your attention only on pieces you personally can do, and you will accomplish several important things: (1) your stress goes way down because you see and accept your lack of control; (2) your energy, focus, and capacity to perform improves because you will not be distracted from doing your best at what is yours to do; and (3) your happiness, whether things go as you prefer or not, will increase markedly as you realize you did everything that is in your control.

This practice has equal benefits for the practice of law and for personal life. If you take the minute or two to make the two lists (control and no control) about something that is stressing you at work, you will likely conclude that pretty much anything about a client, opposing counsel, judge, jury, etc. is beyond your control, although you will seek to influence them in appropriate ways. What they do, say, believe, or choose is their business. Even the most critical factors in a case, the facts and the laws that apply to it, are beyond your control. Accept that for these and many other reasons the outcomes of your cases are not yours to control. This frees you to work with as little worry and as much energy and focus as possible, letting the rest unfold as it will. This approach applies equally to issues that family members, friends, and others have. It is healthy to care and to do your best, and equally healthy to not stress about someone else's choices. The Tao Te Ching says it simply: "Do your work, then step back, the only path to peace."

Once you stop stressing about what you don't control, you can focus on what you do control. If you made the two columns, you probably came to the same conclusions as many others: What you control is all about YOU. These are the areas where you exert freedom of choice, such as your own motives, words, and actions, so the associated stress is slight and of brief.

Because the list of things you control is so short and brings your focus directly back to your own attitudes and actions, you will quickly learn to apply this technique. Do the analysis once or twice on paper; then just begin noticing negative or stressed feelings. When anxiety, frustration, worry, etc. are dominating, ask yourself, *"What am I focusing on right now?"* It will usually be something that you do not control, because that always generates a feeling of frustration or angst. Then shift your attention to something more useful and settling, something that is strictly yours to do. It might involve the situation of concern or another area of interest where you can actually do something constructive. This shift in attention serves to decrease your sense of stress and lead to more clarity about the next thing you could do for greatest benefit.

A SINGLE GUIDING PRINCIPLE TO UNDERSTAND YOUR NEEDS AND BECOME YOUR BEST

I want to leave you with one overarching principle that explains all of this research about lawyers. It is clear that our happiness is all about personal relationships of different kinds—our relationship to ourselves, to others, and to our work. In order to thrive, we lawyers need a pervasive sense of connectedness that encompasses all of the important areas of our lives. If you briefly reflect on these key relationships with regularity and continue to take modest steps to nurture your connectedness with your self, others, and work, you will feel, do, and be your best. Whatever your other successes, stay tuned to this sense of connectedness. When you notice some possible lapse in integrity, intimacy with others, or meaning and enjoyment at work, deal with it honestly and directly, in practical ways. Remaining aware of these most important realities in your life will minimize pain and maximize gain on the levels that matter most to lawyers.

As you proceed through this book, I know you will find many more ideas and areas of knowledge to further your effort to be the very best you can be. All best wishes to you!

APPENDIX: ADDITIONAL WELL-BEING FACTORS

Figure 1.2 sets forth many additional well-being factors and their quantified benefit for lawyer happiness. The factors are listed in decreasing order and in tiers based on their importance. Note that the external "success" factors discussed in this chapter (and shown with light lines in Figure 1.1, the bar chart) appear in Tier 4, while the human relational factors that you have reflected on (shown with dark lines in Figure 1.1) appear here in Tiers 1 and 2. New categories of factors are also included: personal and life choices in Tier 3 and demographics in Tier 5. If you would like to consult the entire study, you can download it at SSRN.com (search: L. Krieger, *What Makes Lawyers Happy?*). Please feel free to contact me with any thoughts or questions (lkrieger@law.fsu.edu).

FIGURE 1.2 *Well-Being Factors and Correlations*

		SWB
Tier 1	Autonomy	.66
	Relatedness	.65
	Competence	.63
	Internal Motivation	.55
Tier 2	Autonomous Support	.44
	Intrinsic Values	.30
Tier 3	Vacation Days	.23
	Children	.20
	Married	.18
	Exercise	.18
	Alcohol Use	−.12
	Prayer (Religious Affiliation)	.07
Tier 4	Income	.19
	School Debt	.19
	Class Rank	.12
	School Rank	.05
	Law Journal	.00
	Made Partner	.00
	Billable Hours	−.10
Tier 5	Age	.17
	Other Demographic	.00–.03

CHAPTER 2

Lawyering as a Spiritual Path

The Importance of Balance and Reflection

Elizabeth Bader

Editor's Note: This book would not be complete without Elizabeth's Yoda/Buddha voice. I have personally experienced her joyous wisdom over many years and am honored to call her a friend. We met in the early 1990s as part of California's "holistic" law exploration. Her chapter reminds me of a story from a psychologist friend, Jacob Herring, who did extensive work with lawyers and law firms. Jacob said that many lawyers had reflective practices of some kind but never shared that they did because they feared being labeled "weak." The opposite is true. It takes strength and discipline to cultivate a useful reflective practice. Elizabeth explains that because law practice inevitably raises profound questions about our values and who we are, it is essentially a spiritual path, one that requires the development of the capacity for balance and reflection.

Lawyers routinely deal with human greed, ego, and selfishness, including, perhaps most importantly, their own. To deal with this, we need a life that includes both balance and reflection. Balance helps maintain a positive connection to life and to others. Meditation and reflective inquiry help us stay in touch with our sense of truth and who we really are. Rethinking our relationship to ambition is also necessary so we can find the role within the legal profession that is best suited to who we are. These and other points are discussed in this chapter.

Elizabeth Bader's career as a lawyer, mediator, and conflict resolution coach spans 30 years. She has also been a committed reflective practitioner for 40 years. Elizabeth has developed a unique approach to mediation based on her insight that "ego" or "face" issues are often the key psychological issues that create conflict and impede settlement. Her award-winning publications, which integrate law, psychology, neurobiology, and spirituality, have won her high praise within the legal and psychology professions, both here and abroad. Prior to becoming a mediator, Elizabeth was an appellate litigator who successfully argued cases before the California Supreme Court and the Ninth Circuit. To connect with Elizabeth and to learn more about her practice, please go to her website (http://www.elizabethbader.com/).

Many years ago, I represented a man with multiple sclerosis in a disability-related case against a public entity. Even with his faltering voice and body, this man emanated dignity, strength, and kindness. When I lost his case, I laid my head down on my desk and cried.

In a classic example of overconfidence,[1] I had not anticipated the loss. My tears were the result of having my hopes for him—and, implicitly, myself—shattered.

In retrospect, I see this case as an early inkling that in the course of my career, I would confront human suffering, evil, and many other difficult facets of life. It would sometimes be quite painful.

In this chapter, I share some of my thoughts on this challenge and how to deal with it.

WORKING WITH HUMAN NATURE: A LAWYER'S DIFFICULT TASK

It is well known that many lawyers are unhappy. Many drink. Many kill themselves.[2]

It is certainly true that each individual's psychological problems contribute to these tragic statistics. However, the crisis in the profession also arises out of a spiritual problem—one that relates directly to what we do as lawyers.

By "spiritual problem" I mean (1) a fundamental human dilemma, (2) that cannot be resolved solely by psychological means (3) but may be worked through or transcended through spiritual or reflective practices, perhaps in conjunction with psychological strategies.

THE CRISIS IN THE PROFESSION AS A SPIRITUAL CRISIS

Just as some in the medical profession have begun to question why their profession has historically avoided questions related to physicians' encounters with death,[3] *it is time for the legal profession to recognize that lawyering calls into question our relationship to suffering, to each other, to life.*

Like physicians who must deal with illness and death every day, lawyers routinely deal with human greed, ego, and selfishness. Then, there is our own selfishness and our own egotism—perhaps the most painful parts of this dilemma. When a lawyer continually strives to "win" while others lose, human goodness and human connectedness can fade into oblivion. A person may gain the world but lose his soul.

---

1. I have spoken and written extensively on overconfidence, and other issues of "face," self-esteem and self-identity in conflict resolution. For example, *see* "The Psychology of Mediation: Issues of Self and Identity and the IDR Cycle," 10(2) Pepperdine Dispute Resolution Law Journal 183 (2010), and "The Psychology and Neurobiology of Mediation," 17(2) Cardozo Journal of Conflict Resolution 363 (2016). For a full list of publications, see http://www.elizabethbader.com/publications-list/.

2. *See* Rosa Flores & Rose Marie Arce, *Why are lawyers killing themselves?* CNN (2014), https://www.cnn.com/2014/01/19/us/lawyer-suicides/index.html.

3. *See* Altul Gawande, *What Doctors Don't Learn About Death and Dying*, ideas.ted.com (2015), http://ideas.ted.com/death-and-the-missing-piece-of-medical-school/.

A LIFE OF BALANCE?

The crucial issue becomes, then, how to maintain one's positive and vital connection to life and to others while serving in a role where one must consistently deal with the worst in human nature and, sometimes, in oneself.

As sages throughout the ages have counseled us, the answer is to seek a life where the positive parts of life continually renew and refresh us. *Balance* is not only necessary for mental health, as many have argued, but also for a life that honestly confronts but is not destroyed by spiritual challenges.

STUCK ON "ON"?

Unfortunately, balance is impossible unless we re-evaluate some of the goals and values widely shared by those in the profession. This is because there is actually a physiological limit to our capacity to shift on demand into relaxation when our real goal is to "win," to be "the best," or to "succeed."

Lawyering and competition arouse the sympathetic nervous system, the part of the nervous system that governs fight and flight and self-protective responses. If the nervous system is stimulated continually over a long period of time, we become more or less permanently stuck in a state of arousal and stress. We become "stuck on ON," as some experts have put it.

Stated in spiritual terms, the notion that with more and more effort, we will become the "best" or the "winner" in life's contests is an illusion. If we become "stuck on ON," it is difficult to engage in balanced, strategic thinking and action— the only kind that is truly effective. More importantly, it also leads to a life of unhappiness.

THE IMPORTANCE OF SPIRITUAL AND REFLECTIVE PRACTICES

The inner strength to remain balanced in the midst of conflict requires the inner power to act according to our sense of truth regardless of external pressures.

This inner power is what the ancient Chinese called *te,* a word which means both virtue and power. Our *te* will not be there when we need it unless we have cultivated it advance. For this, an ongoing, committed, reflective, and spiritual practice is necessary.

MEDITATION

The sublime practice of meditation can bring balance by focusing us on the present moment in a compassionate, nonjudgmental way. It also brings balance by soothing nervous system arousal. However, there are some caveats.

First, for some people, especially those who have experienced trauma, meditation may result in serious impairment or even breakdown. The work of Willoughby Britton at Brown University is beginning to bring this problem to light with regard to mindfulness meditation.[4] This issue has also been recognized by some leaders in the meditation and mindfulness community.

Also, in our secular society, there is a tendency to divorce mindfulness meditation from its roots as a spiritual practice. It then becomes McMindfulness, merely a therapeutic self-help technique. Self-help techniques may, of course, be useful. But if we use them to avoid deeper issues, in the long run they are counterproductive.

When one returns mindfulness and other types of meditation to their ancient, deeper roots, one comes again to the importance of being present, but also the importance of knowing oneself and acting with integrity in the midst of life.

REFLECTIVE INQUIRY

A very useful practice that can be done while we are functioning in the world is what I call *reflective inquiry*. In this practice, we engage in an open-minded inquiry into what is happening in the present moment without judgment. This is a form of meditation within the midst of life.

Example: A defendant in a high-stakes, multi-party case I was mediating became furious with me after receiving the opening offer. He blamed me for what he saw as defects in the offer.

Remaining calm externally, I asked myself: *What is happening here?*

The answer came in a flash. His anger was not about the offer, it was about *him*. He was concerned about a potential loss of face in front of the other defendants.

Acting on this insight, I took him through the nuts and bolts of the offer while showing him great respect in front of all. It turned out the offer was acceptable to him after all. We moved on.

For me, this moment was life-changing. It showed me the power of issues of ego, self-esteem, and self-identity in mediation, which formed the basis for my later work in mediation and elsewhere. It changed how I related to other people in my life as well.

RETHINKING AMBITION

> Do not be a corpse of fame.
>
> —Chuang-Tzu[5]

While reflective inquiry is a moment-by-moment practice, it is also important to examine, on a larger scale, why we want to achieve what we set out to achieve and what price we are willing to pay—or to exact from others. In other words, we need to think critically about our own ambitions.

---

4. On Willoughby Britton's work, Tomas Rocha, *The Dark Knight of the Soul*, THE ATLANTIC (2014), http://www.theatlantic.com/health/archive/2014/06/the-dark-knight-of-the-souls/372766/.

5. *See* the translation in Robert Santee, *The Zhuangzi, A Holistic Approach to Healthcare and Well Being*, in LIVIA KOHN, LIVING AUTHENTICALLY: DAOIST CONTRIBUTIONS TO MODERN PSYCHOLOGY (2011).

Here, it is important to modestly but objectively assess our own strengths and vulnerabilities. One way to do this is to use one's law practice as a mirror. We can ask ourselves: "Which parts of my law practice do I honestly enjoy, or at least find meaningful and fulfilling and worth the expenditure of my time and effort?" A corollary inquiry would be: "Which parts of my practice do I find most stressful and difficult?"

It is important to suspend self-judgment during this inquiry. Getting wrapped up in who we think we "should" be will make it more difficult to be objective.

One important indicator is our sleep patterns. For example, *insomnia* suggests that one's system is too delicate or too stressed to recuperate from each day's practice of law. It is important to heed, not override, the warning and perhaps make changes to how one practices law.

When change is necessary, often we must endure a significant period of what William Bridges calls a "neutral zone" — a period when we do not know what to do to come to our "new beginning." If we are able to tolerate this "not knowing," ultimately, we may end up in a place that is closer to our hearts. Meditation and reflective inquiry are key practices that help us to develop the capacity to tolerate this kind of ambiguity.

COMMUNITY AND CONNECTION

Legal skills, while important, are rarely if ever enough to get us through the difficult challenges associated with practicing law. In large part, it is our relationships with others that see us through and make it worthwhile.

On a functional level, sympathetic nervous system arousal can be modulated by the part of the nervous system that is engaged when we relate to others in a socially positive manner. In other words, connecting with others has a powerful balancing effect.

Staying connected and valuing one's personal relationships is thus a key to balance. Finding a community that is nourishing can also help counteract the sense of isolation we may feel as lawyers engaged in lives of competition.

However, here as elsewhere, it is important to engage in a balanced way. For example, it is important to avoid excessive idealism about any group, no matter how welcoming it appears to be. Otherwise, we simply fall into another form of overconfident, unrealistic, even "cult-like" thinking.

CONCLUSION

When I broke the news to my client that we had lost his case, he was gracious.

Here was another lesson. I had imagined myself doing something for *him*. Yet it was he who bestowed the final gift on me.

In later years, as I have gone through ups and downs in my practice as a lawyer, mediator, and conflict coach, it has always been my commitment to reflective practice that has seen me through difficulties and allowed me to be of most service to others.

Unfortunately, when I started out on the path of lawyering, there was little to no recognition of the spiritual or existential difficulties inherent in the practice of law or of the importance of self-reflection. As a result, I had to learn many lessons through the time-consuming process of trial and error.

Now it is time for lawyers and the legal profession to recognize the need to address these issues early on in lawyers' careers as part of our ongoing dialogue about lawyer wellness and effectiveness.

CHAPTER 3
Mindful Lawyering

Professor Nathalie Martin

Editor's Note: I have never met Nathalie. She was the co-author of *Yoga for Lawyers* (ABA, 2014). When the first named author did not respond, I tracked her down. I'm glad I did. She does a wonderful job of taking what many traditional lawyers might think of as "woo-woo" and brings the ideas and practices down to earth. Her work in a major law school adds credibility to this growing movement. In terms of adopting new practices, as law is to business (a few years behind), law schools are to law practice. In this chapter, she digs into a variety of practical actions you can easily and quickly implement in your busy life.

We can all be more thoughtful about how we live our lives, which are filled with endless distractions. These distractions can leave us frazzled, with little time to contemplate what is most important to us in life. Mindfulness practices help us decrease stress, improve focus, and gain insight into the true meaning of our lives. These practices range from formal daily meditation to small but powerful informal mindfulness practices that we can use throughout our day. This chapter introduces the reader to a few of these practices and the reasons to consider adding these practices to an already busy life.

Nathalie Martin is the Frederick M. Hart Chair in Consumer and Clinical Law at University of New Mexico School of Law, where she teaches commercial and consumer law, as well as mindfulness and professional development. As a long time yoga practitioner, yoga teacher, and meditator, Nathalie is part of a growing movement to teach mindfulness and emotional intelligence in the law school classroom. This movement makes explicit that the interpersonal side of lawyering is critical and that many lawyers need help finding purpose or meaning in their work. Nathalie is the author of *Lawyering from the Inside Out: Learning Professional Development through Mindfulness and Emotional Intelligence* (Cambridge University Press) and *Yoga for Lawyers: Mind-Body Techniques to Feel Better All the Time* (ABA, with Hallie Love).

> To attain knowledge, add things every day,
> To attain wisdom, remove things every day.
>
> —Tao Te Ching

Author Paul Wilson claims that we need cultivate just *one* skill in order to be mindful: the skill of thinking about just one thing at a time.[1] This one skill is a gold mine for lawyers because the ability to focus on one thing at a time fosters intense brain power and creativity. Additionally, if the one thing you are focusing on is a person—for example, a client—learning mindfulness can give you an edge in the field of law.

Mindfulness techniques have been used over thousands of years to bring about a sense of peace. This sense of peace can lead to periods of intense and deep concentration, enhanced productivity, a heightened ability to think through complex problems, and, of course, a calm, peaceful state of mind. Although two of the concepts just mentioned, deep intense thought, on the one hand, and a calm state of mind, on the other, may seem at odds, they are not. Rather, when we are stressed, stress hormones interfere with concentration by flooding the brain with cortisol and making it impossible to "think straight."[2] For this reason, mindfulness techniques can enhance one's ability to "think like a lawyer"—a mindful, clear-thinking lawyer, that is.

In March 2017, *Time* published a special edition of its magazine entitled "Mindfulness: The New Science of Health and Happiness." In that edition, *Time* claims that if we even get a little bit better at being mindful, we can benefit in crucial ways. *Time* is not the only news source talking about mindfulness. Chatter about mindfulness is everywhere. Sources like the *Wall Street Journal*, the *New York Times*, the *Huffington Post* and others feature regular stories about mindfulness. Touted as something new that can change your life, mindfulness has been around for centuries. As one source recently noted, "Mindfulness is not just for type-A CEOs, traders, and venture capitalists looking for fast-track success. It is a rich practice that can be as simple or as complex as you want it to be—a tactic for being productive at work, acting more present in your relationships, or moving closer toward [meaningful] relationships."[3]

Regardless of whether you previously associated mindfulness with fast-track career progress or something completely different, this chapter explains what mindfulness is and how it can help you. It also describes a few simple ways to get started with a mindfulness practice. Mindfulness includes seated meditation, as well as other less formal mindfulness practices, but all mindfulness practices aim to help you live in the present moment and focus on just one thing at a time. Living in the present and being able to focus on one thing at a time makes most of us happier, healthier, and more productive.

Jon Kabat-Zinn, the father of the modern mindfulness movement, founded the Stress Reduction Clinic at the University of Massachusetts Medical School in the late 1970s. Since that time, Kabat-Zinn has trained over 18,000 people in his Mindfulness Based Stress Reduction (MBSR) program. The MBSR program is designed to assist with chronic pain, heart disease, anxiety, psoriasis, sleep problems, and depression.

---

1. Paul Wilson, THE CALM TECHNIQUE 25 (1987).

2. C. Kirschbaum, O.T. Wolf, M. May, W. Wippich, and D.H. Hellhammer, *Stress and Treatment Induced Elevations and Cortisol Levels Associated with Declarative Memory in Healthy Adults*, 58 LIFE SCIENCES 1475 (1996).

3. *The Mindfulness Meditation Guide*, YOGA JOURNAL, http://www.yogajournal.com/article /meditation/mindfulness-meditation-guide/.

Mindfulness helps with physical problems and with severe recurring pain, but can also help everyone find intense focus and answers to some of life's deeper questions.

DEFINING MINDFULNESS

British meditation teacher and author Paul Wilson similarly describes meditation, the main portal to mindfulness, as "just being."[4] Wilson adds:

> When you learn how to live only in the moment, when there is nothing to distract you, when you are not tied to the past or anxious about the future, when your mind and your emotions are your servants rather than your master, your consciousness (your awareness) is in the most perfect state possible. This state is simply 'being.' Meditation is about *being* not *doing*.[5]

Again, mindfulness is present awareness of one's thoughts as they arise and minute-to-minute awareness of one's existence. As Kabat-Zinn further explains, life is full of moments, not just years and decades.[6] He asks if we can stop and be present, even for one moment, and goes on to say:

> A good way to stop all the doing is to shift into the "being mode" for a moment. Think of yourself as an eternal witness, as timeless. Just watch this moment, without trying to change it at all. What is happening? What do you feel? What do you see? What do you hear?[7]

THE SCIENCE OF STRESS

Mindfulness can help us focus, but it is best known for its capacity to reduce stress. Some stress can be motivating, but most lawyers have much more stress in their lives than they need. In prehistoric days it was necessary to be able to run from saber-toothed cats and other dangers. Life depended on being able to run from danger and engage all possible strength and power to do so. This physiological condition is known as "flight, fight, or freeze."

In the modern world, we enter the flight, fight, or freeze condition in response to both large dangers, like the saber-toothed cat of caveman days, and also smaller stressors that are not life or death. As a result, we stay more or less in constant flight or fight mode, which damages our bodies and makes it hard to think clearly.

This constant stress causes minor health risks, such as sleeplessness, weight gain, and reduction in overall health. It weakens the immune system so that other health threats are exacerbated, and can then lead to major health problems, such as heart attacks, cancer, and disabling accidents.

We also put on weight when under too much stress. The body produces more insulin, which increases appetite, decreases will power, increases fat stores, and increases the fat and inflammatory chemicals pumped into the liver. This creates a resistance to insulin, which makes the pancreas create more insulin, which in turn increases appetite even more. Talk about a harmful feedback loop.

---

4. Wilson, *supra* note 1, at 13.
5. *Id.*
6. Jon Kabat-Zinn, FULL CATASTROPHE LIVING 26 (1990).
7. Jon Kabat-Zinn, WHEREVER YOU GO, THERE YOU ARE 11 (2005).

The biggest occupational hazard of stress, however, is decreased brain function. The hormones released into the brain while we are stressed out affect memory and the ability to think and write clearly and speak articulately. You've no doubt noticed this phenomenon in your own life. You are prepared for a meeting or hearing, but stress makes you forget what you are doing. You choke in front of a judge because of something your opponent says. Stress makes us dumber and also ages our brains.

THE SCIENCE OF MINDFULNESS

Mindful practices like yoga, meditation, tai chi, and chi gong enhance mental and physical well-being, overall happiness, and cognitive abilities. Regarding meditation specifically, Eileen Luders at UCLA's Lab of Neuro Imaging has found that meditation increases gray matter in the brain, creates stronger connections between brain regions, and reduces age-related brain thinning.[8] In 2012, she reported finding mindfulness meditation to be associated with larger amounts of gyrification, the process of creating folds in the cortex. Gyrification is thought to allow the brain to process information faster, which is particularly relevant to the work we do as lawyers.[9] Mindfulness can rewire neurological pathways to create long-term benefits in health and wellness. This rewiring can improve physical as well as emotional health.[10] It also can foster emotional intelligence, allowing one to react to difficult situations in ways that enhance one's own well-being and the well-being of others. Above all, as one recent study of GRE scores shows, mindfulness techniques improve thinking and focus.[11]

PUTTING MEDITATION AND YOGA IN THE BROADER CONTEXT OF MINDFULNESS

Seated meditation is the granddaddy of all mindfulness practices but by no means the only mindful practice. The concept of mindfulness is much broader than meditation, as the tree of contemplative practices shows in Figure 3.1.[12]

You might wonder how the benefits of yoga and meditation compare. Both practices bring value to the practice of law, and yoga is a form of moving meditation. Yoga is easy on the brain and easy to practice mentally. Yoga helps make the mind feel at ease without giving the mind's usual chatter much thought. Yoga's benefits

---

8. Scott Rogers and Jan Jacobowitz, MINDFULNESS AND PROFESSIONAL RESPONSIBILITY 27 (2012).

9. *Id.*

10. *Id.*

11. Michael D. Mrazek, Michael S. Franklin, Dawa Tarchin Phillips, Benjamin Baird, and Jonathan W. Schooler, *Mindfulness Training Improves Working Memory Capacity and GRE Performance while Reducing Mind Wandering*, 24(5) PSYCHOLOGICAL SCIENCE 776–781 (2013), available at http://pss.sagepub.com/content/24/5/776. This study found that mindfulness training improved both GRE reading comprehension scores and working memory capacity while simultaneously reducing the occurrence of distracting thoughts during completion of the GRE and the measure of working memory. *Id.* These results suggest that cultivating mindfulness is an effective and efficient technique for improving cognitive function, with wide-reaching consequences.

12. Tree of Contemplative Practices, used with permission from CMIND, THE CENTER FOR CONTEMPLATIVE MIND IN SOCIETY, available at http://www.contemplativemind.org/practices/tree.

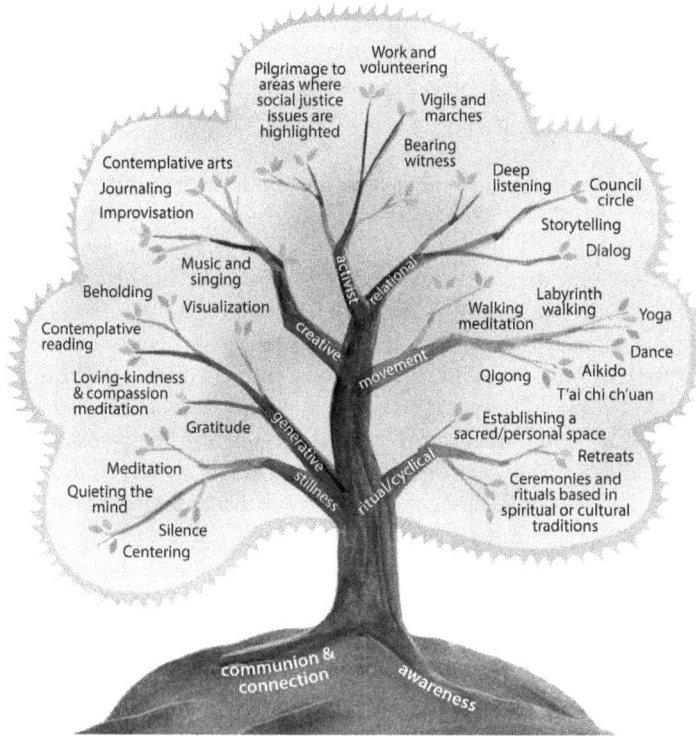

FIGURE 3.1 *The Tree of Contemplative Practices*
(Copyright © Center for Contemplative Mind in Society, used with permission; image found at www.contemplativemind.org/tree.)

make a small but lasting impact on life. Yoga practice is easy to sustain because it feels good in the body. The mind comes along for the ride.

While meditation is beneficial, a regular meditation practice can be harder to sustain than a moving yoga practice. Because lawyers often live from the head up and have incredibly active minds, it does not come easily to most of us to sit and seemingly do nothing. Often we are not sure meditation is doing anything.

You've heard the phrase, "Don't just sit there, go do something." In meditation, we purposely do not get up to go do something. We just sit there. We initially meditate because the benefits of seated meditation have been scientifically proven in endless settings and contexts. We continue doing it because we begin to feel the subtle shifts in our lives.

Dean Emeritus and Professor Charles Halpern, a former Arnold & Porter attorney, notes in his book *Making Waves and Riding the Currents* the first time he ever experienced meditative moments. It was in a canoe on the lakes of northern Ontario. These experiences later led him to a more formal meditation practice, which he claims altered his life and law practice in measurable, positive ways. As he explains:

> I found that in the midst of turmoil I was able to respond to strong pressure with less anger and reactivity. I was able to see things more clearly. I was able to empathize with a broad range of people and identify the things we shared.[13]

_____
13. Charles Halpern, MAKING WAVES AND RIDING THE CURRENTS 5 (2008).

Each of us can return to points in our lives when we had an awakening—an insight that suggested that the world was larger than what we had thought it was. These incidents don't show up on our résumés and we rarely discuss them at work but they permanently change our lives for the better. Meditation facilitates these changes.

I do a brief seated meditation most days and believe the practice benefits anyone who keeps it up. I find that it changes the quality of my day, and I really miss it when it doesn't get done. While more is better, a little medittion goes a long way. In one study, lawyers who meditated every day for 21 days for just six minutes a day (or .1 on a time sheet) reported significant benefits, including the expected calmness and improvements in coping and also the ability to get more work done in less time.

In my experience, many meditating lawyers find meditation through yoga. The benefits of meditation can outweigh those of yoga poses alone, however, so it is worth establishing a formal meditation practice to see if it helps you. Before describing how to do that, the next sections describe some lighter mindfulness techniques. These are like yoga—easier to sustain and with subtler benefits than a formal seated meditation practice. Everything adds up, however. Remember that life is a marathon, not a sprint. Explore some of these options and see what they do for you. Start small.

PRACTICING EASY MINDFULNESS

Mindfulness is a broad umbrella. It includes anything that allows you to put your thoughts on pause, clear the mind, and focus on one thing at a time. We can practice mindfulness while walking, waiting on the phone, waiting in line at the supermarket, driving, walking or running in nature, birdwatching, or just pausing for a moment anywhere. We can chant mantras, journal, or just focus on the breath.

Early Buddhists meditated to calm the mind and to discover the meaning of life, which they accomplished by focusing on the breath. The breath is pretty amazing and is always with us, as Scott Rogers, director of the Mindfulness Program and the University of Miami School of Law, explains.[14] Watching and counting the breath is my own go-to mindfulness practice. Like Rogers, I watch and count my breath throughout my day. I describe a few simple mindfulness practices below. Give each one a try and see how you feel.

1. Basic Breath Mindfulness Practice

To start your mindfulness practice, try this simple breath exercise: Breathe deeply and note how you feel. Focus on the breath, and as thoughts arise (and they will), acknowledge them and let them go, bringing your attention back to your breath. Remember that the brain can only focus on one thing at a time, so rather than trying to eliminate a thought, worry, or trouble, focus instead on your breath, thus giving your mind something simple to do.

Do this focused breathing practice throughout your day from time to time and also try this technique for a set period of time, in a seated meditation. I like to do my seated meditation when I first wake up. I also pause throughout my day and focus

---

14. *Mindfulness in Law Program*, Miami Law, http://www.law.miami.edu/academics/mindfulness-in-law-program.

on my breath for a moment or two. This is no big complex "practice," just a few minutes in the morning and a pause here and there. If you don't meditate already, this is really all you need to know to get started. You can add minutes as you get more comfortable, building up time like you would with physical exercise.

2. Five-Count Breathing or Square Breathing

Sit up straight in a quiet place, any place. It can be a park bench, a classroom chair, or a car. Put your phone on "do not disturb," set your timer for six minutes, and calm down. Let out all the breath. Let any thoughts or worries go right out with that preparatory breath. Inhale deeply and, when you exhale, count in your head, "one." Keep breathing and count each exhalation until you reach five. (There is no magic in five breaths, but we often hold yoga poses for five breaths, so this number of breaths may be familiar to you.)

Once you reach five, start over, counting each exhalation again. Keep going for six minutes. Stay focused on your breath. If another thought arises (which it probably will even though you are counting), acknowledge that thought and let it go. Bring your attention back to your own breath.

A little later in your day, try the five-count technique again. Try it when you are standing around or waiting in line. Just count to five on the exhalation here and there. Keep breathing slowly and you'll feel great.

Tomorrow, try to practice this breathing for another six minutes. Notice subtle changes in your thought processes as you dabble a bit here and there. Just get out of your own way and let things be. Through this light practice, you are attempting to replace some of your usual ruminating with this five-count breathing to slow down those thoughts. We have between 12,000 and 60,000 thoughts a day, and 80% of those are negative.[15] If you watch your thoughts, you may discover that the vast majority of your down-time thinking consists of a negative feedback loop in which your thoughts focus on the past (often regrets) and the future (often worry) rather than the present. In my experience, it takes far less time to pause and enjoy a mindful moment than that we spend continuing with our rapidly looping negative thoughts.

While it is certainly our job as lawyers to watch out for what could go wrong for our clients, when we beat ourselves up about our failures and worry about personal future catastrophes that may not even happen, we sell ourselves short. See if this breathing can help you beat yourself up less.

3. Variation on Lion's Breath Yoga Pose

Take and count ten long deep breaths in and out, and really sigh each one out on the exhale. Make it loud and fun. Count them and keep your focus on these breaths. As other thoughts arise, acknowledge them and let them go, bringing your attention back to your breath. How do you feel? Is anything stopping you from doing this three, four, five times a day?

---

15. William Ury, GETTING TO YES WITH YOURSELF 27 (2016).

4. Deep Belly Breathing

Deep belly breathing improves every function in the body. It also calms the mind. To try it, lie down or sit up tall, and put your hands on your belly. Focus on your belly. Breathe as deeply as you can into that belly and then exhale.

You can even imagine that you are breathing in love and beauty, and breathing out anything that you no longer need. For the left-brained, skeptical, or science-inclined readers, recognize that deep belly breathing is also a wonderful way to activate our parasympathetic nervous system.

Next, see if you can pause and practice this deep belly breathing throughout your day. Next, do it when you are nervous. Finally, try it when you are angry—before you say or do anything.

5. Other Light Mindful Practices

Google has a mindfulness program for employees, and one of their teachers is Mirabai Bush, no doubt named after the poet saint Mirabai from seventeenth century India. According to Bush, we can practice mindfulness at work in many small ways that add up a great deal.[16] You can try these simple pause techniques throughout your day. In addition to your formal seated meditation, try to pause throughout your day every time one of these happens:

The phone rings (which can lightheartedly be called the bell of awareness)
You touch a doorknob
You ride an elevator
You take the stairs
You use the restroom
You wait in line

Each time you take your chosen pause, note your breath and let it help you stay present in the moment, in a nonjudgmental way.

MAJOR MINDFULNESS: FORMAL MEDITATION PRACTICE

Formal meditation practice is technically no different than the short and simple techniques described above. It is just longer, and usually occurs at a designated time and place. Although the formal practice is not technically different from mini-mindfulness, the results are more dramatic. It reminds me of the saying attributed to the Buddha, "If you want to find water, do not dig six one-foot wells; dig one six-foot well instead." So it is with formal meditation practice. A little is wonderful, and more is better.

If you start a formal practice, being in a designated place puts you into your meditation frame of mind. So to get started, find a regular place to practice or "sit." You can sit in a chair or on the ground. If seated on the ground, elevate the hips three to six inches on blankets or pillows. When you sit down, release the weight of your hips and legs fully into the pillows or chair. Be comfortable but aware.

---

16. Mirabai Bush, Working with Mindfulness CD, available at Key Step Media, https://www.keystepmedia.com/shop/working-with-mindfulness-audio-exercises/#.Wh7UCoWcFn0

Choose a certain time of day, and choose to sit for certain amount of time. If you miss it for some reason, try to do it later in the day, thinking of your practice as a gift to yourself and something to look forward to. While a longer "sit" goes further, see how it feels to sit. In the beginning, few people can sit for more than a few minutes at a time. You can work up to more if you like it. Set a timer and, while there, either:

Focus on your breath, counting your breath as described above;
Focus on a piece of nature out a window;
Focus on an object, such as a bracelet, or your own heart; or
Repeat a mantra, something that speaks to you.

Meditation on an Object

Many people set their timer and sit in their formal meditation place and then focus on an object that reminds them of peace and beauty. This can be a religious object, a piece of jewelry, or anything else you like. You can also focus on a flame from a candle, or try this wonderful Flame of the Heart meditation adapted from Tias Little's *Yoga of the Subtle Body*:

Sit comfortably in your special spot. Lift the sides of your trunk and spread the heart space wide. Imagine the chest and heart getting wider and wider. Close your eyes and visualize a flame inside the middle cave of your heart. Notice the rhythm of your breath and imagine the heart flame burning steadily. As thoughts distract you, the flame will start to get dimmer, and it may even seem that it has gone out. If it does, light it back up, and keep focusing on that flame. Watch as the flame gets brighter with your concentration, and dimmer as you get distracted. Stay here for your set amount of time, watching the flame. Imagine the steady flame and the radiance and glow of that beautiful flame as you keep your attention on it. Sense the joy that comes from that steady, undisturbed flame.[17]

Mantra Practice

My favorite type of formal meditation practice is mantra practice, which I practice daily, sometimes during my sit, but always throughout my day. I have been somewhat afraid to suggest mantra practice in my work with lawyers because it seems too odd or new age for some.

I am emboldened, however, by Jeena Cho and Karen Gifford's excellent book *The Anxious Lawyer*. Their book contains an eight-week meditation program in which a new technique is introduced and practiced each week. The results are recorded in a journal. The weeks start with a body scan, then move on each week to following your breath; following your thoughts; a *metta* or loving-kindness meditation; a forgiveness meditation; a self-compassion meditation; and, in weeks six, seven, and eight, a mantra practice combined with some of the other practices.

To start a mantra practice, you first choose a mantra. You have many options, including an English mantra, a chakra seed sound mantra, or a classical Sanskrit mantra. I have tried them all and it is a matter of personal preference. In some ways, it doesn't matter what you choose. The mantra just gives the busy mind something to do.

---

17. Tias Little, Yoga of the Subtle Body: A Guide to the Physical and Energetic Anatomy of the Body 193 (2016).

Mantra practice is simple once you have chosen a mantra. You learn the mantra and repeat the mantra for either a set period of time or for 108 repetitions per day. Many religious traditions ask that rituals be performed a certain number of times, and in the Indian Vedic tradition, which I studied in yoga school, the number 108 has mystical and religious significance. The number 108 is two times around the Catholic rosary, which has 54 beads. It is six times the number 18, which has special significance in Judaism. You can do your mantra for more than 108 times, and even after your formal "sit," throughout your day. Once I have sat for at least ten minutes, I don't worry about the number. I know that I have done more than 108 repetitions.

According to Paul Wilson in *The Calm Technique*, it is simplest to choose a mantra and stick with it forever.[18] On the other hand, don't pressure yourself. You might need to experiment a bit. Don't stress; just have fun. Remain light and calm as you repeat the mantra. Don't grip the mantra; just repeat it playfully.[19] Mantra practice is fun because it is easy. You don't need to try to think, to not think, or to do anything else. You just repeat the mantra. I was taught to repeat my mantra out loud; both Cho and Gifford, as well as Wilson, suggest you repeat it silently. It is up to you and you can mix and match. Just do the mantra.

Cho and Gifford claim that mantra practice is especially good for improving concentration. They also claim that mantra practice connects us to inner joy. Perhaps that is why I love it. One of my highest goals is joy. Interestingly, Cho and Gifford say joy is hard for most lawyers to access.

Choosing a Mantra

1. English Mantras

It is probably easiest to start with an English mantra, one that addresses an issue of importance to you or one that you work toward in your life. My yoga teacher, Kali Om, works hard and needs to remind herself to relax, so she uses "relax and enjoy." I struggle to focus on the positive, so I often use "I am surrounded by love and beauty." Lawyer and yoga teacher Bonnie Bassan works with self-acceptance, in both others and herself, so she likes, "I have enough, I do enough, I am enough." My husband Stewart is working on physical health and strength, so his mantra is "Every day is a step, will it be backward or forward?" Interestingly, when Stewart started working with his mantra, he had never even heard of a mantra or a mantra practice. It was just an affirmation that kept him going. You too may already be unknowingly engaging in a mantra practice.

English mantras can also be more generic. For example, Cho and Gifford suggest the English mantra "let go" and Paul Wilson likes "calm."

While English mantras are easy, no muss, no fuss, with nothing to memorize, you might enjoy a seed sound or Sanskrit mantra simply because these ancient mantras have been in use in meditation for so long.

2. Seed Sound Chakra Mantras

There are many chakra model variations, but the one most well known in the west has seven major energy centers or *chakras* (pronounced just as it looks, not with a "sh" sound) running roughly from the base of the spine to the top of the head. The

---

18. Wilson, *supra* note 1, at 54.

19. Jeena Cho and Karen Gifford, THE ANXIOUS LAWYER 167 (2016).

health of each energy center influences our emotions, physical health, and mental clarity. Each is associated with a one-syllable sound, as listed below.

- "LAM"—chakra 1 (root)
- "VAM"—chakra 2 (sacral/navel)
- "RAM"—chakra 3 (solar plexus)
- "YAM"—chakra 4 (heart)
- "HAM"—chakra 5 (throat)
- "OM"—chakra 6 (third eye/brow)
- "OM"—chakra 7 (crown)

You can chant these seed sounds in order, or do a bit of research on which aspect of yourself you might need to build up a bit and just chant that one seed sound. This web site has a video you can chant along with, if you want to hear the whole sequence: *Bija Mantras—The Sounds of the Chakras: LAM VAM RAM YAM HAM OM* http://ar-yoga.com/2011/10/bija-mantras-the-sounds-of-the-chakras-lam-vam-ram -yam-ham-om/.

Repeating the seed sounds can help you reach a deeply meditative state. If you like, you can also focus on the region of the body that each seed sound is associated with as you say the seed sound, but this is not necessary. Again, just have fun!

3. Sanskrit Mantras

For thousands of years, yoga practitioners and devotees have chosen ancient Indian mantras to use in meditation. Sometimes, a mantra is passed on to the yoga student from a guru and used for life. Another approach is to choose a mantra that is associated with a particular power or intention and repeat that mantra 108 times a day for 40 days in order to bring that intention into your life. The principle is that if you focus enough on something, you will get what you want. In mantra practice, we focus by letting go of linear thinking and just chanting.

Many people believe that doing a 40-day mantra practice, also called a chant, can move or shift a current problem or condition. Although many of the Sanskrit mantras call upon the powers of Indian "deities," you are not asking Indian deities to do the moving. Rather, you are using the mantra to harness the energy you need to move the problem or condition yourself. I have found mantra repetitions to be powerful. There are mantras for everything, even finding love. For more information on Sanskrit mantras, take a look at *Healing Mantras*, by Thomas Ashley-Farland.

Why do we chant for 40 days? No one is sure but the number 40 seems to have religious significance. Jesus went into the desert to meditate for 40 days. Moses went in for a little longer, for 40 years, and Noah's big storm lasted 40 days and 40 nights. The 40-day mantra practice has been used by yogis for thousands of years. After a few days of chanting you will notice the absence of noise in your head. Some people claim that they even see better or sharper after the 40-day mantra practice.

A Sampling of Sanskrit Mantras

1. One example of a Sanskrit mantra is the mantra for Ganesh, that elephant-like Indian deity you often see in Indian restaurants. Ganesh is the remover of obstacles, so this mantra is a common 40-day mantra, as well as a common

personal or lifetime mantra. After all, most of us have a few obstacles that could be removed. Here is how it goes:

> Om gam gana pataye namaha

2. For an open heart, and to bring joy, you can try this one, suggested in Cho and Gifford's *The Anxious Lawyer,* which means "open to the jewel of the lotus":

> Om mani padme hum

3. You can use this very simple Sanskrit mantra, also suggested by Cho and Gifford in *The Anxious Lawyer:*

> So hum

So hum means "I am that." This ancient mantra is said to bring about ultimate self-knowledge and growth. If you try it, you'll find it to be both simple and healing, a nice combination. To use this one in a traditional way, say *so* on the inhale and *hum* on the exhale. As you repeat *so,* inhale and imagine a line of energy drawing up the front of the body from the root of the spine to the area between the eyebrows. As you repeat *hum,* exhale and imagine that energy running from the area between the eyebrows down to the back to the tailbone.

DEVELOPING YOUR PRACTICE

In this chapter we have reviewed the science of stress, as well as many of the benefits of mindfulness. We then provided a description of a variety of mindfulness practices, including small practices such as pausing throughout one's day and practicing breathing exercises or mantras during the work day while performing other tasks. We also described variations of formal seated meditation practices, which have been used over the centuries to calm the mind, improve focus and concentration, and bring us closer to our true selves.

While anyone can benefit from *any* mindfulness practice, developing a formal seated meditation is most likely to help you achieve positive changes in your life. We end with simple, step-by-step suggestions for beginning a formal meditation practice:

1. Get in the right frame of mind. Be light. Don't look at this as another obligation, but as a chance to create space in yourself and your life.
2. Gain domain knowledge by briefly practicing one or two of the variations on mindful practice described here—for example, five count breathing, deep belly breathing, or a mantra repetition.
3. Find a place in your home, and perhaps at work as well, where you can practice daily for a set period of time. Try to stay with it for at least a month without deciding if it is doing anything for you. Any habit takes at least 21 to 30 days to develop.
4. Pick an amount of time to start with and add minutes each week. For example, start with six minutes, and add six minutes at the end of each week. By the end of a month, you'll be at 24 minutes.

5. Do the practice. Keep in mind that every day is different and consider those differences part of the practice. Sometimes you'll be bored. Sometimes your mind will wander. Sometimes the "sit" will be easy. You don't have to love it. You don't even have to like it. You just need to do it.
6. Keep a little journal by your side and write down how you feel as you exit your meditation practice.

You are accomplished. You know you can do this if you choose to, and the empirical research behind these practices makes it wise to give it a try. While you are at it, develop your informal practices, like counting and watching your breath throughout your day, when the phone rings, when you touch a doorknob, when you ride an elevator or take the stairs, or when you wait in line. Remember, a little goes a long way.

CONCLUSION

Remember that mindfulness practices vary greatly, as the Tree of Contemplation shown earlier in this chapter indicates. Mindfulness practices include tai chi, chi gong, yoga, chanting, singing, journaling, and many other activities. After reading this chapter, if you want to dive deeper into mindfulness, you can explore taking the eight-week MBSR class Jon Kabat-Zinn has designed. These classes are offered in most geographic areas around the country and will introduce you to a large variety of mindfulness practices. I have taken the course myself, as have many of my friends of all religious and political persuasions. In other words, this course is not for hippies but for regular working people like us.

If you want to learn more about formal meditation, which is one of the cornerstones of mindfulness, take a look at the detailed meditation book by Jeena Cho and Karen Gifford entitled *The Anxious Lawyer*. In this American Bar Association publication, Cho and Gifford do a wonderful job explaining how meditation can help us and also how to do it. If you are interested in mindfulness as it applies to legal education, I strongly recommend *Making Waves and Riding the Currents* by Charles Halpern.

Mindfulness practices have stood the test of time for a reason. While not every practice is for everyone, there are many practices beneficial to anyone who uses them consistently. The only people who cannot benefit from these practices are those who do not practice. I wish you the best of luck finding the right practice for you.

CHAPTER 4
Transform Lawyer Well-Being into a Team Sport

Anne Brafford, Esq., MAPP

Editor's Note: As the Chair of the ABA Law Practice Division Well-Being Committee, Anne had to be committed. Her contribution here is invaluable. Her suggestions are specific "to-dos" that generate happier lawyers, as reflected in Larry Krieger's opening chapter. She provides specific strategies that people leading legal organizations can implement, and they can use those same strategies to "manage their bosses." The fact that happy lawyers are more productive lawyers ought to lessen resistance and motivate changes in leaders' behavior. Furthermore, leadership does not have to come from the top. It can come from anywhere!

Historically, lawyer well-being strategies have focused primarily on how to toughen up lawyers to enable them to withstand the muck storm often brought on by their jobs. These individual strategies are very important. But research shows that it's even more effective to focus on organizational strategies that fix problems that harm lawyer well-being in the first place. Legal organizations play an enormous role in whether lawyers feel engaged or depleted and burned out. In other words, lawyer well-being should be viewed as a team sport. How can organizations get started? Four science-backed strategies are offered here.

Anne Brafford is the Chairperson of the American Bar Association Law Practice Division's Attorney Well-Being Committee, is a member of the National Task Force on Lawyer Well-Being, and is involved in multiple other national and local level attorney well-being initiatives. In 2014, Anne left her job as an equity partner at Morgan, Lewis, & Bockius LLP after 18 years of practice to focus on thriving in the legal profession through Aspire, her educational and consultation firm. She has studied with world-class experts in positive psychology and organizational behavior while earning a Masters of Applied Positive Psychology from the University of Pennsylvania and in her current PhD program in positive organizational psychology at Claremont Graduate University. For more strategies on lawyer well-being and organizational thriving, look for her book *Positive Professionals: Creating High-Performing, Profitable Firms Through the Science of Engagement*, published by the American Bar Association.

Before reading any further, can you do me a favor? I'd like you to pause for a moment and bring to mind two things. First, think about a personal high point as a lawyer—a time when you were at your best, feeling really jazzed, engaged, and proud. Seriously—it'll only take a few moments. Okay, got one in mind? Good. Now think about the surrounding details. What occurred? What personal strengths and skills did you use? Who were the people and what were the surrounding circumstances that contributed to your accomplishment?

Now, turn to the darker side. Just for a second. (I don't want to spoil your good mood.) Think of a low point you've had as a lawyer. Bring to mind a specific example in which you were outraged, disappointed, or disgusted. How did you personally contribute to the situation? How did other people or events contribute to it or to your ability to bounce back? From these experiences, what did you learn that might help you replicate the good or avoid the bad?

When we succeed, it's easy to congratulate ourselves on our awesomeness without fully appreciating all of the people and circumstances that helped us get there. As for the low points, it's often easy to totally blame ourselves for those too. But are the most difficult situations those that we alone have caused or can handle best on our own? Are individual skills, strengths, and resilience enough for us to be our very best and to persevere through rough patches? Or are our surrounding circumstances, resources, and support mechanisms just as important—if not more so? My guess is that, for most of you, high points and low points and how you responded to both were heavily influenced by your circumstances. As poet John Donne famously wrote (and Jon Bon Jovi famously sang in "Santa Fe"), "No man is an island."

When legal professionals talk about ways to enhance "lawyer well-being," they often treat lawyers like islands. They most often propose strategies to toughen up individual lawyers or boost their individual skills. They focus on individual lawyer resilience, stress management strategies, mindfulness meditation, emotional intelligence, psychological capital, physical and mental health, and other individual-focused strategies and programs. These all are very important to lawyer well-being, and I advocate for them too.

But our focus on individual strategies often overlooks an elephant in the room: toxic work cultures. Lawyers would not need to be so tough if they were not regularly pelted by storms of noxious muck in their workplaces and professional institutions. When a TV meteorologist reports the local weather while getting shelled by a wild hail storm, do you think to yourself: "What he needs is a sturdy helmet and a flak jacket so he can hang in there and really take a beating"? Or do you think along with me: "Why are you standing out in that storm, you nut job?" Why would we try to armor him up when it makes much more sense—and will be more effective—to change his circumstances? For people to be their best, a supportive context is essential. Lawyers are most likely to be able to fulfill their potential when their workplace and professional cultures help them thrive. Lawyer well-being should be a team sport.

It's understandable why we focus mostly on individual strategies to promote lawyer well-being. Trying to make people tougher seems easier than changing the entrenched organizational and institutional structures that are causing the problems. Some are so embedded in the system that they've become invisible to us. It's time to throw a spotlight on them. This is so because organizational research consistently has shown that contextual factors play a bigger role in worker well-being than individual traits, skills, and strengths.

What are "contextual factors"? They encompass everything in our social surroundings. They include things like our job characteristics as well as social and organizational aspects of our work, such as how much autonomy we have, our supervisors' leadership styles, support from our colleagues, meaningfulness of our work, opportunities for development, clear feedback, and many others. Specific examples relevant to lawyers include a colleague offering to cover a hearing for you, a supportive leader giving you advice about your development, or a supervising partner entrusting you with significant responsibility for which you feel ready.

Think about it this way: If a goldfish is living in a bowl of polluted water, it doesn't matter how tough and resilient the little guy is. Eventually, he'll float to the top, belly-up, after slowly suffocating in the murk. It's not realistic to focus only on individual-level strengths and skills without also cleaning up the pollution and enriching the environment. Research shows that the best approach to well-being is to incorporate both types of strategies—those that focus on both the individual and the context or organizational surroundings.

There are many things law firms and other legal organizations can do to start detoxing their environments and cultivating a culture where lawyers can thrive. The overall goal is to remove obstacles when possible and to build a structural support system that enables growth and pathways to success. I offer four tips in the following sections on developing contextual strategies to boost lawyer well-being.

1. DEVELOP EFFECTIVE LEADERS

Effective leaders are absolutely essential to lawyer well-being efforts. Leaders with the most contact with lawyers (e.g., supervising partners) have the biggest impact on their work experience—driving almost 70 percent of workplace perceptions. Effective leaders contribute to better performance, work engagement, job satisfaction, and retention of valued people.

Toxic leaders do just the opposite. They can also seriously damage workers' health. Bad leadership is linked to depression, anxiety, emotional exhaustion, and burnout. Multiple studies also have linked supervisors' bad behaviors to an increased risk of heart disease, heart attack, and death. Yes, *death*. The bad behaviors studied in this research might surprise you. They include fairly common behaviors like playing favorites, criticizing unfairly, failing to provide information or listen to problems, failing to explain goals or praise good work, not assisting with professional development, and not showing that they cared.

Because leaders so strongly influence whether lawyers have energizing or draining work experiences, ignoring leader development will doom lawyer well-being initiatives. And nearly all lawyers are leaders in some capacity—even junior lawyers who work with paralegals and secretaries. Whatever their level, most supervise and motivate others and are watched closely by staff and more junior lawyers for cues about standards and expectations. From a developmental perspective, it's best to start shaping good leadership skills as early as possible and before less effective habits and patterns take root.

2. CULTIVATE THE EXPERIENCE OF MEANINGFUL WORK

Report after report about Millennial lawyers say things akin to, "Millennials want to work—they're happy working—but they want to find meaning in work." And don't we all secretly agree? Many of us decided to go to law school with some hope of creating a fulfilling, meaningful career in which we generally felt happy, healthy, and satisfied. Is that how you felt when you started law school? Do you still feel that way?

When I speak and write about lawyer well-being, I almost always include something about the importance of feeling that our work is meaningful. And, often, multiple lawyers talk to me afterwards about their struggle with this very issue. One very successful senior law firm partner recently told me that it was an issue that has kept him up at night.

For many of us, our jobs are not just a source of income. We want to be part of something that matters and contributes to a greater good. I went to law school because I wanted to help make the world a better place—I wanted to serve an important purpose. That same desire also was a big factor in my decision to leave the practice of law several years ago. My life as a litigator defending big companies in employment disputes was challenging and interesting. But my sense of meaning and purpose had steadily disintegrated. The chief reason that I returned to graduate school in organizational psychology was to investigate the possibility of shaping workplace culture. That could have sustained me and other lawyers like me that share a longing to feel that we're valued, valuable, and making an important contribution to the greater good.

Law firm and other organizational leaders can play an important role in fostering a sense of meaning and purpose in the workplace. Experiencing our work as meaningful means that we believe that it matters and is valuable and that it contributes to personal growth and the greater good. It has significant personal and organizational benefits. For example, meaningful work is the biggest contributor to work engagement and impacts physical and mental well-being. It also is positively associated with job performance and job satisfaction and is negatively tied to feelings of alienation at work, turnover, and stress.

The energizing effect of meaningfulness stems from people's strong desire to feel a sense of both impact and recognition. Impact refers to a feeling that we're making a difference in the world. We want to feel that "my work matters." Recognition refers to signals we receive from the world that our presence matters—we want to feel that "I matter." The psychological experience that "I matter" and "my work matters" generates a sense of meaningfulness—which helps fuel work-related well-being.

An important way that leaders in the legal profession play a role in this issue is by influencing others' perceptions through what's called "framing." Framing is simply how we present information. Presenting the same information to people in different ways triggers different emotions and thoughts. For example, a patient may agree to surgery when the doctor says, "You have a 90% chance of surviving," but not when she says, "You have a 10% chance of dying." This is so even though the statements are logically equivalent. Law firm leaders can use framing techniques to positively shape the way lawyers view their work—they can frame work to accentuate meaningfulness.

Opportunities arise every day to cultivate the experience of meaningful work for everyone around us. We can take every opportunity to reinforce the significance of other lawyers' daily work. For example, we can highlight the impact of others' work by:

- Drawing attention to how their work benefits others—clients, other lawyers, the firm as a whole.
- Making sure they have challenging work that allows them to use a variety of skills and strengths and to grow and learn.

- Highlighting how an assignment can build their skills and meet their goals.
- Explicitly telling them why their contribution is important. When people perceive that their work is pointless or valueless, their motivation plummets.
- Explaining how their work fits into the project's larger framework. Avoid "drive by" assignments where lawyers are assigned a task with no knowledge of its significance or how it fits in the bigger puzzle.
- Ensuring they know the outcome of projects in which they participated. Radio silence in response to completed work projects should be outlawed.
- Regularly connecting them with clients in situations in which clients explain how they have benefitted from the lawyers' work. By realizing the impact of our work on others, we become more likely to invest time and energy into the tasks that will help them.
- Articulating a mission or purpose for the firm that is not solely focused on revenue-generation. People are much more motivated in the long term when they feel that their work has intrinsic value—that it helps people or makes the world a better place. After extensive research, the authors of the best-selling books *Built to Last* (Jim Collins and Jerry Porras, HarperCollins, 2002) and *Good to Great* (Jim Collins, HarperCollins, 2001) concluded that a key feature of financially successful, enduring companies was that they pay attention to vision, values, and core purpose that goes beyond profit.

These strategies focus primarily on enhancing the perceived impact of work—the sense that "my work matters." Equally as important to the experience of meaningful work is the sense of recognition—that "I matter." Those strategies are discussed next.

3. CULTIVATE CULTURES IN WHICH LAWYERS FEEL VALUED AND VALUABLE

Our work-related well-being and decisions about whether to fully invest ourselves at work depend a lot on whether we feel a sense of recognition—that we're valued, valuable, and needed. Everyone searches for ways to feel important and special at work. Do we feel like we're making a difference? Are we taken for granted? When little is asked or expected of us, when little is invested in us, and when we're treated as if we're unimportant, the result is that we feel that we don't really matter. And this feeling will destroy engagement and well-being.

There are multiple psychological reasons why positive interactions, expressions of gratitude, and the like are important to well-being, engagement, and organizational success. I'll discuss a few here to help explain why this well-being strategy is so important.

First, **a sense of belonging and being cared for** is an extremely important part of feeling that we're valued and valuable. It is a basic human need that must be satisfied for optimal functioning and health. It impacts many aspects of functioning—including cognitive processes, emotional patterns, behaviors, and health and well-being. High-quality connections with others also are critical to organizational functioning because work gets done (or not) through people and their social channels. If those channels break down due to poor-quality connections, lawyer well-being and organizational success will suffer.

Second, we humans are highly sensitive to **cues about our social value**. We continually scan for—and are bombarded by—cues about whether others value us and our work. We make rapid judgments and automatic, often unconscious decisions about whether to try to connect with or withdraw from people giving off these signals. You can think of everyone you encounter as having two powerful antennas protruding from their heads that are affixed with a red and green light. These "sociometer" antennas scan constantly for cues about self-worth. Signals of rejection trigger the red light. Signals of acceptance trigger the green light and give a positive jolt to self-esteem. We fit all of these bits and pieces of signals together like a puzzle that give us an overall view of whether we belong and are valued—which significantly impacts our self-confidence, motivation and well-being.

Third, people also monitor what's called their **effort-reward balance**. If they feel like they're giving more than they're receiving, their motivation and well-being will take a tumble. Positive interactions that include recognition and gratitude are forms of reward that weigh heavily in the effort-reward balance—even more than money. These types of behaviors communicate a genuine acknowledgment, approval, and appreciation for work well done. They include heartfelt communications that notice and acknowledge a person's value and significance. When leaders engage in simple positive acts like saying thank you, praising performance, or giving compliments, workers feel more positive emotions, job satisfaction, emotional attachment to their jobs, and well-being.

Fourth, **frequent bouts of positive emotions** that trigger even a mild uptick in mood are essential to engagement and well-being—and people are a common trigger for both positive and negative emotions. The problem for lawyers is that their work often entails an onslaught of negativity. It's part of our jobs to pay attention to everything that might go wrong. On top of that, we regularly face setbacks and annoyances—we lose motions, cases, and clients; opposing counsel are exasperating; colleagues can be jerks; judges can be disinterested; and on and on. To exacerbate the situation, much research shows that bad is stronger than good: bad events produce stronger emotional reactions and have longer-lasting effects on our emotions and behaviors. To counterbalance the outsized impact of negative emotions, we need to have three to five times more positive ones.

Law firms' fast-paced, pressure-cooker cultures can pose obstacles to positive interactions that make people feel valued. For example, a 2008 study asked big firm associates how their working conditions could improve. The top responses included that partners lacked collegiality, did not express appreciation, and treated them as if they were fungible.[1] In short, partners conveyed that associates *did not matter.*

Lawyers' reports of lack of respect and courteousness comport with nationwide surveys showing that workplace incivility is on the rise. Incivility is defined to include low-intensity acts of disrespect like sarcasm and rudeness, whether or not the conduct is intentionally malicious. Chronic incivility is corrosive. It depletes followers' energy and motivation, increases burnout, and inflicts emotional and physiological damage. It also diminishes productivity, performance, and helping behaviors. Recommendations for what to stop doing and what to start or continue doing are listed in the following sections.

---

1. Ingo Forstenlechner & Fiona Lettice, *Well Paid but Undervalued and Overworked,* 30 EMPLOYEE RELATIONS 640–652 (2008).

Behaviors to Stop Doing

- Rudeness and sarcasm
- Embarrassing or belittling others
- Using a condescending tone
- Treating others like they're invisible
- Taking others for granted
- Eye-rolling or other dismissive body language
- Micro-managing others
- Losing your temper
- Intimidating others

Behaviors to Start or Keep Doing

- Say please and thank you
- Make special efforts to be helpful
- Praise job performance
- Give compliments
- Treat others with dignity
- Foster a sense of belonging
- Act in caring ways
- Listen and avoid interrupting
- Be truly present and genuine
- Convey others' value
- Aid the success of others
- Be empathetic
- Solicit and act on input
- Give access to valuable resources
- Use appropriate tone
- Treat others as equals
- Give credit when it's due
- Support autonomy

As one example of my own green light firing up, I vividly recall showing up to my office one morning as a law firm associate after weeks of little sleep and a lot of stress as we prepared for trial in a thorny employment case. We settled the case the day before trial. On my desk waiting to greet me the next day was the biggest bouquet of blooming pink flowers that I've ever seen and a thank you card from the supervising partner. She never took me for granted. She didn't take the view that no thanks were necessary for someone just doing their job. The result? I would've run through fire for her.

4. EXPAND LAWYERS' SENSE OF CONTROL AND AUTONOMY

Perceiving a sense of control and autonomy also is enormously important for lawyer well-being. When we lack it, we're vulnerable to burnout, depression, and alcohol abuse. Having a high level of job demands and responsibility with little control is a toxic combination. On the other hand, autonomy fuels well-being. A recent study of over 6,000 lawyers[2] working in a wide variety of legal jobs found that, of all factors studied, autonomy had the strongest relationship with lawyer well-being. The positive link between autonomy and well-being was large—three times larger than the association between income and well-being.

Why would this be so? First, stress is less distressing when people feel that they have choices and are able to take action to meet challenges. Control reduces ambiguity, enhances predictability, and allows people to plan their own lives. On the other hand, people who are robbed of autonomy, are bossed around, or who are micromanaged feel that their unique contribution doesn't really matter. Autonomy helps people feel respected, valued, and valuable.

Skeptics may object to the idea that lawyers can have any real sense of control over workload and schedules. Courts set short deadlines, opposing lawyers file emergency motions, clients continually have time-sensitive needs, and so on. If we really want to get at the source of lawyer distress, we might seriously question the current structure of the legal practice and whether it can be altered to support well-being while maintaining a high standard of excellence and client focus. Since overhauling such procedures and practices will take decades, we can focus on what we can do in the meantime to make the situation better, even if not ideal.

For example, how many emergency projects for associates are caused by partners' poor time management or neglect? How many times do partners consult with associates or junior partners before agreeing to court or client deadlines that can ruin Christmas, a child's ball game, or a family vacation? I could go on, but you get the picture. These types of things happen sometimes. When they become chronic, they communicate lack of respect and devastate lawyers' sense of control and autonomy.

So how can you get started with better supporting lawyers' sense of control and autonomy? Here are four ways to do so.

Grant Independence Commensurate with Ability. Among the best ways to support autonomy is to allow as much independence and discretion as lawyers' level of experience and competence allow. I was lucky to work with many high-performing associates, and I asked one recently what she found most engaging and energizing when we worked together. She listed a string of things that made her really "feel like a lawyer" early in her career—court appearances, depositions, witness interviews. She helped me learn that, when we grant trust and autonomy, people often live up to it. When we don't, we teach them that their contribution isn't valued and that they should simply do the minimum required while awaiting our commands and re-writes.

Use Participatory Leadership. Using participatory decision-making strategies is another way to support autonomy. When leaders use this style, they are open to others' suggestions, solicit input, and spur open discussions for identifying new solutions. When people are involved in making decisions, they feel more autonomous when carrying them out. People who are left out of decision-making have a higher risk of burnout.

Participatory decision-making can engage all levels of lawyers, including decisions impacting partners and other senior lawyers. As part of a law firm leadership project, I asked a group of partners to describe features of the best and worst firm leaders. The dominant theme was that good leaders openly share information and give opportunities for meaningful input into significant decisions and bad leaders don't. The stories of bad leaders hoarding information, blocking participation, and

---

2. Lawrence S. Krieger & Kennon M. Sheldon, *What Makes Lawyers Happy?: A Data-Driven Prescription to Redefine Professional Success*, 83 GEORGE WASHINGTON LAW REVIEW 554 (2015).

announcing surprise decisions were filled with disgust and frustration—the kind of negative emotions that harm well-being and can lead to burnout.

Allow Flexibility. Flexibility in where and when followers do their work also helps boost their sense of control and autonomy. Technology has dramatically enhanced the potential for such flexibility, making telecommuting both feasible and desirable because it provides greater autonomy and job satisfaction.

Many law firms still have not embraced the full potential for flexibility because they worry that lawyers will shirk their responsibilities if allowed to work from home. Recent research should help allay these concerns. A 2015 study that crossed industries found that telecommuting did not harm workers' performance—and, in fact, boosted it. They found that the grant of expanded autonomy was at the root of the effect.[3]

Workers felt grateful for the trust and autonomy granted to them by their organizations and so reciprocated with greater energy that positively influenced their performance. This comports with my own experience as a law firm partner when I freely allowed telecommuting by lawyers who worked with me. My experience was that the trust I invested was rewarded with trustworthiness. They were highly responsive and continued to do excellent work—at a time and place that was more tailored to their lives.

Avoid Coercive Language. When making work-related requests, partners and other law firm leaders can respect followers' autonomy by using words of influence rather than coercion. Dwight D. Eisenhower defined motivation as "the art of getting people to do what you want them to do because they want to do it." This is an excellent description of how leaders support autonomy while getting things done. How can we put this into practice? Research shows that five leader behaviors are particularly effective at supporting others' autonomy when communicating work requests.

Autonomy-Focused Behavior	Example
1. Use language that doesn't sound controlling or coercive. (Avoid bossiness.)	"It would be really helpful if you could ___" rather than "Have this to me by tomorrow."
2. Take others' perspectives and acknowledge their feelings.	I'm sorry about this short turn-around time. I know it's a pain and I'm sorry about that.
3. Give rationales for requests.	"The client just asked for an update by tomorrow" rather than "I know it's Friday afternoon, but this needs to be done tomorrow."
4. Tailor motivation strategies to account for others' individual interests, preferences, and work-related values, and to boost their confidence in their abilities to be effective and master new skills.	I wouldn't ask just anyone to do this, but I know you can handle it. And the upside is that it might give you a chance to take a deposition.
5. Maximize others' sense of choice and self-initiation.	I know it's getting late and it's totally fine if you want to go home and work on it there. What time do you think is reasonable to get me a draft?

---

3. Ravi S. Gajendran, David A. Harrison & Kelly Delaney-Klinger, *Are Telecommuters Remotely Good Citizens? Unpacking Telecommutings Effects on Performance Via I-Deals and Job Resources,* 68 Personnel Psychology 353–393 (2014).

While autonomy-oriented strategies require that we invest a little extra time and effort, research indicates that it's worth it. They will pay off by enhancing motivation and well-being.

CONCLUSION

Lawyer well-being is not a solo sport, and the expectation that lawyers will survive if they simply grow a thicker skin is not realistic. Firms wanting to build and keep high-performing teams should take seriously their responsibility for contributing to an environment in which lawyers can thrive. Most of the ideas in this chapter require only a bit of time and cost little but provide a good start toward building thriving organizations filled with lawyers able to be their best.

CHAPTER 5
Using Emotional Intelligence to Promote Lawyer Wellness

Dr. Larry Richard, Esq., PhD

Editor's Note: A book about lawyer well-being would not be complete without Larry Richard's contribution. He is the pre-eminent expert on lawyer behavior. He is also a dear friend whom I have known for over 35 years. We both stopped practicing law at the same time with the idea of looking for ways to make a contribution to what we each thought was a somewhat dysfunctional and critical aspect of society. Working with Larry, I have seen how he uses empirically based behavioral assessment tools that lawyers accept and relate to as vehicles for changing individual behavior and organizational culture. This chapter introduces a kind of intelligence all lawyers might cultivate.

In this chapter, I explain the origins and discovery of the psychological construct known as emotional intelligence (EI). I present the evidence that EI is a separate quality from the more traditional form of intelligence. I explain why EI is a strong predictor of effective leadership, coping with change, and building relationships, three important and interconnected outcomes. Finally, I offer some strategies for lawyers to learn each of the four EI skills, and suggest that in doing so, they will increase their capacity for both physical and emotional wellness.

Dr. Larry Richard is recognized as the leading expert on the psychology of lawyer behavior. A graduate of the University of Pennsylvania Law School, Dr. Richard was a litigator for ten years before earning his PhD in Psychology from Temple University. Since then, he has gathered and analyzed personality data on thousands of lawyers. In 2011, he launched his own consulting firm, LawyerBrain LLC (www.lawyerbrain.com), which has provided consulting services to many of the top law firms and major corporate law departments in the areas of leadership, change management, and talent selection and development.

It's the end of a long day for Harry. He is eager to get home and sleep in his own bed, for a change. The line at the security checkpoint in the airport is long, and, wouldn't you know it, Harry is randomly selected for a full search. "I'll miss my flight," he whines to an unsympathetic TSA agent.

Exiting the checkpoint, he rushes to the nearest screen to see what gate his flight departs from, and then he sees the dreaded message: CANCELLED. He reads it three times, just to make sure it is indeed his flight. There is no mistaking it.

He practically gallops to the airline service desk, hoping to find an alternative flight home.

He's seventh in line. The next few moments in Harry's life will show us whether Harry has really high or really low emotional intelligence (EI). If his EI is low, we may expect to see him start spewing angry invective at the airline agent before he even gets to the counter. He may become enormously frustrated, agitated, and irritated. As a result, he may end up distorting what he is told, or not even hearing it. The solutions he is likely to think of will mainly be coercive in nature.

By contrast, if his EI is high, he may calm himself by adopting a mindset of acceptance and empathy: "I can't change the situation, so I might as well be as pleasant as possible when I talk to the gate agent. I'm sure the agent is under a lot of pressure, and it won't help me one bit to add to it."

This example is made up, and it illustrates just a small slice of EI, but it illustrates a very real point—emotional intelligence matters greatly in everyday life.

What is emotional intelligence? Where did it come from? And how can it help lawyers in coping with change, uncertainty, and stress? Can it improve wellness? Is it learnable? In the pages that follow, we'll answer all these questions.

Emotional intelligence is a term coined by two psychologists, Jack Mayer and Peter Salovey. In 1988, during the presidential election that was taking place that year, Mayer and Salovey had an epiphany that came from watching the presidential bid of Senator Gary Hart, the then-front-runner on the Democratic side, completely melt down when photos were revealed that showed him to be having an illicit affair on a boat named "Monkey Business." (You can't make up stuff like this!)

Hart suffered a reversal of fortune politically, and had to drop out of the race. Up until then, he had been viewed as intelligent, photogenic, popular, charismatic, and as having a very good chance of winning the election.

Dr. Mayer was an intelligence researcher. He studied the cognitive behavior of individuals. Dr. Salovey was an emotions researcher. He studied the role that emotion plays in everyday life. They happened to be together when they heard the story about Gary Hart on TV. One of them reportedly turned to the other and asked, rhetorically, "How is it possible for someone so smart to do something so stupid?!"

That moment led them to consider that perhaps classic intelligence—what we measure as intelligence quotient (IQ)—might be a completely separate skill from "emotional intelligence," a term they coined. Is it possible, they wondered, if there are certain measurable skills that involve using emotions intelligently, skills that people have or don't have, independent from how smart (IQ) they are?

They also wondered: If this set of skills exists, has it already been studied and labeled, or did they discover a new dimension of human psychology? If it exists, can it be measured? Can it be learned or is it innate? And does it matter—that is, are people who have higher EI any better at certain things than people who have lower EI?

Not long after this incident, they did some research in the literature, and wrote an important article, published in a professional journal, proposing the idea that human beings may possess four competencies, collectively called "emotional intelligence."[1] Those competencies are:

The ability to identify and accurately label emotions—in one's self and in others. This is a form of "self-awareness." Do I pay attention to my emotional inner life? If so, can I recognize a particular emotion at the time that I experience it? Can I accurately label it? Am I mindful enough to realize when a particular emotion emerges, or do I only realize it later, or not at all?

The ability to use emotions to regulate thought. Psychologists have discovered that "thoughts" and "feelings" are not opposites, as we once thought, but rather, both are necessary to make sound decisions. Recent neuroscience research shows that the emotional regions in our brain are wired to connect with the intellectual (thought) regions of our brain. Those with greater EI skill in this second competency understand that emotions can facilitate thought—for example, they know that if they want to do a task that requires creativity, then shifting into a positive, even playful, mood will enhance their creativity; or, if they want to do some work that requires attention to detail, a slightly sad, negative, "down" mood will actually boost their attention to detail.[2]

The ability to understand emotions. This includes what we commonly call "empathy," but it also includes other elements. For example, when someone expresses a complex emotion, do you understand the component emotions? When someone behaves in a certain way, or reacts to an event in a certain way, are you skilled at accurately inferring what emotion must have caused them to react that way? Can you accurately predict how another person might react when faced with a particular situation? This cluster of skills includes empathy in the conventional sense plus the ability to understand the emotions of others in a sophisticated way. Such an understanding aids us in interacting successfully with others, and in figuring out the best way to influence them, a skill that's particularly useful for lawyers in general and even more so for those in leadership roles.

The ability to regulate your own behavior. This includes both the ability to express an emotion, even though it might be difficult for you, as well as

---

1. Note that the model that I'm describing here is based on the research of Mayer and Salovey. There are two other widely respected models of emotional intelligence—one proposed by Daniel Goleman, who wrote the book *Emotional Intelligence,* and one proposed by Reuven Bar-On, who authored a test called the EQ-i. All three models are in wide use today, and there is considerable overlap among the models, and yet there are differences. For simplicity's sake, this chapter confines itself to the Mayer-Salovey model, which is strongly supported by empirical research. *See* Salovey, P. & Mayer, J. D., *Emotional Intelligence,* Imagination, Cognition, and Personality 9, 185–211.

2. The reverse is also true—thoughts can generate emotional states. For example, pessimistic thoughts can generate a depressive mood. *See* Marc A. Brackett, Susan E. Rivers & Peter Salovey, *Emotional Intelligence: Implications for Personal, Social, Academic, and Workplace Success,* 5 Social and Personality Psychology Compass 88–103 (2011); available at http://ei.yale.edu/wp-content/uploads/2013/09 /pub184_Brackett_Rivers_Salovey_2011_Compass-1.pdf; Joseph P. Forgas, *Don't Worry, Be Sad! On the Cognitive, Motivational, and Interpersonal Benefits of Negative Mood,* 22 Current Directions in Psychological Science 225–232 (2013); available at http://dx.doi.org/10.1177/0963721412474458, https://www.scientificamerican.com/article/be-sad-and-succeed/.

the ability to decide not to express an emotion even though you feel it. An example of expressing a difficult emotion might be the situation where somebody annoys you, and it's appropriate under the circumstances to assertively ask them to stop. Some people have difficulty doing so. The emotionally intelligent person has learned how to overcome their own reticence and can up-regulate certain emotions. An example of not expressing an inappropriate emotion might actually look very similar to the preceding example—suppose a senior partner in your law firm does something that angers you in a meeting, and further suppose that this same senior partner has a big say in determining your discretionary compensation. You may, at that point, wish to down-regulate your emotion, that is, to figure out a way to acknowledge what you're feeling—to yourself—but to not express it to the senior partner at that moment.[3]

Since the publication of that early article, hundreds of scientific studies have been conducted on EI, hundreds of professional journal articles have been written, and dozens of authoritative books have been written on EI.

From all this scholarly work, we've learned the answers to the questions that Mayer and Salovey posed:

- Emotional intelligence is indeed a new construct, as opposed to being a mere label for something we already knew about.
- The four skills are learnable. (Although, as with any skill, some people are better at learning them than others, and some will never learn them.)
- EI can be measured. Mayer and Salovey constructed a very good test called the MSCEIT—Mayer Salovey Caruso Emotional Intelligence Test—that measures EI. It is a "skill-based" test, which makes it hard to "fake." In other words, it doesn't ask questions like a personality test might, where you think you know what the answer is "supposed" to be. Rather, it gives you "emotional" problems to solve and either you know the right answer or you don't. There's no faking it. For example, they may show a photograph of a person's face and ask you "How much sadness—on a scale of 1 to 5—is this person expressing?"
- And most important, EI does indeed correlate with, and even predict, certain important behaviors, such as the ability to cope well with change, the ability to lead others, and the ability to form and successfully maintain relationships.

How do lawyers score on the MSCEIT? The test provides an overall EI score as well as several subsidiary scores. The overall score is reported using a scale that's identical to the way that traditional intelligence ("IQ") is reported: a score of "100" is considered "average"; two-thirds of the public score between 85 and 115. (This is called the "standard deviation" statistic.) Let's say that an individual gets an overall MSCEIT score of 130. This represents a very high score, and it would reflect a high

---

3. Research shows that "suppressing" a negative emotion can actually be harmful and is not very effective anyway. A person still reacts in ways that tip off others that they are experiencing the negative emotion (like "anger"). A more successful strategy is to "reframe" the situation, i.e., to genuinely adopt an alternative, believable narrative that explains your election not to express that emotion at that time. That's actually a much healthier way to handle the situation.

level of emotional intelligence. By contrast, an individual scoring 70 would have very low emotional intelligence. Scores among the general public are distributed along a classic bell curve, with most scores falling between 85 and 115. Over the years, I've tested about 1200 lawyers with the MSCEIT, and their average score is 98.1, which is slightly below the average of 100.

Considering that emotional intelligence is a set of learned skills, this is not surprising at all:

- Most lawyers are not interested in learning about emotional intelligence.
- Most law schools and law firms don't teach it nor do they typically coach for it in their development programs.
- Most law professors don't intentionally role model it.
- Most law firms and law departments don't intentionally encourage its learning or reward people when they demonstrate it.
- Nor do they generally penalize lawyers who don't exhibit these skills (except in extreme cases).
- It's not generally included as a criterion in most compensation systems in law firms.
- Most law firms and law departments don't systematically include EI skills as a criterion when they hire new lawyers.
- We generally don't learn these skills by accident, but only if we're interested and if we are exposed to someone who effectively teaches or role models the skills.

Despite this, it's surprising how many lawyers expect to score higher on the MSCEIT than they actually end up scoring.

HOW CAN YOU USE THESE SKILLS TO IMPROVE YOUR OWN WELLNESS?

Let's review the four basic EI skills along with some tips about how to learn or improve each of them:

1. **The ability to identify and accurately label emotions.** Psychologists have determined that the skill of recognizing and labeling emotions in yourself and the skill of recognizing and labeling them in others is essentially the same skill. Therefore, one promising strategy for learning these skills is to increase your acuity in reading the emotions on the faces of others with whom you interact. I have had great success using the materials of Dr. Paul Ekman, a well-known and widely respected psychologist who has devoted his career to the science of reading facial expressions of fundamental emotions. He has designed a do-it-yourself learning system, which he sells on his website, that can teach you to recognize the seven most common emotions. Once an individual learns to read emotional "micro-expressions," you have that skill forever. I have found that lawyers who learn to read these seven emotions tend to generalize their learning and become better all around at reading and identifying emotional expressions in others, as well as better at recognizing the same emotions in themselves.

2. **The ability to use emotions to regulate thought.** There are two parts to this skill—the first part is understanding what mood states[4] are best for generating particular cognitive results. For example, as I noted earlier, if you are about to begin a task that calls for creativity, the best mood is a positive emotional state, particularly a playful or humorous mood. So you may want to identify two or three recurring cognitive processes that you find yourself using regularly, and then ask yourself what mood seems to put you into the best mental state to achieve that result. If you can't figure it out yourself, try observing others doing that task really well, and see what kind of emotional state they're in when they perform that task at their best. The second part of the skill is learning how to enter that mood state on demand. Using our "creativity" example, how might you get yourself into a positive mood? In classes I've taught to lawyers, here are some of the answers they've given to this question:

   a. Listen to my favorite upbeat music.
   b. Go for a walk in my local garden.
   c. Physical exercise—play basketball, go running, etc.
   d. Talk to a friend who is generally in an upbeat mood or who has a positive, happy personality.

   I'm sure you can think of other examples. Once you enter the appropriate mood state, assuming you've been accurate in your selection, the cognitive task becomes easier.

3. **The ability to understand emotions.** This calls on the skill of "cognitive empathy"—that is, understanding *intellectually* what is motivating another person, how they think or feel about something, or how they might react to a particular event. Research[5] shows that you can learn to more accurately understand the motivations of others (a) by reading well-written novels, especially those that accurately portray human emotions and that put their characters into common situations that reveal honest human nature and (b) by watching well-written, well-cast, and well-directed movies that do the same thing—show characters dealing with common human dilemmas that reveal their emotional state. The key in both techniques is to read books or watch movies that critics have praised for their honest, accurate portrayal of human nature.

4. **The ability to regulate your own behavior.** To learn self-regulation, there are several steps:

   a. First, think of a recurring situation in which you want to do a better job of regulating your emotions. It can either be a situation where you want to up-regulate (i.e., to get better at expressing a difficult emotion) or a situation where you want to down-regulate (i.e., to get better at electing not to automatically express an emotion that might get you into trouble).

---

4. Think of "mood" as an emotion extended over time.

5. Pam Belluck, *For Better Social Skills, Scientists Recommend a Little Chekhov*, THE NEW YORK TIMES (2013), https://well.blogs.nytimes.com/2013/10/03/i-know-how-youre-feeling-i-read-chekhov/.

b. Next, replay in your mind a recent actual event that took place. It should be an event where you didn't self-regulate this particular emotion as well as you wish you had. Then replay it again, but imagine your memory is like a movie, and try to slow it down so that when you get to the part right before you express (or fail to express) the emotion in question, you can "stop the action." What you want to notice is what's going on in your mind and your body. Tune into your thoughts first—what thoughts ran through your head just before the critical moment? Some people are very aware of their every thought; others barely notice that an internal monologue is taking place. If you're in the latter category, tune in, listen, try to hear what your mind is serving up. Your thoughts matter. And learning how to tune into those thoughts, and then change them, can be very powerful.

c. Also tune into your body. Every emotion is "embodied"—it produces physiological symptoms. For example, if you're trying to regulate anger, you might notice that right before you express anger at someone, you become aware that you clench your teeth, or that the muscles in the back of your neck tighten, or you close your hand into a fist, or your heart beats faster, etc. Notice these "precursor" symptoms. Generally, once an emotion is in the process of being expressed, it's hard to regulate it, but if you can identify the physiology of the moment *just before* its expression, there is a much better chance of successful regulation.

d. Next, replay the scenario again, but this time, as soon as you hear any of the precursor thoughts or feel any of the precursor symptoms, redirect your mind to react in the more regulated way that you are wishing for (i.e., either expressing the difficult emotion, or reframing the emotion that you would normally express). For example, to use the anger example, as soon as I hear a precursor thought ("Why that #@!%!—how dare he say something like that!") or I feel my chest tighten or my lips get tense, I can say to myself, "I have a choice here—I can notice my anger without needing to actually express it." You may also benefit from adding thoughts that reframe the event that triggered your anger—e.g., "I know this makes me mad because it feels like XX disrespected me, but maybe XX is going through his/her own distress" or "Maybe XX didn't mean to disrespect me." This step can be challenging for some lawyers because it requires both empathy and compassion, and some scholars have asserted that law school training diminishes these aptitudes.

Every one of these four EI skills can be helpful in coping with change, uncertainty, and stress. In the first place, an individual who becomes adept at even one of these skills naturally becomes more tolerant and understanding in situations that don't go his/her way.

Second, when you work on improving these skills, it produces a state of greater emotional balance, what some would call a feeling of being more "centered."

Third, recent neuroscience research shows that when individuals experience positive emotions, it boosts their immune systems. Practicing EI skills also allows you to adopt a more optimistic mindset as you move through life, and an optimistic mindset has been linked in research[6] to (to name just a few of the documented benefits):

- Greater longevity.
- Lower blood pressure.
- Fewer cardiovascular incidents.
- More satisfying and successful relationships.

Finally, and most importantly, when you improve EI skills, you increase your capacity to form authentic, healthy relationships, the centerpiece of well-being for most people. In fact, the growing research on "social connection" shows that building such relationships and maintaining them are just about the most important thing a human being can do. Strong ongoing social connections have been linked to:

- Greater life satisfaction.
- Greater work satisfaction.
- Longer, healthier, and more satisfying relationships.
- Greater longevity.
- A strengthened immune system.[7]

As in most other things, improving EI behavior is not an "all or nothing" proposition. Rather, every little bit helps, and the more improvement you achieve, and the more of the four EI competencies you master, the greater the payoff you will experience. Good luck in your journey towards greater emotional intelligence.

---

6. *See,* for example, Martin E. P. Seligman, LEARNED OPTIMISM (1992); Barbara L. Fredrickson, POSITIVITY: TOP-NOTCH RESEARCH REVEALS THE 3-TO-1 RATIO THAT WILL CHANGE YOUR LIFE (2009); Ciro Conversano et al., *Optimism and Its Impact on Mental and Physical Well-Being,* 1 CLINICAL PRACTICE & EPIDEMIOLOGY IN MENTAL HEALTH 25–29 (2010); Deborah D. Danner, David A. Snowden & Wallace V. Friesen, *Positive Emotions in Early Life and Longevity: Findings from the Nun Study,* 80 JOURNAL OF PERSONALITY AND SOCIAL PSYCHOLOGY 804–813.

7. *See,* for example, George E. Vaillant, TRIUMPHS OF EXPERIENCE: THE MEN OF THE HARVARD GRANT STUDY (2015); Dean Ornish, LOVE AND SURVIVAL: THE SCIENTIFIC BASIS FOR THE HEALING POWER OF INTIMACY (1999); Matthew D. Lieberman, SOCIAL: WHY OUR BRAINS ARE WIRED TO CONNECT (2015); Barbara Fredrickson, LOVE 2.0: HOW OUR SUPREME EMOTION AFFECTS EVERYTHING WE THINK, DO, FEEL, AND BECOME (2013).

CHAPTER 6
Resilient and Ready
Tools for Adapting to Stress and Change in the Law

Paula Davis-Laack, JD, MAPP

Editor's Note: Resilience is a critical skill for the legal profession. Paula gets specific about the unique challenges lawyers face because of the nature of the work. Burnout and substance abuse are endemic and the cause is often the drive to be a better lawyer. Specific proven tools can be powerful lifelines for a sinking professional. That's why they are included.

Law firms and organizations need lawyers and talent who can think critically, develop business, and solve problems based on the way clients live and work today. Without a fully engaged, high-performing and resilient pool of talent, law firms and organizations cannot grow and thrive. Resilience, the capacity for stress-related growth, and resilience skills provide additional tools that lawyers need to successfully cope with these stressors. Resilience is built through a set of core competencies that enable mental toughness and mental strength, higher performance, strong leadership, and tenacity. Resilient people give up less frequently when they experience setbacks.

Paula Davis-Laack, JD, MAPP, is a former practicing lawyer turned consultant and stress and resilience expert. Paula earned a master's degree in applied positive psychology from the University of Pennsylvania and helped to train thousands of Army soldiers and their family members in resilience skills as part of her post-graduate work. Her articles on stress and resilience-related topics appear regularly on her blogs in the *Huffington Post, Forbes, Fast Company,* and *Psychology Today.* She is the Founder and CEO of the Stress & Resilience Institute, a training and consulting firm devoted to helping law firms and lawyers prevent burnout and build their resilience to stress (www.pauladavislaack.com).

The question I'm most often asked by people is this: "You used to be a lawyer, and now you help busy professionals build stress resilience. How did you go from practicing law to doing that?" The answer is that I burned out seven years into my law practice. During that time, I noticed that I was becoming less effective at managing my stress, was chronically physically and emotionally exhausted, overly cynical, and felt ineffective as I lost confidence about where I fit into the profession. It wasn't until I left my law practice and began to study the impact that stress has on busy professionals that I realized that this "thing" I had experienced had a name—burnout. In order to fully recover, I had to learn new skills to help me better understand my high-achieving ways, and that included increasing my resilience to stress. Resilience skills helped me to actively grow from the challenges and adversities I experienced and continue to help me today. Here is why resilience is such a needed skillset in the legal profession.

WHY THE LEGAL PROFESSION NEEDS RESILIENCE

1. The Legal Profession Is Different, and It's Changing

The continuous change that is present in the legal profession is adding to the already high levels of stress that lawyers experience. Clients continue to demand flexible billing arrangements and different methods for getting legal work done, and more attorneys are demanding flexible work arrangements to better integrate work and life. This has given rise to alternative business models like secondment firms and virtual law firms. Firms are also exploring how artificial intelligence—the development of computer systems able to perform legal tasks normally requiring lawyer involvement—can help them complete client work more quickly and cost effectively.

The legal profession is different from other professions. Law is often a zero-sum environment involving high-stakes matters with a winner and a loser; lawyers often have to take on tough clients and ask sensitive questions in court, sometimes in a way that conflicts with their values but is required to zealously represent a client; communication can be adversarial, and even regular conversations are treated as arguments to be won, a style that easily carries over to staff and family with negative consequences; and many firm cultures emphasize profits per partner and extrinsic rewards over meaning and well-being.[1]

2. Well-Being Decreases in Law School and Continues to Decrease in Practice

The loss of personal well-being among many lawyers starts in law school. Research shows that before law school, future law students are as emotionally healthy as the general population; however, just six months into law school, levels of well-being crash and anxiety and depression levels increase dramatically.[2] More troubling, levels of anxiety and depression among law students have been found to remain signifi-

---

1. Adapted from work done by David N. Shearon about the specific challenges lawyers face in the legal profession and how the legal profession is different.
2. G. Andrew Benjamin et al., THE ROLE OF LEGAL EDUCATION IN PRODUCING PSYCHOLOGICAL DISTRESS AMONG LAW STUDENTS AND LAWYERS 225, 240–247 (1986); Kennon M. Sheldon and Lawrence S. Krieger, *Does Legal Education Have Undermining Effects on Law Students? Evaluating Changes in Motivation, Values and Well-Being*, 22 BEHAV. SCI. L., 261, 271 (2004).

cantly elevated even two years after graduation.[3] Lawyers and law students also have significantly higher levels of stress, stress symptoms, alcohol abuse, social isolation, and marital dissatisfaction.[4] These statistics were again supported in a 2016 study conducted by the ABA and Hazelden Betty Ford Foundation, which found higher than average levels of depression (28%), anxiety (19%), and stress (23%).[5] More troubling were the findings showing that younger lawyers in their first 15 years of practice, working in private firms, had the highest risk of problematic drinking, with 31% of this specific group identified as problem drinkers.[6]

3. Stress and Burnout Are Real Challenges in the Law

Occupational stress has been shown to be significantly associated with both personal and work-related burnout among lawyers.[7] Lawyers who spent the majority of their time working on civil and criminal matters felt more fatigue and exhaustion not only from their legal work, but also from the stressful and negative interactions with their clients.[8] Another study of public defenders found that 37.4% of them scored in the clinically significant range of burnout.[9] Lawyers experiencing burnout were found to be less committed to the organization, reported lower identification with organizational goals, and were less willing to exert effort to achieve those goals.[10]

Professionals who are burning out are more prone to errors, have lower levels of well-being, lower retention rates, higher turnover, and lower morale.[11] One study showed that for each one point increase in a person's exhaustion score on the Maslach Burnout Inventory ("MBI"), there was a commensurate 5% increase in the likelihood of that person reporting an error; for each one point increase in a person's cynicism score on the MBI, there was a commensurate 11% increase in reporting an error; and for each one point increase in a person's personal efficacy score on the MBI, there was a commensurate 3.6% decrease in likelihood of reporting an error.[12]

Resilience has been shown to help prevent and alleviate burnout in a number of studies.[13] Law firms and organizations need lawyers and talent who can think critically, develop business, and solve problems based on the way clients live and work today. Without a fully engaged, high-performing, and resilient pool of talent, law firms and organizations cannot grow and thrive.

---

3. *Id.* at 246.

4. Todd David Peterson & Elizabeth Waters Peterson, *Stemming the Tide of Law Student Depression: What Law Schools Need to Learn from the Science of Positive Psychology*, 9 Yale J. Health Pol'y L. & Ethics, 357, 359 (2009).

5. Patrick R. Krill, Ryan Johnson, & Linda Albert. *The Prevalence of Substance Use and Other Mental Health Concerns Among American Attorneys*, 10(1) J. of Addiction Med., 46–52 (2016).

6. *Id.*

7. Tsai Feng-Jen, Huang Wei-Lun, & Chan Chang-Chuan, *Occupational Stress and Burnout of Lawyers*, 51, J. Occ. Health, 443–50 (2009).

8. *Id.* at 449.

9. Andrew P. Levin, et al., *Secondary Traumatic Stress in Attorneys and Their Administrative Support Staff Working with Trauma-Exposed Clients*, 199(12) J. Nerv. Ment. Dis., 946–55 (2011).

10. Susan E. Jackson, Jon A. Turner, & Arthur P. Brief, *Correlates of Burnout among Public Service Lawyers*, 8(4) J. Occ. Behav., 339–349 (1987).

11. Gail Gazelle, Jane M. Liebschutz, & Helen Riess. *Physician Burnout: Coaching a Way Out.* 30(4) J. Gen. Internal Med. 508–513 (2014).

12. Tait D. Shanafelt, et al. *Burnout and Medical Errors among American Surgeons*, Annals of Surgery (2009).

13. Michael P. Leiter & Christina Maslach, *Interventions to Prevent and Alleviate Burnout*, in Burnout at Work, 145–167 (Michael P. Leiter, Arnold B. Bakker & Christina Maslach eds., 2014).

HOW TO BUILD RESILIENCE

Resilience is your capacity for stress-related growth, and resilience skills provide the tools a lawyer needs to successfully cope with the stressors outlined previously. Resilience is built through a set of core competencies that enable mental toughness and mental strength, optimal performance, strong leadership, and tenacity. Resilient people give up less frequently when they experience setbacks.

Resilience thrives when you focus on building skills in the following categories, captured by the acronym FOCUS:[14]

F: Flexible, accurate, and thorough thinking—what is often referred to as "mental toughness";

O: Other people matter—fostering high-quality relationships with others;

C: Connecting to something bigger—identifying clear sources of meaning and motivation;

U: Utilize positive emotions—developing a positive emotional balance so that negative emotions aren't the only emotions utilized; and

S: Self-care—taking time to recharge your batteries both at work and outside of work.

Each component of the FOCUS model is explained in more detail in the following sections along with a sample skill to try.

F: Flexible, Accurate, and Thorough Thinking

To develop resilience, you have to understand how you think about adversity, stress, and challenging situations. Your "inner critic" drives a number of counterproductive thinking styles, such as catastrophizing (the downward spiral style of thinking you may experience during a stressful event), having a fixed mindset (the belief that your talents and abilities are fixed and aren't able to be grown in any way),[15] and other thinking traps (jumping to conclusions, mind reading, consistently blaming yourself when things go wrong, or consistently blaming other people or circumstances when things go wrong). The good news is that you can learn how to identify and correct counterproductive thinking styles and convert your "inner critic" into your "inner coach" to develop a more flexible, accurate, and thorough thinking style under stress.

SKILL TO TRY: When you are stuck thinking in a counterproductive way, ask yourself one of these questions to help you reframe your thinking:[16]

1. How will I feel about this a year from now?
2. What specific evidence do I have to support this thought?
3. What would I tell my friend/partner/child if he or she was in the same situation?
4. What impact is this thinking having in my life?

---

14. This is my own model of resilience after researching the topic for my master's thesis at the University of Pennsylvania.

15. Fixed and growth mindsets are the work of Dr. Carol Dweck—she summarizes her research in the book *Mindset*.

16. Judith S. Beck. Cognitive Behavioral Therapy: The Basics and Beyond (2nd ed. 2011).

O: Other People Matter

Developing high-quality relationships is critical to a happy, healthy, and resilient life. High-quality relationships have four key characteristics (and have been positively associated with feeling psychologically safe at work):[17] they are empowering, they provide a sense of trust, you can be your authentic self, and they are respectful.

Solid work relationships also translate into quantifiable gains in performance. Workplace friendships are one of the strongest predictors of productivity, and those who say that they have strong, supportive colleagues at work get sick less often, are more focused, are more loyal to their organizations, and change jobs less frequently.[18]

SKILL TO TRY: The most basic skill to help you build more effective relationships is the 10/5 rule. If you're within ten feet of another person, look at them and acknowledge that you see them; if you're within five feet, say hello. While this may seem silly and even simplistic, try it. I bet you move through work and life either distracted or tethered to some type of electronic device, so I suspect you'll find this harder to put into practice than you might think.

C: Connecting to Something Bigger

This component of resilience enables meaning and motivation. Engaged employees perform better on a daily basis, and the higher a person's level of engagement, the higher their objective financial returns.[19] Higher employee engagement translated into higher client satisfaction and loyalty, greater profitability, and more productivity.[20]

The quickest way to get lawyers motivated at work is to provide them with opportunities to experience autonomy, competence, and connection on a daily basis.[21] Law school professor Lawrence Krieger and psychologist Kennon Sheldon have done extensive research on lawyer motivation and well-being. Most recently, they analyzed data from over 6,200 lawyers and law students to discover what really drives and undermines well-being and engagement.[22] What they discovered is that the external factors that are often emphasized in the legal world—grade performance, income after graduation, law school rank, and law journal membership—were either not correlated at all or only very weakly correlated with long-term well-being.[23]

---

17. Abraham Carmeli, Daphna Brueller, & Jane E. Dutton. *Learning Behaviors in the Workplace: The Role of High-Quality Interpersonal Relationships & Psychological Safety.* 26 Syst. Res. 81–98 (2009).

18. James K. Harter et al. (2016) *The Relationship between Engagement at Work and Organizational Outcomes: 2016 Q12 Meta-Analysis.* Here is the link to download the report: http://www .workcompprofessionals.com/advisory/2016L5/august/MetaAnalysis_Q12_ResearchPaper_0416_v5 _sz.pdf

19. Arnold B. Bakker. *An Evidence-Based Model of Work Engagement,* 20 Current Directions in Psychol. Sci. 265–269 (2011).

20. James K. Harter, Frank L. Schmidt, & Theodore L. Hayes. *Business-Unit-Level Relationship between Employee Satisfaction, Employee Engagement, and Business Outcomes: A Meta-Analysis.* 87(2) J. of Applied Psychol. 268–279 (2002).

21. Edward L. Deci & Richard M. Ryan. *The "What" and "Why" of Goal Pursuits: Human Needs and the Self-Determination of Behavior.* 11 Psychol. Inquiry 227–268 (2000). Deci, Ryan, and their colleagues have researched the building blocks of motivation and engagement for more than three decades. As such, there is a substantial body of science supporting these three psychological needs.

22. Lawrence S. Krieger and Kennon M. Sheldon. *What Makes Lawyers Happy? Transcending the Anecdotes with Data from 6200 Lawyers.* 83 George Washington Law Review 554 (2015). Available at SSRN http://papers.ssrn.com/sol3/papers.cfm?abstract_id=2398989.

23. *Id.* at p. 24.

Experiences of autonomy, connection, and competence were found to have the highest correlation with well-being.[24]

Despite the law firm emphasis on external rewards and profits per partner, adults don't typically derive long-term meaning from extrinsic goals. In one study, adults with intrinsically motivated goals reported higher levels of life satisfaction and well-being and lower levels of anxiety and depression upon goal attainment. The adults with extrinsically motivated goals reported higher levels of anxiety and depression upon goal completion. They thought achieving these "profit" based goals would make them happier, and in the end, it didn't.[25]

Meaning matters in other ways as well. People who believe that their lives have meaning and purpose share a whole host of healthy benefits: they are happier, feel more in control over their lives, feel more engaged at work, and report less depression and anxiety and less workaholism.[26]

SKILL TO TRY: Create a bigger-than-self goal, which can also be done as a team exercise. A bigger-than-self goal is less about the objective goals you have like working a set number of billable hours; rather, it's more about how you see yourself within your community (which could mean in your firm, family, or larger community). Ask yourself what is it that you want to contribute and how you want to make an impact. When people are connected to bigger-than-self goals, they are more hopeful, curious, grateful, and inspired. Not surprisingly, they also show greater well-being and satisfaction with their lives.[27]

U: Utilize Positive Emotions

Resilient lawyers proactively build their positive emotionality through the use of humor, relaxation techniques, and optimistic thinking.[28] Additional studies showed that positive emotions predicted increases in both resilience and life satisfaction, and being able to utilize positive emotions during adversity may help buffer against stress and restore more productive coping habits.[29]

SKILL TO TRY: Set aside time every month for attorneys to share recent accomplishments as a group. Lawyers are trained to think about who's at fault, who's to

---

24. *Id.* at p. 25. The precise correlations are as follows: the correlation between autonomy and well-being is .66; the correlation between connection and well-being is .65; and the correlation between competence and well-being is .63.

25. Christopher Niemiec, Richard M. Ryan, & Edward L. Deci, *The Path Taken: Consequences of Attaining Intrinsic and Extrinsic Aspirations in Post-College Life.* 73(3) J. RES. PERSONALITY 291–306 (2009). *See also* Daniel H. Pink, DRIVE: THE SURPRISING TRUTH ABOUT WHAT MOTIVATES US 142–143 (2009).

26. Bryan J. Dik, Zinta S. Byrne & Michael F. Steger. PURPOSE AND MEANING IN THE WORKPLACE (2013).

27. Jennifer Crocker & Amy Canevello, *Consequences of Self-Image and Compassionate Goals, in* ADVANCES IN EXPERIMENTAL SOCIAL PSYCHOLOGY Vol. 45 232–273 (Patricia Devine and Ashby Plant eds., 2012). *See also* Kelly McGonigal, THE UPSIDE OF STRESS (2015). Dr. McGonigal uses the term "bigger-than-self" goals in her book.

28. Michele M. Tugade & Barbara L. Fredrickson (2004). *Resilient Individuals Use Positive Emotions to Bounce Back from Negative Emotional Experiences,* JOURNAL OF PERSONALITY AND SOCIAL PSYCHOLOGY, 86(2), 320–33.

29. Michele M. Tugade, Barbara L. Fredrickson & Lisa Feldman Barrett (2004) *Psychological Resilience and Positive Emotional Granularity,* JOURNAL OF PERSONALITY, 72(6) 1161–1190.

blame, and what to do to mitigate a client's risk. This constant problem-focused mentality is good lawyering, but can negatively impact everything from well-being to relationships.

S: Self-Care

The Ideal Worker culture (the creation of our modern day workplace where people are expected to be totally dedicated to their jobs and always on call, forcing people to choose to prioritize their jobs ahead of other parts of their lives) is burning people out at faster rates and zapping them of the precious energy and engagement they need to sustain their careers over the long haul. The Gallup organization surveyed more than 10,000 people to determine whether they were "fully charged"—getting regular doses of meaning, interactions, and energy at work. When asked to reflect about their day yesterday, only 11 percent of their sample reported having a great deal of energy.[30] Our collective lack of recovery is costing companies more than $60 billion a year.[31]

Daily recovery from work is crucial to maintain high levels of well-being, performance, and resilience. Recovery from work is defined as the process by which a person's functioning returns to pre-stressor levels and work-related strain is reduced.[32] It's not enough to go home and take a break. Optimal recovery is a combination of both internal recovery (the short breaks you take while you're at work) and external recovery (how you spend your time after work, on the weekends, and on vacation).[33]

SKILL TO TRY: Become a self-protective giver. Lawyers who frequently give of their time and talents can quickly find themselves confronting generosity burnout, unless they put some boundaries in place around their giving. A recent study found that selfless teachers saw significantly lower student achievement scores on year-end assessments (they exhausted themselves trying to help everyone with every request).[34] Successful givers prioritize requests for help, address their own needs (no more skipping lunch to help someone else), look to help multiple people with a single act of generosity, and chunk their giving into dedicated blocks of time.[35]

THE BENEFITS OF A RESILIENCE APPROACH

Resilience doesn't guarantee that you will be successful in every situation, but your capacity for recovery will be greatly increased such that you shift into adaptive behavior much more quickly when you encounter stress or a challenge.

---

30. Tom Rath, Are You Fully Charged? 7 (2015).

31. Shawn Achor & Michelle Gielan, *Resilience is about How You Recharge, Not How You Endure.* Harvard Business Review (June 24, 2016).

32. Wido G.M. Oerlemans, Arnold B. Bakker, & Evangelia Demerouti, *How Feeling Happy during Off-Job Activities Helps Successful Recovery from Work: A Day Reconstruction Study*, 28 Work & Stress, 198–216 (2014).

33. Evangelia Demerouti et al., *Daily Recovery from Work-Related Effort during Non-Work Time*, 7 Occ. Stress & Well-Being, 85–123 (2009).

34. Adam Grant & Reb Rebele, *Generosity Burnout.* Harvard Business Review (February, 2017).

35. *Id.*

The benefits of learning resilience skills as a method to become a more complete leader and lawyer, develop better work/life integration, manage challenge and stress, and prevent burnout are many. When you are more resilient:[36]

- You can tolerate change, stress, uncertainty and other types of adversity more effectively than those with lower levels of resilience. You develop healthier coping strategies and are therefore more likely to mitigate the impact of stress and adversity.
- You are more self-efficacious; meaning, you believe that you can produce results, achieve your goals, and feel effective in your life. You have a sense of agency and believe that problems can be solved as a result of your own efforts. This mindset helps to buffer against developing a "giving up" mentality and learned helplessness.
- You are more motivated to achieve in many different areas of life and are flexible in your ability to adapt to challenges, adversity, and changing life circumstances.

RESILIENCE WORKS

1. Success in the Legal Profession

Lawyers and law firms report different types of improvements after resilience training. Several firms I've worked with have implemented a gratitude wall: an area within the firm or a specific practice group to track thank-yous and team wins. These firms report that attendance at practice group meetings is higher and the attorneys look forward to sharing recent accomplishments—successes that would otherwise go unreported or unnoticed.

Numerous attorneys have emailed me to report closer relationships, particularly at home with family members. In addition, I have lost count of the number of lawyers who report that they are sleeping better because they are also remembering good things that happen during their day instead of constantly focusing on negative events or what went wrong. As lawyers get better at recognizing counterproductive thinking, they report lower levels of catastrophizing and have a better understanding of their thinking traps and how to reframe counterproductive thoughts. They have reported that they bounce back quicker from stressful situations and feel more confident taking stretch assignments.[37]

2. Success in the Military

We don't often think of the military as a place for progressive human management tools. It is. For more than three years, I had the privilege of teaching and training resilience skills to drill sergeants, non-commissioned officers, officers, and their

---

36. Andrew E. Skodol, *The Resilient Personality in* HANDBOOK OF ADULT RESILIENCE 112–125 (John W. Reich, Alex J. Zautra, & John Stuart Hall eds., 2010).

37. These results are summarized from thousands of emails, evaluation form responses, and personal discussions with workshop participants and professional development executives at dozens of law firms throughout the United States.

spouses as part of the Army's Comprehensive Soldier and Family Fitness program ("CSF2")[38] in partnership with the University of Pennsylvania. CSF2 is the Army's program to provide all Army community members with the psychological resources and skills to cope with stress and adversity and thrive in their lives. CSF2 has been able to scientifically validate the importance of resilience to performance and the effectiveness of resilience training for its soldiers. Here are some of the findings to date:[39]

- Officers who had higher levels of resilience were more likely to be promoted ahead of schedule, assigned the toughest jobs, and achieve the rank of Brigadier General (a one star general) or higher.
- Soldiers receiving resilience training reported higher overall emotional fitness, good coping ("When I get stressed out, I problem solve"), engagement ("I would choose my current work again if I had the chance"), friendship ("I have someone to talk to when I'm down"), and lower levels of catastrophizing ("When bad things happen to me, I expect more bad things to happen").
- Units with resilience trainers had significantly lower rates of substance abuse diagnoses and diagnoses for mental health issues, such as depression and anxiety (in some cases, the reduction in these diagnoses was as high as 60%).

CSF2 continues to expand its resilience training offerings to include a course for spouses of soldiers, a new executive course for high-ranking soldiers, and a course for teens. Ultimately, the CSF2 course was designed to create more resilient leaders in the military. While the stressors might look different in the law, law firms would be well-served to think about how training programs, like resilience, could enhance the leadership capacity and capability of their lawyers by specifically addressing the challenges lawyers face each day.

3. Success with Adults Generally

Many of the skills in the Army's resilience training course were adapted from the Penn Resiliency Project ("PRP"). The PRP has been evaluated in more than a dozen controlled studies. While some inconsistent findings have been reported, the studies suggest that PRP significantly reduces symptoms of depression and anxiety and helped participants perform better. In the studies that included long-term follow-ups, PRP resilience skill effects were found to last for two years or more.[40] More recent meta-analyses have demonstrated that resilience training is a useful means of developing mental toughness and well-being.[41]

---

38. For more information on the Army's CSF2 initiative, please visit http://csf2.army.mil.

39. To review a summary of these outcomes, please visit http://armymedicine.mil/Documents/CSF2InfoSheet-Mar2014.pdf. *See also* the following summary of both the empirical and popular media papers and articles of the CSF2 program at https://ppc.sas.upenn.edu/services/resilience-training-army.

40. Steven M. Brunwasser, Jane E. Gillham, & Eric S. Kim, *A Meta-Analytic Review of the Penn Resiliency Program's Effect on Depressive Symptoms*, 77(6) J. OF CONSULTING AND CLINICAL PSYCHOL. 1042–1054 (2009).

41. Ivan T. Robertson et al. *Resilience Training in the Workplace from 2003 to 2014: A Systematic Review*. 88 J. OF OCC. AND ORG. PSYCHOL. 533–562 (2015).

As outlined in this chapter, resilience is built through five specific pathways captured by the acronym FOCUS. Additional quick strategies to build your resilience include:

- Using a mindfulness technique called STOP, an acronym that stands for "Stop, Take a breath, Observe, Proceed." It's meant to be used as a quick time out to increase your self-awareness and self-regulation.[42]
- When you feel stuck or overwhelmed, ask yourself where you have a measure of control or influence in the situation.[43] This question helps to activate purposeful action.
- Track your Job Demands (aspects of your job that take consistent effort and energy) and Job Resources (aspects of your work that are motivational and energy-giving).[44] Do you have enough Job Resources to maintain your resilience and not burn out? If no, what is missing and how can you incorporate it?

Challenge and change are here to stay in the legal profession, and stress is not going away. Building the resilience of your organization—and the lawyers and other professionals in it—makes good business sense.

---

42. Bob Stahl & Elisha Goldstein, A MINDFULNESS-BASED STRESS REDUCTION WORKBOOK 60–61 (2010).

43. *Supra* note 16.

44. Arnold B. Bakker, Evangelia Demerouti, & Ana Isabel Sanz-Vergel *Burnout and Work Engagement: The JD-R Approach*. ANN. REV. OF ORG. PSYCHOL. & ORG. BEHAV. 389–411 (2014).

CHAPTER 7
The Lawyer in the Lotus
The Benefit of Yoga for Lawyers

Professor Nathalie Martin

Editor's Note: This book would not be complete without a chapter about yoga. I remember when Ropes and Gray began doing yoga classes in their library almost twenty years ago. Nathalie does a great job of sharing yoga philosophy in a way that resonates with my friend Maren Showkeir's book *Yoga Wisdom at Work*. More important, she introduces *stealth* yoga exercises you can do in and around your office. That's a way to generate well-being that you can begin right now!

People have been practicing yoga for over 5,000 years. The original reasons to practice yoga, to find peace and connect to the divine and to one's true nature, are as useful today as they were 5,000 years ago. This chapter introduces the history of yoga, the science behind its benefits, and the various forms of yoga practiced today. It is designed to help readers who are considering yoga find the right practice and reap the many benefits of this unique form of moving meditation.

Nathalie Martin is the Frederick M. Hart Chair in Consumer and Clinical Law at University of New Mexico School of Law, where she teaches commercial and consumer law as well as mindfulness and professional development. As a long time yoga practitioner, yoga teacher, and meditator, Nathalie is part of a growing movement to teach mindfulness and emotional intelligence in the law school classroom. This movement makes explicit that the interpersonal side of lawyering is critical and that many lawyers need help finding purpose or meaning in their work. Nathalie is the author of *Lawyering from the Inside Out: Learning Professional Development through Mindfulness and Emotional Intelligence* (Cambridge University Press) and *Yoga for Lawyers: Mind-Body Techniques to Feel Better All the Time* (ABA, with Hallie Love).

The goal of yoga science is to calm the mind, that without distortion,
it may hear the infallible counsel of the Inner Voice.[1]

—Paramahansa Yogananda

As lawyers, most of us are very busy people. We make choices every day about
how to spend our precious time, even if those choices involve mundane things like
whether to walk the dog, go to the gym, have another cup of coffee and a quiet
moment to ourselves, or return to a list of seemingly endless phone calls. This chapter
explains why yoga may be worth your time as well as how to start a yoga practice.

As a lawyer, law professor, long-time yoga practitioner, and yoga teacher, I have
witnessed yoga's transformative powers many times. These powers still surprise and
delight me. Perhaps that's because here in the west, we are conditioned to think of
yoga primarily as way to a way to stretch out and unwind. Yoga is very good for
that, and also to build strength and flexibility. Yet yoga can also help us in other
ways. Yoga philosophy is rich with lessons for the lawyer, or for anyone in a service
profession.

Yoga philosophy is a tremendous teacher. It helps us learn to be kind both to
ourselves and to others. After all, we are all connected. Yoga posture practice, or
asana, meaning the physical practice of yoga, helps us get in touch with our bodies,
our feelings, and other people.

Lawyers can use help with these interpersonal skills. According to a recent American Bar Association study, over 60 percent of clients polled had negative reactions to
their lawyers, even though the clients felt their lawyers were smart and knowledge-
able about the law. In fact, the more contact a client had with his or her lawyer, the
lower the client's opinion of the lawyer.[2] When asked to explain, clients said again
and again that lawyers seemed to lack care and compassion. Clients reported caring
more about feeling listened to and cared for than about the quality of the legal skills
of their lawyer. In other words, "caring is as much a part of the legal profession as
intelligence."[3]

This chapter discusses both of these interrelated aspects of yoga—first yoga philosophy and then the physical practice. It describes in some detail where yoga came
from and how it has been used successfully, before describing how to get started
practicing yoga.

INTRODUCTION TO YOGA: MORE THAN JUST PRETZEL POSES

Judging by the explosive growth in yoga in the western world (including the United
States), one would think yoga was relatively new. In fact, yoga is one of the oldest
practices in history that is used to calm and clarify the mind. The sheer longevity of
the practice gives yoga added credibility.

Over 5,000 years ago, an Indian sage named Patanjali wrote the first yoga
text, the *Yoga Sutras*. These sutras contain an eight-part philosophy of life and
self-improvement program that includes ethical principles, observances, yoga poses

---

1. Yogananda, AUTOBIOGRAPHY OF A YOGI (2007).
2. Douglas O. Linder & Nancy Levit, THE GOOD LAWYER SEEKING QUALITY IN THE PRACTICE OF
LAW (2014).
3. *Id.*

(*asana*), breath control, withdrawal of the senses, focused concentration, meditation, and if we get there, enlightenment. The *asana*, which we tend to associate with all of yoga here in the west, were originally devised solely to prepare Indian devotees for meditation.

The word *yoga* comes from a Sanskrit word with meanings that include "to bind, yoke, or join." In physiological terms, yoga means to join the body with the mind. In broader philosophical terms, yoga explicitly acknowledges our union with all other living beings and with the entire universe. According to yoga philosophy, yoga is not what joins us with all other living beings. Rather, we are already all joined—already one. While it is hard to document where and when he said it, Albert Einstein purportedly discovered this scientific principle in 1905, as he explains:

> A human being is a part of the whole called by us "universe," a part limited in time and space. He experiences himself, his thoughts and feelings as something separated from the rest, a kind of optical delusion of his consciousness. This delusion is a kind of prison for us, restricting us to our personal desires and to affection for a few persons nearest to us. Our task must be to free ourselves from this prison by widening our circle of compassion to embrace all living creatures and the whole of nature in its beauty.[4]

According to both the quotation attributed to Einstein and ancient yoga teachings, we exist only in relation to the world, including other people, so we have no separate existence in any real sense. We are completely and inseparably connected on a physical, mental, and emotional level with all other beings. This reality of connectedness explains why we feel terrible after we treat another person badly.

The idea that we are all connected differs from the ideas behind many western religious traditions, which often separate rather than join people together. Consider, for example, how many wars have been fought in the name of religion. Yoga, however, is not a religion at all. Yoga philosophy and *asana* can be practiced by people of all faiths or no faith at all.

Nevertheless, yoga philosophy does suggest that we refrain from harming other living beings; that we act truthfully; that we refrain from stealing, hoarding, and envy; and that we live a purposeful life. These restraints or ethical principles are similar to those espoused by most major religions of the world, but in yoga there is no shame. We avoid these harmful practices because through connectedness, when we harm others, we harm ourselves at the same time.

YOGA'S PRACTICAL APPLICATIONS

As the discussion above suggests, yoga is not just exercise. Yoga, when practiced mindfully, has the capacity to open us up both emotionally and physically, to help us see the world through fresh eyes, to slow us down, and to bring us in closer contact with our true selves. Yoga is a big help to lawyers because it helps us become more self-aware. Yoga also frees us from linear thinking and helps us become better lawyers by making us more creative. Finally, yoga gets us in touch with our bodies, which helps us experience emotions more fully and form more meaningful relationships with others.

---

4. Albert Einstein, 1905.

For many years, in my own practice, I considered yoga a physical practice, solely a stress reliever with some emotional benefits. Even when considered this way, yoga is great. From the very first practice, I slept better and got in better touch with my emotions. When I later also began to embrace yoga philosophy, yoga helped me on a deeper level. I achieved better outcomes at work and in my personal life due to enhanced self-awareness and enhanced emotional intelligence. Yoga makes me feel better about myself and about life. While yoga has now spread off the mat into life in general for me, even the initial physical benefits of yoga are incredibly beneficial and easy to achieve. Below, I explain how yoga has changed in recent years, some of the more tangible benefits of yoga, and how to get started if you are new to yoga. The chapter ends with ways you can practice yoga in the office and throughout your day.

HOW YOGA HAS CHANGED IN RECENT YEARS

In the past ten or so years, the West's relationship with yoga has shifted. Yoga has become dichotomous—more extreme in two directions. In some settings, such as many gyms and hot yoga studios, yoga has become more athletic and more competitive. In these settings, the focus is on fitness and exercise. While I am not opposed to fitness by any means, these classes do not feel like yoga to me. They feel like exercise classes in which yoga poses are offered as part of the exercise. Examples of this trend include Power Yoga, Piyo, Yogalates, Yoga Spin, and so on.

On the other hand, yoga's broader healing powers have recently been recognized in many unconventional settings. We have seen an enormous growth in non-profits that bring yoga to prisons; to veterans, soldiers, and military families suffering from PTSD; to homeless men and women; and to school-aged children in stress or trauma. For example, the nonprofit Warriors at Ease trains teachers to teach yoga and meditation to service members, veterans, and their families,[5] as does the Give Back Yoga Foundation.[6] Similarly, the founder of The Prison Project, realizing that many prisoners suffer from multiple traumas that are hard to treat, describes his project's goals as follows:

> Yoga as a mindfulness practice is our tool for reengaging prisoners with their bodies to restore the connection between mind, heart, and body. We use a yoga practice to develop the whole person, increase sensitivity toward oneself and empathy for others. By putting the men and women back in touch with their bodies, they begin to care more about themselves and understand the harm they have caused.[7]

Yoga has become a popular way for women to transform their lives in the West Bank and even to help people in refugee camps throughout the world. Hospitals around the country use yoga to aid in the healing process, both physically and mentally.

Yoga has been particularly beneficial in schools. The non-profit Bent on Learning, which brings yoga to New York's inner city schools, notes that one study showed a 93 percent decrease in violence and aggression as a result of yoga in school programs, and another showed higher test scores and improved emotional responses.[8]

---

5. Active Duty & Veterans Find Resources, WARRIORS AT EASE, http://warriorsatease.org/.
6. GIVE BACK YOGA FOUNDATION, http://givebackyoga.org/.
7. THE PRISON YOGA PROJECT, https://prisonyoga.org/.
8. BENT ON LEARNING, http://bentonlearning.org/research/.

Scientific research on the benefits of yoga is plentiful. For example, homeless women who are exposed to yoga have reported feeling at home in their own bodies for the first time. Victims of sexual assault report similar results from yoga, as do prisoners and soldiers returning from war. In other words, the power of yoga to transform lives and heal us has been rediscovered thousands of years after yoga's birth.

YOUR YOGA PRACTICE: GETTING IN TOUCH WITH THE BODY

Most people in the west try yoga to feel better physically. I initially practiced yoga for the simplest of reasons; it made me feel great.

Lawyers frequently live from the head up. Many of us overwork the mind and mostly ignore the body; what most of us need is to work the body harder and the mind less. We need to move around much more while also clearing the mind. Clearing the mind calms it and makes it more efficient and effective at problem-solving. It improves concentration, focus, and creativity.

This is where *asana* or pose practice comes in handy. Regardless of the type of yoga class we take, a unique feeling of stillness comes over us at the end of an *asana* practice. If you try it, you will feel the stillness set in. You will feel different from when you walked in, and not just from the workout. You will feel rested in a more gestalt way. Unlike other group movement classes, there is no competition and no place to go or be, and no particular goal other than being present. Ideally, we are able to live in the present moment during the entire class and keep focused on the poses. The practice restores rather than exhausts. The focus is on the present, not the past or the future, and we finally get an opportunity to enjoy life and live it.

Asana practice stops the mind from racing and nudges us into calm. The mind feels rested because resting the mind is part of all *asana* practice. Paradoxically, we are moving but also stopping the chatter. Stopping the mind chatter but moving the body allows us to easily reset. This pause clarifies our thinking and makes us more efficient, not to mention more self-aware and empathetic. *Asana* is a form of moving meditation. Perhaps not surprisingly, then, *asana* is a frequent gateway to more contemplative practices such as seated meditation and chanting.

CHOOSING A YOGA PRACTICE OR CLASS

So how do people begin yoga practice? Many of us start taking yoga at the gym. While I did this myself, and it sent me on the path of yoga, gyms can be odd places to practice yoga. The energy can be competitive and fitness-focused. There will likely be few things said at the beginning about yoga philosophy and few heartfelt messages about personal growth. The classes are often just poses. The classes also may be taught by fitness instructors who specialize in other things, such as spinning or muscle conditioning or sculpt classes. Nevertheless, the gym is one place to start your practice.

Another place to start practicing *asana* is with DVDs or online classes. My husband Stewart and I did this for a long time. We then began interspersing the DVDs with studio classes. This makes it possible to practice a bit every day without going to a studio every day. If you choose to practice with DVDs or online courses, it is best to go to a studio once in a while to make sure your form is correct, which brings me to the topic of studio classes.

Studio classes are critical to developing a practice. But how does one find a good studio? Word of mouth is one good way. Studios pop up all the time and they are of varying quality. Studios that have been in business for a long time are better for beginners than brand new studios. New studios are often filled with new teachers and beginners need to practice with experienced teachers to avoid injury.

Regardless of the studio you try, ask about the experience of the teachers before you buy a package at any studio. You need to feel comfortable and trust the studio and the teacher in order to get anything out of a yoga class. For example, I am 57 years old. I have been in classes with very new teachers who encouraged me to do things that I knew would not be good for me. We know our own bodies better than anyone else.

When first taking studio classes, try to pick a restorative, beginners, fundamentals, basics, alignment, or Yoga 1 class. Sometimes these classes are also called hatha, gentle, or slow. Avoid vinyasa, flow, mixed level, intermediate, Yoga 2 or 3, hot yoga, or power yoga, at least at first. Above all, once in the class, listen to your own body. Stretching and expanding is good, pain is not.

Try a few different teachers, too. When you meet a teacher, think about your overall impressions of him or her. Also think about your own intention in taking the class. What is it that you hope to get out of it? Do you want to be pushed physically? Do you want significant interpersonal growth, which requires receiving feedback on poses and other aspects of the practice? Or are you mostly looking for an encounter with a teacher with an open heart and an ability to develop self-acceptance? In my own classes, my goal is to help everyone feel better about themselves during the class and to help each person learn something about themselves. I tend to appreciate this open-hearted approach in the classes I take, rather than a 'tough love' approach. All classes aim to help you live in the present. Experiment and see what speaks to you.

Finally, don't be surprised if emotions come up while you are practicing, even in a group setting. Sometimes people even shed a tear or two. This is a normal way to let those emotions work their way through your body—but fear not. You don't need to cry to be a yogi!

STEALTH YOGA AROUND THE OFFICE

In addition to your studio classes, you can also practice stealth yoga all day, even in your office. It is fun to practice in ways that are not visible to others, but again, there is no shame in yoga. Practice if it makes you feel good and don't worry what others think. You might start a yoga revolution!

Here are a few suggestions for office yoga. If you would like to explore more poses and see some photographs of them, consider purchasing my American Bar Association book with Hallie Love, *Yoga for Lawyers: Mind-Body Techniques to Feel Better All the Time.*

Upright not Uptight

One thing that longtime yoga practitioners (called yogis if male, yoginis if female, and yogis if mixed company) consistently have is perfect posture. Yogis make it a point not to slouch, even when not in yoga class.

Start your yoga practice very simply by sitting upright and not slouching in your chair. Recall that yoga poses are called *asanas* and each one has a Sanskrit name ending in *–asana*. An example is triangle pose, or *trikonasana*. Yoga teacher and author of *Yoga of the Subtle Body* Tias Little jokingly calls our most common everyday pose "slump-asana."[9] As he says, we practice it for hours a day! We need to work extra hard to avoid slump-asana.

To do this, put a pillow or a blow-up lumbar roll under your low back at the base of your chair, as well as your car seat. While at work, if you can, sit on an exercise ball for part of your day too. You can buy a stand-up desk or, if you really want to go for it, explore getting a treadmill desk. Just be sure you have another place to sit with a colleague or client so that you aren't towering way above your visitors.

Take a Walk on the Wild Side

- Stand up and walk around every hour or so.
- When you begin, scrunch your shoulders and roll your neck to let go of some tension.
- Then stand nice and straight in a position we call "mountain pose," with your shoulderblades down your back, chest open, head over shoulders, shoulders over hips, and hips over ankles.
- Keep those shoulderblades and collarbones down and the chest lifted as you walk about.
- Use this opportunity to talk in person rather than email—or just walk or run the stairs.
- While you are coming and going, practice five-count breathing.
- Feel the openness and optimism as you focus on your breath.

Develop Your Inner Desk Dog

- Stand up near your desk with some space behind you.
- Put your hands on your desk and walk your feet back until your forearms are resting on the desk and your back is straight, parallel with the floor.
- Stretch your glutes (your buns) back as far as you possibly can. Imagine the tip of the tailbone rising to meet the sky.
- Breathe deeply and stretch back, allowing the back to become parallel with the floor and the head and neck to be a natural extension of the spine.
- Keep the back nice and straight. Hold the pose for five deep breaths and come up. Do this three times.

Twist and Shout

Actually, there is no need to shout, but twisting the body massages the internal organs and promotes digestion. It also feels amazing.

- Sit in your chair with your back straight and your hands on your knees.
- Then bring your left hand to your right knee and place the right hand somewhere on the chair behind you.

---

9. Tias Little, Yoga of the Subtle Body: A Guide to the Physical and Energetic Anatomy of Yoga (2016), 86.

- Keep the shoulders down and the chest lifted.
- Take a nice deep breath and twist to the right, allowing the twist to originate at the lower ribs and work all the way up to the shoulders, eventually looking over your right shoulder.
- Stay there for five cleansing breaths.
- After that, on exhale, slowly allow the head to come back to center.
- Then allow the rest of the body to follow. Switch to the other side. Sweet!

For a second twist that also stretches out the shoulders:

- Start in the same upright position with your hands on your knees.
- Hinge forward at your hips, keeping your spine neutral.
- Place the right forearm on the inside of the right leg and press the knee outward just a bit. Reach the left arm out to the left and up, keeping the shoulders back.
- Give it five sweet deep breaths.
- Sit up and switch sides. Enjoy!

Hip Hip Hooray

Remember that emotions are experienced in the body, not the mind. The mind only experiences the thoughts associated with an emotion. For every negative emotion, even one we are not aware of, there is a physiological response—often pain, tightness, and constriction. One place we store negative emotional energy, such as anger, anxiety, and sadness, is in the hips.

- To set that energy free, start in that same upright seated position, hands on knees.
- Reach down and hold your right ankle. Place the right ankle above the left knee.
- Sit up nice and tall, with your shoulders back and your chest lifted.
- Gently hinge forward at the hip crease with a neutral spine. Do not force the right knee to drop; it may be very high, but that just means you need a good hip stretch. (Make sure you feel sensation in the hip or thigh, not in the knee. You may even hug the knee in toward you if that helps you avoid knee strain.)
- Gently twist your ribcage to the right and the left, releasing that tension in the hip.
- Hold for five breaths and switch to the other side. Feel the release!

Do Something Fishy

- Move any pillow out of the way if there is one at the back of your chair.
- Start in the same upright position described above, hands on knees, shoulders back, chest lifted.
- Form fists with your hands and place those fists at the base of the back of your chair, where the seat and chair back meet.
- Press your weight firmly into those fists and press the elbows into the chair, arching the back into a seated backbend.

- If it is comfortable, look up towards the ceiling. If not, look forward with the back arched.
- Give it five deep breaths and enjoy this seated version of the yoga "fish pose," which is thought to cure a long list of ailments. Whether it does or not, it feels great!

Lift Exhaustion and Your Legs

Consider practicing 'legs up the wall pose' when you are really exhausted. I did it preparing to give a talk in Paris, before which I had flown all night. It did the trick.

- Close your door. Set your phone to "do not disturb," and then set the timer to go off in five to ten minutes.
- Find a piece of empty wall space in your office.
- Sit next to the wall with your right hip and shoulder almost touching the wall and your legs stretched out on the floor next to the wall.
- Then lie down on your left side and, rolling onto your back, lift the legs up the wall.
- Your spine and head will be lying on the floor. Your glutes should be touching or close to the wall.
- If it is more comfortable, you can place a cushion or folded blanket under your sacrum (where your spine meets the back of your hips).
- Stay here for five to ten relaxing minutes. This restorative yoga pose can make you feel as if you just took a nice long nap; you emerge refreshed and clear-headed.
- While there with your legs up the wall, engage in five-count breathing until the alarm goes off.
- If thoughts arise, and they will, acknowledge them and let them go, bringing the attention back to your breath.

Sigh It Out with Lion's Breath

This one is a little funky, I know, but please try it. It could become your favorite. You can also look this pose up online if you want to see someone doing the pose. Just search "seated lion's pose."

- Move away from your desk as you are going to swiftly move your head and upper body forward in this deeply cleansing and satisfying pranayama (breath work) pose.
- Start in the same upright position as the other seated poses, with hands on knees.
- Arch your back, inhale deeply, open your mouth, stick out your tongue, lean forward swiftly and let out a huge "HHHHAAA" sound.
- Do this four, long, enjoyable times and see how cleansed and clear you feel. Go ahead—spit it out!

This pose rids us of negative emotions and detoxifies the head and neck. I did this pose in the bathroom of the U.S. Senate before some Banking Committee testimony I recently gave. It calmed me down and allowed me to send only positive vibes to people on both sides of the aisle.

CONCLUSION

I suppose it is obvious that I love yoga. While yoga doesn't cure every problem in the world, it does make it easier to deal with life's problems. For me, yoga means smoother sailing through life, and an ability to swim with rather than against the current.

As you develop your yoga practice, try to stay open to whatever other challenges and growth opportunities your yoga practice brings you. You've heard about many of the physical and mental benefits of yoga, but the benefits of yoga don't end on the mat. We practice yoga to be calm, strong and flexible, but yoga can also help us find the inner voice that points us toward our greater purpose. Being a lawyer can be one of the most fulfilling jobs on earth. I hope that through your developing yoga practice, your law practice and the rest of your life can become richer. At first the shifts yoga creates are subtle, but over time they can be momentous, assuming you are open to wherever your practice takes you.

CHAPTER 8
Healthy Brands Win

Katy Goshtasbi, JD

Editor's Note: I met Katy a few years ago when I was presenting at the ABA Law Practice Division Leadership Conference. She liked what I was saying about personal presence. When I found out what she was doing, and the transition she had made from being a securities lawyer, I was intrigued. A big part of the intrigue was that I had both done a great deal of work on my personal brand and thought it important enough to develop an ABA Annual Meeting Program around it with John Mitchell, another one of the authors in this book. Branding as Katy shares it is much more about personal identity than marketing. Yet, as she explains, it's a very effective and powerful attractor.

Developing your own intentional brand is directly tied to your well-being. By being intentional about your message, you reduce stress on yourself and boost your confidence. This change alone is instrumental to well-being. You also increase your emotional resonance by being happier. In this way, others find you more attractive—as a human and as a lawyer. This shift impacts well-being directly as well. Branding is a marathon and not a sprint. A healthy brand takes time to develop. Nothing great is created overnight or in a vacuum. Healthy branding is an iterative process that takes time, patience, creativity, and willingness to be curious.

Katy Goshtasbi is a former securities lawyer where she practiced for 14 years at the SEC, in a law firm, as a federal lobbyist, and in-house. For a decade now, she has run a global brand development company. She collaborates with lawyers to develop brands and brand cultures that attract clients and attention and allow each lawyer be less stressed and happier. She has authored *Personal Branding In One-Hour For Lawyers* (ABA Publications, 2013) and will Chair the ABA Law Practice Division in 2018–2019.

Finally, a renewed focus on lawyer health and wellness, and so the writing of this book. For so long the assumption was that a successful lawyer referred to substantive success within the practice of law. Then the perspective shifted to health in terms of substance abuse and suicide. As we now know, the statistics suggest a deeper perspective on lawyer health. Our success as lawyers is deeply tied to our strength as well-rounded and healthy human beings.

What does wellness have to do with marketing and branding yourself as a lawyer? Simply put, healthy brands win. What does this mean? Branding once meant logos and traditional marketing notions. Those days are long over—for lawyers and everyone else.

A person's brand is our relevant attributes and strengths, how we choose to communicate those attributes to our audience, and then how the audience perceives this message and brand.

If the goal is to develop business and be seen, heard, and promoted, then we, as the person, are the most important component of this "brand" equation. Not what we do as lawyers, but who we are as humans. Would you buy a car missing a tire or a pair of shoes that were missing a heel? Probably not. For the same reason, no one wants to hire a lawyer who does not have a healthy brand presence and message, based on a healthy sense of self.

From this process, the evolution of brand culture within a law firm setting grows and matures. Every firm has a brand culture, whether intentional or not. This brand culture is based on each individual lawyer's brand values. Brand values are based on each individual lawyer as a person. A firm's brand culture exists no matter what. An effective firm brand culture includes each lawyer's brand values, developed with intention and focus.

HEALTHY BRAND PRESENCE

Who Are You?

We can probably agree that it is much easier to focus on our functional and substantive legal practice than to focus on who we are as people. After all, we've been trained to be good lawyers and we know how to do so. We are comfortable with our substantive work.

The tougher part is to be courageous and take a look inward to figure out who we are—who we are as a person. This inquiry has little to do with our work as a lawyer. It is an inquiry into individual memories and ideas and beliefs as we have evolved as a human. Essentially, it's about looking at the story of you, your autobiography, and seeing what life experiences have made you who you are today—as a person and as a lawyer. For instance, my immigrant status informs much of my world and actions. It's so very personal. It's a process that can be therapeutic, fun, scary, and very necessary.

Why does this matter to the practice of law, a lawyer's brand, and getting business as a lawyer? It's about authenticity and trust. Brands that are authentic are trusted. When we trust, we engage and hire. This trust builds and grows off our emotional needs and gut feelings. If we do not effectively know you and feel a connection with you emotionally, then we are not likely to engage with you, hire you, promote you, etc. The deeper and more intimate the emotional connection, the better your brand works—the higher recall we have for you and the more memorable you are for us.

From this process of figuring out who you are, you are able to establish an optimal framework for explaining why you are good at what you do substantively, why we should care, and how we can develop a relationship with you.

Support

The biggest struggle in building a healthy brand presence based on the inquiry of who we are is taking a leap of faith to believe this process is relevant. As lawyers, we could be better at marketing ourselves in many respects. Throw into the tasks of marketing strategy a deep dive into memories and our individual pasts? For most of us, this is a place we don't want to go and, in fact, hope to forget.

The first step is finding a support mechanism to meet your goal. Since this process is simple to understand, but not always easy to do, support is fundamental. This support could take the shape of colleagues, friends, peers, family, and/or consultants trained in this discipline. The goal is to stay open and know that this process works best when there is collaboration spawned from a support system to keep us accountable and to encourage us to keep going.

Stress and Self-Confidence

What impedes a healthy brand presence? One answer is stress. Research has shown a direct, inverse correlation between stress and your personal brand. The higher a person's stress, the lower the self-confidence and the less effective the personal brand value. No one wants to be around someone who is stressed, much less hire them and pay them good money!

These days it seems everything stresses us out. An astounding number of cell phone users stress out when their phone battery is low. Part of this is generational. Yet, part of this is about a culture that has been created with more reasons to stress. Stress is sexy. It seems we feel important when we can say we are stressed because we are busy and wanted and useful.

Common marketing wisdom shows that our audience does not buy what we do for a living (i.e., our legal substantive knowledge). They buy based on how they feel about us as people. Emotions outweigh content. The only emotion that really sells anything is happiness. The product industry has mastered this concept. As professionals, we have a long way to go on this notion.

So how do we reduce our stress and increase personal brand effectiveness? Here are five obvious yet hard to practice concepts that are a MUST for everyone. Practice these techniques to focus and reduce the negative effects of stress.

1. **Meditate or sit still.** The more one does, the faster paced we tend to become. We all notice the busy pace of others. We tend not to like it because we have enough of it in our own lives, so it doesn't attract us. A fast pace based on stressful living means our brand is seen as messy and unfocused. Unfortunately, we are not used to being still anymore. We tend to find ways to create busyness in our lives because we are, in a way, addicted to that pace. Find ten minutes (at least) each day to sit in silence and do NOTHING. This process will help you focus, and you come across as more credible.
2. **Keep a gratitude list/journal.** The more grateful we are about the everyday things in life, the better our lives. Recall, the goal is creating HAPPY personal brands for all lawyers. Projecting a happy personal brand that others want to follow requires us to first feel happy. End of story.

3. **Take inventory.** Sit down once a quarter and review your calendar. Do you really need to be doing all the activities on your calendar? Does each activity optimize your life? Does the activity make your soul sing? Do you get business as a result? Does your personal brand shine with the activity? Be honest. No one is grading you but you.

4. **Paint it RED.** At least three times a week, do your best to paint it red. In situations where you are not sure what to say or how to interact with people, be HONEST and sincere and tell them the exact truth or reasoning behind your mindset and/or activity. Watch the weight get lifted and stress come down. These are the personal brands that shine because of impactful and direct communication.

5. **Be kind.** Being kind boosts our self-confidence because we have done something nice for another and feel good about ourselves. Being kind attracts kindness. Being kind boosts your personal brand and relieves your stress. This is easier said than done. Just being aware of when you are kind and when you are not is a great start. Don't forget to be kind to yourself. This is not "mushy" or "touchy feely" advice. This is simply how humans respond best to stimulus—through kindness rather than fear.

Being kind also requires us to build our "empathy" muscle. Spend ten minutes each day being self-aware of whether each interaction we have with others or with ourselves is from a place of empathy.

Healthy Brand Message

Once the discovery of "Who You Are" has been made, then the process of shaping this information into a message to share with the world begins. If we skip the first part, the messaging part is four times as difficult and 99 percent less effective. Why? The foundation for the healthy brand message has not been set. In brand development, the notion of "the two Cs" are very important—clarity and consistency. If we are not clear on who we are foundationally, there is no path from which a healthy, consistent, and effective brand message can evolve.

The term "healthy" here refers to a brand message that is true to who we really are and aspire to be as a person. When the message is healthy, it has authenticity and comes from a place of genuine integrity. The message lands on the target audience with ease and grace and sinks in. The result is that the audience responds well, naturally. From there, anything is possible.

Process in Action: Example from the Trenches

How does all this come together? Take the example of a client law firm. Let's call them XYZ firm. XYZ came to us looking to scale their brand and culture. They were stagnating after having grown to over 100 lawyers, yet repeatedly dropping down to around 80 lawyers. This signaled some apathy among their lawyers—if attrition was high, then employees were not feeling valued nor understanding their place at the firm. This also accounted for why revenues were stagnating.

Their chief culture officer fully admitted to not understanding how to scale growth. What she understood was that growth required a healthy brand culture for the entire firm. This brand culture had to be based on a stable brand for each individual attorney.

The first step was laying down a stable foundation for the firm. This required working with each individual attorney to unearth his or her unique brand. We looked at a baseline of where each one was and where each one wanted to go. We delved into their personal stories to gather enough data to develop their brand and message, uncovering why they were invested in their practice and clients.

We assessed strengths and taught the lawyers how these strengths were their true tools to success. These strengths were unique and, combined with their individual stories, sold them to others. We armed lawyers with more tools for their toolbox, such as to how to manage their brands by being self-aware of how they were coming across to others and dealing with the ups and downs of practicing law. We collaborated with each lawyer to understand where he or she fit into the firm and his or her financial and overall impact on the firm brand. The final step was to take these individual brands and create practices to develop the entire firm brand culture. This led to the brand messaging and content for firm marketing.

Within six months of this process, revenues increased. Why? Morale increased because each lawyer understood his or her individual contribution to the firm. As a result, productivity and engagement were up. This meant that business development naturally increased. Because a strong firm brand culture was developing, the mood in the firm was elevated. Not only did this lead to higher billable hours and revenues, it lead to happier and healthier lawyers.

CONCLUSION

Developing your own intentional brand is directly tied to your well-being. By being intentional about your message, you reduce stress on yourself and boost your confidence. This change alone is instrumental to well-being. You also increase your emotional resonance by being happier. In this way, others find you more attractive as a human and as a lawyer. This shift impacts well-being directly and attracts people to you.

Branding is a marathon and not a sprint. A healthy brand takes time to develop. Nothing great is created overnight or in a vacuum. Healthy branding is an iterative process that takes time, patience, creativity, and willingness to be curious.

Start one step at a time, go slow, be kind to yourself and realize you are doing foundational and groundbreaking work. This process not only benefits your business and career, it benefits you personally and benefits the world on a larger scale than you know it. Most importantly, remember the happiness part and have fun in the process. Otherwise, what's the point?

Part II
Self-Management

CHAPTER 9
Increasing Well-Being
Minimizing Self-Sabotage and Maximizing Self-Empowerment

Diane Costigan, MA

Editor's Note: Tools, tools, and more tools! That's what Diane is all about. I've known Diane for almost 20 years. I've watched her go from junior professional development associate to law firm consultant back to becoming the first in-house full-time coach in a rapidly expanding large law firm. She cares about people and uses her martial arts background and discipline to help people get from here to there as she has done with herself. She lays out in meticulous detail how we get in the way of getting to where we want to be and how we can empower ourselves to get beyond what's in the way. Stay mindful and follow the steps and process. Step by step, one foot then the next. You realize you have climbed a mountain!

At some point almost all of us self-sabotage. We get in the way of our own self-proclaimed goals. We say we want these goals but don't take steps that would move the needle in the *right* direction. Other times, we act in ways that propel us in the exact *opposite* direction of where we want to be. Getting in the way of our own goals can compromise our well-being as many of the goals we set are meant to be in furtherance of our well-being, whether it is to exercise, meditate, or sleep more; improve our overall health through diet and lifestyle changes; or find more balance. When we resist these goals, we are keeping ourselves from living healthier, happier, more fulfilling lives. But there is hope. This chapter explores what self-sabotage is, why it can be so hard to overcome, a strategic approach to conquering it, and some self-empowering best practices to help navigate your way.

Diane Costigan has more than 20 years of experience helping lawyers maximize and enjoy their careers. As Director of Coaching at Winston & Strawn LLP and the former Head of the Coaching Practice at Volta Talent Strategies, she has an integrative approach to coaching attorneys on business development, stress and time management, leadership, and executive presence. Diane spent ten years overseeing recruiting, legal personnel, and professional development and training for a global Am Law 100 law firm. Diane is certified in both executive and health coaching as well as Emotional Freedom Technique (EFT/Tapping) and has practiced meditation for nearly 20 years. She is passionate about helping lawyers so that they can excel.

SELF-SABOTAGE: WHAT IS IT AND HOW DOES IT SHOW UP?

Almost all of us self-sabotage at some point in our lives. We get in the way of our own self-proclaimed goals. Goals that we say we want. Goals that we say are meaningful to us, like losing weight, exercising more, and reclaiming time for self-care, or work-related objectives like making partner or bringing in more business. Goals that either directly or indirectly relate to our well-being. We say we want these goals but don't take steps that would move the needle in the *right* direction. Other times, we act in ways that propel us in the exact *opposite* direction of where we want to be. I'm not talking about the occasional one-off mistake or poor choice. Self-sabotage, a self-defeating behavioral pattern, has both scale (how much or how frequently you engage in the behavior) and scope (the depth or breadth of the behavior).

I once worked with a lawyer who had been drinking up to 12 cups of coffee a day (scale) for the past six years (scope). This particular attorney was working on a number of goals, but maintaining a calm demeanor was at the top of the list. In our first meeting, he downed three cups of coffee in an hour. It was clear this was at least one form of self-sabotage that was not only getting in the way of success with his goal, but also his overall well-being.

My role as a coach to lawyers is to help them set and achieve goals that are meaningful to them. That often involves surfacing specific steps, approaches, strategies, and tools they may need to be successful. Most of the time, it will also involve helping them to overcome resistance they may have to actually implementing their coaching plan. You can have the most comprehensive strategy for your goals, but in the absence of taking action, not much will happen.

Sometimes resistance is easy to spot at the beginning of a coaching engagement, and other times it is not apparent until the lawyer is not taking any meaningful action toward their goals. This chapter outlines a coaching approach to help bust through self-sabotage when it is preventing you from progress and implementing self-empowering behaviors and self-talk. I'll walk you through a case study to provide a sense of how self-sabotage manifests itself. We'll also explore a strategic approach to how you can overcome what might be getting in the way of your goals.

Self-sabotage shows up in any number of ways. One of the most common I see among lawyers is an excess or surplus of something—the most frequent is overcommitment or working too much. Other common areas of excess are worry (e.g., constantly worrying about losing your job or worrying about specific aspects of life like your job, relationships, health, etc.), pessimism and analysis-paralysis (e.g., overanalyzing, overthinking, and not being able to make decisions). On the opposite side of the spectrum, self-sabotage can show up as a deficiency or deprivation. Not getting enough sleep, not eating or exercising enough, not getting any down time, and so on.

In dealing with self-sabotage, I often refer to the "Pernicious Three Ps": procrastination, perfectionism, and people pleasing. People pleasing can lead to its close cousin, overcommitment. A common trend I see is that overcommitting to others often goes hand in hand with under-committing to oneself. In many ways, self-sabotage can create its own self-perpetuating system that causes an overall feeling of being stuck and unable to move forward toward one's goals. Feeling stuck is often a telltale sign that self-sabotage may be wreaking havoc on your goals.

To highlight the self-perpetuating system self-sabotage can create, allow me to introduce you to Sarah. Sarah is a high potential, homegrown seventh-year associate who is well respected and well liked by her practice group and firm leadership.

When I asked her what goals she wanted to work on in coaching, she responded in a notably teary delivery, "I want to make partner. But I don't think I can do this anymore." Here's what else I heard from Sarah:

- She feels like her schedule has gotten increasingly out of control over the years, and she's stretched too thin.
- She has a very close relationship with the partners she works with and doesn't want to let them down, so she keeps taking on additional responsibility.
- She always answers phone calls and emails—especially from clients and partners but from associates as well. Many of the partners and the associates on her team often stop by to ask her questions and she feels like she should make time for them. As a result, it seems like she can never get to her own work until 6 or 7pm after everyone has started to shut down, so she ends up staying later than she would like (people pleasing and overcommitment).
- She has difficulty saying no when the firm asks her to do something like join a committee (she's on the Associates Committee and the Women's Committee), serve as a mentor, or do an interview.
- She feels like she's running on fumes. She is not sleeping well and repeatedly hits snooze on her alarm clock each morning to get some extra sleep, even though this results in not exercising and starting her day in a scramble.

Sarah had several *different* types of self-sabotage operating simultaneously and interrelatedly that she wanted to address to get out from under the weight of feeling hopeless, so she could progress toward her goal of partnership. Her core self-defeating behavioral pattern of choosing to put other people's priorities first caused her to have no time and energy to devote to her own. While self-sabotage is an inhibitor to overall success, happiness, and well-being, there is some good news. In many cases, with a strategic, self-supportive, and systematic approach, even the most entrenched self-sabotage can be overcome. For self-sabotage that has deeper psychological roots, however, it is always advisable to work with a mental health professional.

WHY IS SELF-SABOTAGE SO HARD TO OVERCOME?

Self-defeating, counter-intuitive behaviors that compromise goal attainment can be overcome, but it is not easy. It takes time, energy, dedication, discipline, and a strategic approach. Before starting the process, you need to step back and look at a compounding problem. Self-sabotage often creates additional stress in our lives. Not the good kind of stress that challenges us and gives us a boost of adrenaline to cross the finish line. It's the kind that exhausts and depletes us. When we are in energy-depleted states, it can be incredibly challenging to work towards a goal, let alone put in extra effort to breach our own self-sabotage.

Take the case of Sarah. Sarah was grappling with multiple forms of self-sabotage: people pleasing, overcommitment, and lack of self-care. The cumulative effects of each of these on Sarah led to her being chronically stressed, exhausted, and feeling hopeless and disempowered. It also meant that every day she was likely to continue to get in her own way, whether it was snapping at someone who she might need to help or making a careless mistake that would take additional time to correct.

It was clear that Sarah needed to break through these underlying patterns of behavior to succeed her goal of making partner. To do so, she needed some vital resources:

time, energy, and motivation. The resources and plan Sarah needed were at high risk of being compromised by self-sabotaging behavior (like snoozing her alarm clock or convincing herself she didn't have the time). I like to call this *stressotage*: what happens when we try to make changes or improvements while already stressed.

When stuck in patterns of self-sabotage, it can feel as if we can't help ourselves from engaging in the behavior, whether it's having that third glass of wine, eating the second helping of dessert, or skipping exercise in lieu of television time. We can't help ourselves because we're likely stuck in a stress loop without resources or an exit strategy. Because we are stressed, we do not have access to the more creative thinking parts of our brain, so rather than focusing on solutions and possibilities, we only see challenges and problems. (This thinking is endemic to lawyers because seeing problems is what we get paid for, but it's not helpful to our personal ecology!) We may also be stuck in our own disempowering story or victim mentality, reinforcing our perception of a lack of solutions.

All is not lost. We can find those resources. We can develop and implement an exit strategy. We can develop a "beginner's mind" that sees substituting empowering behaviors as a learning process and shift to a more empowering story. The key is to start small, to support ourselves along the way, and to not stop prematurely. In Sarah's case, we started with implementing some small steps to help her regain some energy. The trick was to identify manageable changes that were easy to implement without self-sabotage getting in the way. The big-picture strategy: she would not put someone else's priorities in front of hers; she would not add more things to her overcommitted schedule; and she would not capitulate because she was too tired (which was her typical excuse for her lack of self-care activities).

After some exploration and brainstorming, we landed on helping her get more sleep. And for more than a week, that was the only thing we focused on so that she did not feel overwhelmed. First, we concentrated on helping her get just ten minutes more of sleep. We then worked up to thirty minutes and, ultimately, an additional hour each day. We made a micro-change to the story she was telling herself around sleep. Instead of telling herself "it is impossible for me to get to bed before 12:30 am," she shifted to "I am open to the possibility of getting to bed before 12:30 am." It was a subtle shift, but it gave her more hope and motivation than she had before. As she was more successful with this first micro-change, she was able to continue to shift to an even more positive sleep story. The micro-changes to her sleep routine involved setting an alarm for going to bed and listening to a guided meditation to fall asleep. The more empowering narrative helped energize her enough to start working on the rest of her self-sabotage.

"A-D-O-P-T" A NEW APPROACH—FIVE STEPS TO BREAKING FREE FROM SELF-SABOTAGE

You are likely struggling with self-sabotage if you have been working towards a goal that is still unrealized or have been unsuccessful with a desired behavior change. To break unhelpful patterns of behavior, emotional intelligence concepts of self-knowledge, self-awareness, and self-management are critical tools to leverage. In Sarah's case, she knows that she has the tendency to be a people-pleaser (self-knowledge). She also knows she is most likely to people-please when one of the partners she is close to asks her to do something (self-awareness). It is in those moments that she needs to implement a tool or strategy to avoid people-pleasing (self-management). It's important to remember that changing long-standing patterns of behavior, particularly self-sabotaging ones, is a process that has starts and stops as well as ups and downs. Often, it is helpful to work with a coach who can help you take it in stages. Here are five steps that can help you "A-D-O-P-T" a new approach to conquering your self-sabotage:

1. **Awareness:** You need to be aware of the self-sabotage itself—what it is and how it manifests. Second, you must be aware of and alert to, moment to moment, self-sabotage.
2. **Diagnose:** Gain an understanding of what is causing you to self-sabotage.
3. **Objective:** Counterbalance awareness and diagnosis with your ultimate goal and objective to help connect your efforts to something you value.
4. **Plan:** Bridge awareness and meeting your objective or goal with a strategic plan that closes the gap.
5. **Take Action:** Execute your plan. It's important to take action, even if it is only small steps, to keep the needle moving forward.

Step One: Awareness

It may seem overly simplistic, but acknowledging self-sabotage and identifying the form it is taking is the first step in overcoming it. Sometimes, self-sabotage can be a blind spot—a behavior we engage in without our awareness, like pessimism or passive-aggressiveness. An important aspect of recognizing self-sabotage is cultivating a keen awareness of what triggers the sabotage or, even better, when it is likely to take place. This can be challenging because it is often so ingrained that we don't even notice when it is happening. To overcome self-sabotage, we must shift from engaging in the behavior and self-talk mindlessly to being mindful and *aware* of implementing a new more helpful behavior. The new approach will become internalized—effortless—and the autopilot will be self-serving rather than self-defeating.

Cultivating awareness is itself a process that happens in stages. It can be achieved through intense reflection and introspection, and it can be enhanced and expedited by the use of a coach who can give direct feedback about what she or he observes and collect feedback from other key stakeholders. Coaches can serve as powerful guides to identifying critical self-knowledge, building self-awareness, and brainstorming tools and approaches for self-management. Perhaps best of all, they provide the support and accountability necessary to navigate a change process.

Sarah and I first spent time getting clear on the situations that were most likely to trigger her people-pleasing, as well as some of the *tells* that would help her know she was being triggered. One powerful tell was a heaviness she would feel in her chest every time she had overcommitted due to people-pleasing. Acknowledging the self-sabotaging behavior is a solid step to conscious recognition, but sometimes you don't catch yourself in real time. For example, Sarah would often catch herself people-pleasing after committing to do something she didn't really have time for. This is often where people throw up their hands and proclaim themselves incurable. My question to Sarah was, "So what if you did people-please this time?" The important thing was that she ultimately caught herself and put herself in the process of decreasing unhelpful mindlessness while increasing mindfulness.

Cultivating awareness is often a process of starting backwards. When Sarah found herself self-sabotaging after the fact, we came up with a plan. First, we worked on having her stop wherever she was, acknowledge that she had self-sabotaged, give herself a *do-over* to identify what she would have done differently and then commit to do that the next time she found herself in that situation. Doing so increased her awareness such that she was quickly able to catch herself in real time when she was about to people-please and could use a predetermined tool or strategy to avoid the behavior and make a more empowered choice. Eventually, she was able to increase her awareness, so much so that she knew ahead of time when she was likely to people-please and was able to avoid falling into the trap.

Step Two: Diagnose

Awareness is an important first step, but it is also helpful to pair it with an understanding or diagnosis of why the self-sabotage is occurring. Sometimes, even when we are fully aware that we are about to engage in self-sabotaging behavior, we make the choice to do it anyway. Digging deep below the surface to gain understanding can give you insight into the direction you might take to overcome self-defeating behaviors. Self-sabotage can seem so persistent and hard to overcome because we haven't taken the time to investigate its root cause. Understanding why you might be self-sabotaging unlocks the key to freeing yourself from it. Not doing so leaves you susceptible to it; it remains fully intact despite your best attempts to bust through it.

Here are three questions to ask to start the process of excavating what might be underlying unhelpful behavioral patterns:

1. How is this behavior serving me? It might seem like a counter-intuitive question, but we usually do not engage in behaviors that aren't serving us—even if it is on a subconscious level. Often, it is a pattern that served us well in the past but now is hard to give up. Here are some places to look for further exploration:

   - **Is this keeping me safe?** In Sarah's case, her overcommitment was a pattern from her childhood. She was the only child of parents who both worked, so she was always signing up for activities and social engagements to avoid being lonely. At work, she felt as though her likeability was tied to saying *yes*.
   - **Would giving this up compromise my sense of identity?** I once worked with a lawyer who felt like double and triple checking every piece of work product was a key to his success as a junior associate. As a junior partner with more work and responsibility on his plate, that behavior was compromising his success. Because of his reputation as a perfectionist, he had a hard time giving it up.

2. What am I afraid of? Fear can be a key subconscious motivator for self-defeating behavior. There are a few places to look when it comes to fear and self-sabotage.

   - **Fear of success:** Sometimes success with a behavior change might bring some perceived negative consequences—like having to keep up with the changes. An example is a lawyer who self-sabotages her business development efforts because she's afraid if she brings more work in she won't have time to do it.
   - **Fear of failure:** Of course, the potential for failing at a behavioral change can be enough to keep an unhelpful behavior in place—like resisting a diet because you do not really believe you'll be successful.

- **Fear of loss:** Overcoming a self-defeating behavior might result in you losing something. We talked previously about identity in the case of the perfectionist. Another common theme I see is not wanting to fully work on stress because it provides an excuse if the work product is not fully up to par.
- **Fear of a specific consequence:** There might be a specific outcome to giving up self-sabotage that seems unsavory or scary. For instance, a lawyer may be afraid to work on resolving the issues that are causing him unhappiness in his job because he might then realize he wants to leave the law but feels he can't because he needs to pay off loans. It's safer to keep complaining about his job.
- **Fear of the unknown:** Similarly, it might be safer to stay stuck in an unhelpful behavioral pattern versus having to navigate something new—like being an unhappy practicing attorney but not taking steps to explore a new career or modify the one you have because it is not fully clear what that would look like.

3. What negative or limiting beliefs do I have about myself or the world at large that are keeping this self-sabotage in place? Often, when we drill down on why we might be engaging in a certain behavior, we find a core belief that gets in our way. A recurrent one I see and have worked on myself is imposter syndrome—"I'm not good/smart/capable enough," "There is something fundamentally wrong with me," or "I'm not likeable unless . . .". These types of beliefs can also be external, such as "The world is not safe," "Everything is a struggle," or "Everyone is always out to get me." To uncover any limiting beliefs, listen for the "story" you might be telling yourself about the situation. Again, we can get stuck in our own sob story of self-sabotage like, "I just can't catch a break and get out from under my to-do list." Pay attention to what you say when people ask you how you are doing. Do you typically say things like "crazed" or "stressed"? If so, dig down deeper to see if you are running a belief that needs to be confronted. Alternatively, fill in the following: "What is really going on with my [insert the self-sabotage you are working on] is . . .". In Sarah's case, she ran a limiting belief that she was not likeable. Once we were able to confront that belief and disprove it, she was able to feel more comfortable saying *no* to people when she needed to because she no longer believed her answer had any bearing on whether or not they liked her.

Step Three: Objective

Now that you are aware of your self-sabotaging behavior, a powerful next step in overcoming it is to clarify why it will be valuable for you to do so. In other words, what is your specific objective in overcoming this behavior? Breaking through self-sabotage is hard work (otherwise you would have done it already), so you need to keep your eye on the prize. In Sarah's case, we needed to keep her anchored in the benefits making partner would have for her, so she stayed motivated to keep working on her patterns of people-pleasing, overcommitting, and denial of self-care.

To stay focused and clear on your objective, ask these six questions:

1. Why do I want to overcome this self-sabotage? What value will it bring? What is the cost of not overcoming it?
2. On a scale of 1 to 10 (with 1 being low and 10 being high), how much do I want to overcome this? If this score is a 5 or below, you may need to go

back to the first question, otherwise you may not have the motivation and drive you need to be successful.

3. On a scale of 1 to 10 (with 1 being low and 10 being high), how willing am I to take the steps I will need to take to overcome this? Again, if your score is lower here, it is a clue that there is some resistance that needs to be addressed. Drilling down on all of the aspects in first question of why you want this can help. Additionally, going back to Step 2 (Diagnose) is another good place to look.

4. On a scale of 1 to 10 (with 1 being low and 10 being high), to what extent do I believe it is possible for me to overcome this? This is such an important question, which goes back to the limiting beliefs that often get in our way. If, on a subconscious level, you do not believe you are capable of making your desired changes, or that for external reasons it is not even available to you, it will compromise your motivation and can produce resistance. In short, it will be hard for you to move the needle. To the extent your score is low, ask yourself what you would need for it to be possible. You may need to do some brainstorming and creative problem solving to increase the score.

5. On a scale of 1 to 10 (with 1 being low and 10 being high), to what extent do you deserve to overcome this? Having a low score here may mean that you haven't fully surfaced some limiting beliefs in Step 2. It will be important to do so before embarking on any plan to overcome self-sabotage. This can be a painful question to sit with, but it is important to answer for the needle to move forward.

6. How will I know that I've been successful in overcoming this? Answering this question can provide specific tangible actions you can point to that can a) connect you back to the benefits of overcoming your self-sabotage, b) give you hope that it's doable, and c) give you a standard of measurement for your progress.

Often, if a coachee is not making progress on their self-sabotage, we will revisit these six questions to make sure they have the motivation they need to keep in motion.

Step Four: Plan

Now that you are aware of a limiting pattern of behavior that is getting in your way, and you have an understanding of what you would like to change and your level of motivation to do so, you need to know exactly how you are going to accomplish it. I may seem like I'm stating the obvious but, in my experience (personal as well as professional), many people approach overcoming self-sabotage with a default strategy of "I just need to force myself to not do it anymore." While admirable, that strategy, with its lack of specificity and direction, is likely to fail. What's more, with every failed attempt, it will likely dispirit the person attempting it. And even worse than that, if the self-sabotage is anchored in a limiting belief, such as "I'm not worthy," it will only reinforce the belief and the level of difficulty in overcoming the behavior. We've already seen how insidious and imbedded self-sabotage can become. It can keep people stuck. As the age-old saying reminds us, "If you want to keep getting what you are getting, keep doing what you are doing."

In order to truly break through the behavior, it will be helpful to have a clear, detailed, well-thought-out plan that you can come back to each time you might be susceptible to defaulting to the old behavior—something that will interrupt your old pattern and remind you of the new patterns you are trying to instill. The steps that go into your plan should be specific to and supportive of your context or situation. Referring back to the information you have already sourced through this process is a good place to look for clues. Recall the last time you engaged in the behavior—what were you thinking? What were you feeling? What thought or feeling would be more helpful? What would you need in place to make that switch? The answers to these questions can inform your plan. Some strategies that I have seen work include the following:

> **More of/Less of:** If overcoming your self-sabotage involves something you want to do more of, is there something in your life you would like to do less of—from which you could transfer the time, energy, and attention? For example, if you would like to exercise more and you would also like to be on social media less—one strategy could be to transfer that time to exercise. It might have to happen in smaller steps or involve some pre-work. How much time do you spend on social media? When? How much would you be willing to dedicate to exercise? In Sarah's case, she wanted to sleep more and she wanted to be in the office less. As a starting point, once she made some headway on her overcommitment behavior, she was able to commit to being at the office 30 minutes less one or two days a week and transfer that time to sleep. On the other hand, if overcoming your self-sabotage involves something you'd like to do less of, like drinking alcohol or eating sweets, is there something you'd like to do more of that you could transfer that time, energy, and attention to?

> **Exact Opposite/Approximate Middle:** Overcoming self-sabotage can be fun if you can approach it like a game and with a "beginner's mind"! One such game is to challenge yourself to do the exact opposite of the sabotaging behavior you are about to engage in. For example, if you are about to hit snooze on the alarm clock instead of getting up to go to the gym, challenge yourself to do whatever it is you imagine to be the exact opposite. That might mean actually getting up to go to the gym and doing your work-out as planned or it might just mean getting up and doing something else. Either way, you will have interrupted the pattern, and that is the immediate goal. If the exact opposite is too hard right out of the gate, determine what the approximate middle might be between the behavior you are about to engage and its exact opposite, and choose that instead. For example, you are about to eat dessert when you are trying to cut back on sugar. The approximate middle would be to just eat half of the dessert. This is still moving the needle towards your goal. Once you can make reaching the approximate middle a practice, you can then challenge yourself to do the next approximate middle. Continuing to take this approach will eventually get you to your destination.

> The main thing here is that you have interrupted the pattern and moved the needle more in the direction of your goal, which feels much more empowering and can help you stay motivated. In Sarah's case, when she was asked to take on more work, it was challenging for her to go right to the exact opposite of saying no. Instead, she went to the approximate middle of "Can I get back to you after I've had a chance to review everything I have going on?" In doing so, she broke her default pattern of saying yes. It also gave her time to realize that she, in fact, did not have the time

to take on something else and to craft a thoughtful response that made her feel better about saying no. Often, she was able to suggest an alternative strategy for the partner or suggest the work go to someone more junior as a way to stretch that person and get them more responsibility—a win-win for everyone.

Stage It: It is likely that you may need several different strategies to work through whatever you are working on. And, it may be the case that each strategy has to be approached in stages. For example, Sarah wanted to get back to exercising so we spent some time identifying what her "ideal" goal would look like. For her, the ultimate goal was taking a class at the gym twice a week and going for a run outside twice a week. Considering where she was when we began coaching, that goal was not going to be realistic given her time commitments and energy level. That meant she needed to approach it in stages until she could build up to her ideal. She had to start small and build. While she was working on minimizing her commitments to free up some time and optimizing sleep to free up energy (both of which she did in stages), she set a preliminary and much more realistic goal of getting back to the gym just once a week. That was it—just once a week. That's a strategy I call *pick and stick*. Not surprisingly, this means you just pick one thing out of everything you could be doing to work towards a goal and stick with it. Once you have mastered that one thing, and it becomes your new habit, then you can add another strategy. Once Sarah kept her once a week commitment for three weeks, she was ready to add in one outdoor run. She just kept building from there until she reached her ideal.

This approach is so important, particularly for lawyers who tend to be achievement-oriented and overachieving, which in many ways contributes to their success but can have a dark side. Often when I'm helping lawyers set goals in this context, they will start off with a somewhat unrealistic goal like, "I'm going to start exercising five times a week," or "I'm going to start meditating every day," or "I'm going to stop eating carbs." If you are exercising or meditating zero times a week, jumping to a high number will likely result in failure, which will feel disempowering. It's much better to start with a smaller number, even if that number is one, and build from there.

Tactical, Practical, & Energetic: Again, it is likely that you will be working a few different strategies or approaches while overcoming a self-sabotaging behavior or pattern. In addition to staging your approach, it can also be helpful to look at the types of strategies you are picking. Over the years I've observed that overcoming self-sabotage often requires both tactical and practical steps as well as ones that boost energy. For example, to help Sarah get more sleep, she would do tactical things like setting an alarm 30 minutes ahead of when she wanted to go to sleep. She also began using part of that time to plan out her priorities for the next day. In addition, she would carve out five minutes to write in a gratitude journal, which helped keep her perspective positive by anchoring her in how fortunate she was. She also spent ten minutes per day meditating, which helped calm her nervous system at the end of a stressful day. These two steps helped her energy levels. By helping her to keep a more positive outlook on things and feel more grounded and calm, she was able to stay motivated and energized to do the rest of what she was working on.

Step Five: Take Action

Planning is a key step in the process of overcoming the feeling of being overwhelmed. It can provide a roadmap to help us get to our desired outcome. That said, it is not enough to just plan. Sometimes, planning is the easy part—the part that's interesting, even fun. It's taking action where we fall down, particularly when we are talking about self-sabotage. To quote martial arts master Bruce Lee:

> Knowing is not enough. We must apply.
> Willing is not enough. We must do.

Taking action comes down to leveraging the power of choice. The first step is to be aware that you are in a moment of choice. This can be the hardest part because our lives are busy and we move through them on autopilot. Mindfulness or another form of meditation practice can help you build your awareness muscle. It is also a powerful ally in the battle against self-sabotage. Once you are aware that you are in a moment of choice and close to defaulting to an unhelpful behavior, simply pause and reconnect to your goal. It is about keeping your eye and your focus on the prize. If your objective in Step 3 (Objective) is crystal clear, you have already done a lot of the heavy lifting. From there, it is just a matter of staying mindful of your objective and its value in that moment of choice.

A few helpful strategies to get in and stay in action:

Confronting Questions: Behavioral change is an ongoing, powerful conversation you have with yourself. Sometimes we stop the conversations prematurely. You might have a short conversation with yourself when hitting the snooze button instead of going to the gym. "Do I feel like going to the gym?" If the answer is no, end of story. What is likely to happen is that you might shame or guilt yourself the rest of the day for not keeping a commitment, which is not an empowering conversation. Instead, you can use what I call a confronting question that forces a longer conversation with yourself—a conversation that may end with you actually getting up and going to the gym. Here are three powerful confronting questions that can really help to turn around a moment of choice away from a sabotage behavior toward a more empowering one:
1. First, ask yourself, "Will this choice distract me from my goal or move me in the right direction?" Sometimes that question alone can get you moving in the direction of your goal.
2. If not, ask yourself, "Do I want this choice (an extra nine minutes of sleep) more than I want to keep my commitment to myself (going to the gym)?" You may, in fact, still decide that you'd prefer the sleep, but the question has planted a seed of doubt.
3. You may then follow it up with "How am I likely to feel if I make this choice?"

Chances are, by this point, you've kept the conversation with yourself up long enough to help get you back on course. If not, and you still choose the sleep, that is okay. It is data for you and your coach to process later down the line. Perhaps it means you need to go back and recalibrate your original goal or that you've picked the wrong strategy. Either way, it's part of a larger, longer, and important dialogue with yourself.

You can also create your own confronting question based on what you are working on. If the confronting question is anchored to a goal or core value, it is more impactful. For example, "If I really want X (e.g., more sleep), what is the best choice I can make in this moment to achieve X?" Or, if you are trying to avoid something in your life, try "Will this choice add to my stress/struggle/suffering or will it alleviate it?" or "What is the most important thing I could focus on right now to reduce my stress/increase my well-being/feel better/have more energy, etc.?" If you are avoiding a behavior that would otherwise help you break through your self-sabotage, like not giving feedback to a colleague who is creating an unproductive work environment, one of my favorite questions is, "What is likely to change about this situation in the absence of me taking action/communicating?" Play around with your confronting questions. Make them meaningful to you, the context of your life, and your personality. The more personalized they are, the more you are likely to remember to use them.

Go "Lawyer" on Yourself: Once you've opened up a dialogue with yourself in a moment of choice, you may be more receptive to persuasion. This is a great opportunity to use your lawyering skills. Make your best argument as to why you should stick to your goal and not engage in a sabotaging behavior. Negotiate with yourself if need be. Establish a contract with yourself—sign it even. You've worked so hard in school and in practice to develop these skills to help others. Why not employ them here to help your most important client—YOU?

Pre-pave Success: You've done enough investigation work on yourself and your self-sabotage at this point to know that there are predictable situations where you are likely to default to your old patterns. Use that self-knowledge to pre-pave success for yourself by having a strategy ready to go once your self-awareness in a moment of choice kicks in. Sarah had a particularly hard time saying no to people when they showed up in her office. To pre-pave success, she implemented a very simple strategy of writing down her reminder phrase, "prioritize my own priorities," on a post-it on her desk when anyone would come in her office to ask her for help. Taking this step helped keep her present to her goal of not overcommitting by defaulting to a *yes*. She was also able to implement other pre-planned strategies of coaching junior associates to take ownership and responsibility of whatever it was they were coming to her about so it didn't always end up on her plate.

Another way of pre-paving is to avoid or put boundaries around situations where you are likely to self-sabotage. If there is a food that you have determined is not a healthy choice but you have a hard time resisting, choose not to keep that food in your home. Or create a guideline of having that food as a special treat or X number of times per month, quarter, year, etc. I work with clients who feel they are spending too much time on email or the Internet, which can be a big distraction. You can spend hours in your inbox and yet feel completely unproductive. As a professional in client service, you can't avoid email but you can put some boundaries around it. Sarah was able to implement what I call *priority project time* where she would commit 1.5 hours, twice a day, in the morning and the afternoon, to do nothing but the priorities on her to-do list for that day. She would turn off email alerts, close her door, and not answer her phone, which functioned as a way to wean her off of feeling the need to people please. To feel comfortable doing this, she would immediately turn to emails right after and she also had clear exceptions for certain phone calls that she would take during those times. This pre-paving helped her to be more efficient with her time and move things off of her to-do list.

Systematize: The easier you make it for yourself to actively implement your strategies, the more likely you are to do it. One way to make it easy is to systematize. Create a system out of the steps you need to take and put it on autopilot. I like to say, take the *think* out of routines so you are not as likely to think or talk yourself out of it. That might mean moving your alarm clock away from your bed so you can't hit snooze and having it right next to your pre-packed gym bag (as Sarah started doing) or taking an hour or two every Sunday to prepare healthy meals for the week. You might take time to literally plan all of your meals for the week. Sarah also set up a "Time Management" date with herself every Friday afternoon to make sure her to-do list was updated, review where her time had gone that week, and preview what was on deck for the following two weeks. This enabled her to go into the next week with clarity about what availability she had, which prevented her from overcommitting and helped her to delegate more as necessary. Systematizing is a powerful tool to set yourself up for success.

BEST PRACTICES

Beware of the Push-Through Period, Backsliding, and Resistance

You now have some concrete steps to start turning self-sabotage around. We know that it can be a challenging process, so it will be important to watch out for signs that you are resisting the changes you want to make. Many strategies will yield early positive results like Sarah's sleep modifications, for example. She immediately could see the positive impacts of getting more sleep, so she was motivated to keep doing it. However, sometimes you have to try new strategies and test out new behaviors and experience some lag time before you see significant changes. For example, let's say you decide to lose 15 pounds and you embark on some changes to your diet in addition to starting an exercise regimen. In the first few days, you may be excited by the idea of the changes, which alone can fuel your motivation. You may not see any results during those first few days. Because the changes you are making may feel uncomfortable, unfamiliar, or even unsavory to you, as those days without results continue, you can become less and less motivated. I call this the *push-through period* because if you can motivate yourself to stick with the changes, they will eventually bring results, and the impact of those results will reinforce your motivation.

Making it through this initial push-through period is critical to successfully reaching your goals, yet it is the time when people can give up and revert back to a disempowering, demotivating story like "This is impossible" or "I'll never be able to pull this off" or "People like me just can't lose weight." When those thoughts creep in, it is easy to derail from the new plan and have a setback. (Or the setback happens first in a moment of low motivation, which then reinforces the story.) Either way, it brings you back into the self-sabotage loop. Maintaining your "beginner's mind" here can be critical.

Of course, the push-through period isn't the only time in a behavior change process when you can get stuck. There are other times when you face setbacks, backsliding, or even failure. In my experience, there are a few keys to successfully navigating through any of these periods to keep momentum and stay on track. Let's start with your mindset. When it comes to overcoming self-sabotage, I like to say you have to *friend* yourself out of it, as opposed to what many people do, which is to *fight* or *bully* themselves out of it. Think about it, we've already talked about how limiting beliefs are often a root cause of self-sabotaging behavior, so beating yourself up for inevitable setbacks along the way (setbacks that will occur because you are human) is only going to fuel a disempowering story.

If you employ some self-compassion and understanding that it is not easy to make significant behavioral changes and act as your own cheerleader, that will help shift you towards a more empowering story and maintain your motivation high to keep you in action. Action leads to traction when it comes to goal attainment. When Sarah was first implementing the changes we discussed, there were a few times early on when she just forgot to do something, actively decided not to do it, or made the opposite choice. She would come to our session totally deflated about it, and I would ask her what her best friend would say to her about it. Or what she might say to her best friend if the situation was reversed. The response was always with more compassion and understanding than how Sarah was treating herself. My point in doing so was to remind her that she was human and that we were not looking for perfection in her efforts. Instead, we were looking for movement and/or data. Even the act of realizing that she hadn't implemented a strategy was moving the needle. And making an opposite choice of what she wanted was data for us to feed back into her coaching.

One way to friend yourself out of an unhelpful behavior and into a new one is to reset with your plan each morning. If you've had a setback on a particular day, acknowledge it, process it, see if there is helpful data, but move on the next day. If you catch it in enough time, you can even play around with a real-time reset. In other words, the minute you become aware you've missed an opportunity to implement one of your strategies or you've ended up going in the opposite direction, simply start over, or at least take a small step in the right direction. For example, Sarah once realized she had committed to something she really didn't have time for. Instead of getting angry at herself and feeling hopeless about it, she went back to the person and carefully got herself out of the commitment by suggesting that she would supervise a more junior associate instead.

You don't necessarily want to let yourself off the hook each time you have a setback. Feel the pain and grow from it. Take ownership of it but put it behind you. That said, if you've had a setback every day in a given week, you may need to go back and recalibrate. You might have picked the wrong strategy or are trying to implement it on an unrealistic scale. Having repeated setbacks or feeling in general like the scale is not moving may mean you have to go back to the drawing board and calibrate what you have committed to until you get into motion with it. So: be kind to yourself by resetting each morning while, at the same time, hold yourself accountable by checking in on overall progress at least once a week.

Another great way to friend yourself is to focus less on the setbacks and amplify all of your successes as well as their positive impacts. Focusing on the positive is more empowering and motivating and will help keep you in motion. It can help you feel that what you are striving for is, in fact, possible. Connecting the actions you are taking to a positive impact, like having more time or energy or less stress, can help to reinforce the value of the effort you are putting in. For example, Sarah quickly noticed that when she was able to get more sleep she had so much more energy, which enabled her to get back to exercise and to feel less stressed. Both of these impacts helped her navigate moments throughout her day when she was likely to overcommit by saying yes when she knew she should say no. By overcommitting less, she freed up more time for herself, which helped her get to the gym.

By verbalizing all of these impacts (and recording them in her gratitude journal) she was able to clearly see the connection between the effort she was putting in and the positive impacts of the results she was getting. These *positive-compounding impacts*, as I like to call them, helped keep Sarah's motivation high so that she could not even imagine going back to her old, self-sabotaging ways. It also helped to reinforce her new positive habits to the point where they became more automatic.

If you find yourself in deep levels of resistance, you can go back through the previous steps to get re-grounded in your mission. In addition, here are some resistance-busting questions I like to ask clients and myself to work through blocks:

1. What behavior or self-talk is getting the way or stopping you?
2. Is it the right action or strategy to be taking at this time? (If not, recalibrate.)
3. What is one small next step you would be willing to take?
4. What do you need to have in place to do it?
5. Visualize what success would look like if you did take the action step. How do you feel? What is one benefit?
6. Why am I denying myself this emotion (such as joy, relief, happiness, peace, etc.) and/or this benefit (such as increased energy, more time, less stress, etc.)?

We've covered a lot in this chapter. Some of it might be a bit triggering for you. If it is or if taking this on by yourself seems overwhelming, consider asking a friend or a family member who can be objective and is aligned with your goals for support, encouragement, or accountability. Even better, buddy up with someone who is seeking to make similar changes where you could provide mutual support. In addition, it may be helpful to reach out to a professional who can help. Whether that is a therapist or a coach (executive, life, health), having someone who can partner with you, provide you some tools and most importantly, hold you accountable, can help you help yourself to break these patterns once and for all.

If, while going through the steps highlighted in this chapter, you unearth some deeply entrenched limiting beliefs that may be the result of some type of trauma, it will be important to work with a qualified and credible mental health provider who can help you work through them safely and effectively.

Most important, just get started. I often observe busy lawyers delaying overcoming their self-sabotage. I hear things like, "I'll get back to exercise once this deal is over," or "I'll start meditating after this trial." Delay tactics like this are just adding to the existing self-sabotage. As you probably already noticed, there is never a *good time* to start these things. There may be another big and stressful project as soon as you finish your current one. Plus, we have only been focusing on work related stressors in this chapter. There can be myriad things going on in your personal life that might cause you to want to delay.

You may have also noticed, in the case of Sarah, that while her main goals were career related, many of the self-sabotaging behaviors were a hit to her well-being in two ways. First, they were preventing her from a goal she really wanted, which does not feel empowering or inspiring, and, even worse, they created frustration and despair, which increased her stress levels. Second, her compromised sleep and lack of recovery and exercise were compromising her physical, mental, emotional, and spiritual well-being.

So, be pro-active about your own well-being by taking a positive step in the direction of where you want to be—even if it is a teeny, tiny micro-step. As I'm fond of saying to my clients and myself, "Even ten minutes of something good for you is better than no minutes of something good for you." We all can find ten minutes each day to do something good for ourselves. Start small. Build. Celebrate. Liberate.

CHAPTER 10
Your Best Career Path

Rachelle J. Canter, PhD

Editor's Note: Almost 25 years ago, Shelley was my career coach. She helped point me in the right direction, suggested essential resources, and provided wise counsel. Much water has passed under the bridge since then, and I consider her a close friend to whom I refer people when they need career advice. They always say she is wonderful! Part of how she shows up that way is that, just as in this chapter, she takes a complex arena and reduces it to easy-to-follow, doable steps. That is the mastery of a professional who knows what she is doing. It's the reason she is often called upon to provide career advice and coaching in an outplacement situation. I can't think of a more sensitive career choice point, and she navigates it with elegance.

This chapter outlines ten principles and steps to help you find and follow your best career path by taking time to do the following:

1. make an informed choice;
2. don't let your stories about your career hold you back;
3. manage your career—don't delegate it;
4. create a career plan to guide career moves and choices;
5. build your employability;
6. build your brand;
7. take small steps to create momentum;
8. keep your brand up to date;
9. cultivate emotional intelligence; and
10. conduct periodic reviews to ensure you are still on the right path.

Rachelle J. Canter, PhD, is President of RJC Associates. Shelley has helped hundreds of attorneys make successful career moves within and outside their organizations. She authored a career guide for attorneys and executives, *Make the Right Career Move* (Wiley), and was one of three coaches featured in an *ABA Journal* cover story. She is adjunct faculty for the Women Senior Leaders Program and Women Board Directors programs at Northwestern's Kellogg School of Management Center for Executive Women. Shelley earned her PhD in Social-Personality Psychology from the University of Colorado and is a Phi Beta Kappa graduate of Stanford University with a BA in Psychology.

Choosing and following your best career path is essential to a fulfilling career and life, yet it gets little attention from most lawyers. Think about it: how many lawyers do you know who love their work?

The main reason I began to do career work with lawyers almost 30 years ago was because I knew so many unhappily employed lawyers. I still do. Don't be or remain one of the unhappily employed! Law is a demanding profession and it is not unreasonable to expect that it should be a fulfilling one as well—but it is up to you to do the work to ensure it.

Here are ten steps to your best career path:

1. MAKE AN INFORMED CHOICE

Meghan, like many other law school grads, finished law school with hundreds of thousands of dollars in student loans. Like so many financially encumbered young lawyers, she took a position with a big law firm that offered a lucrative salary to begin retiring the debt.

She went to law school to become an advocate for social justice, but she had to defer her dreams. Despite her interest in litigation, the firm assigned her to the corporate practice, where they had the biggest need.

Five years turned into ten. Meghan liked the compensation but not the work. After so many years in corporate practice, pursuit of her social justice advocacy dreams seemed impossible. The long work hours made it hard to even know where to start, so, like so many other lawyers, she never did. She just put her head down and focused on her less-than-fulfilling career path.

Whether you are five, ten, 15, 25, or one year into your legal career, make time to explore your values, skills, sources of career satisfaction and dissatisfaction, and other career-relevant factors, to lead to a well-reasoned career choice.

Your ideal job may not be immediately available or financially feasible, but clarifying your passions and targets is important so you can follow your dreams. It is never too late: I have worked with lawyers in their fifties, sixties, and beyond to make new career choices that are more aligned with their sense of true calling.

Ask yourself three questions: Are you living up to your potential? Are you making a difference? Is it the kind of difference you want to make? With this general framework in mind, make sure to take advantage of the wealth of books, online resources, and classes to help you make this choice. If you are not making headway on your own, hire a career professional to ensure your career progress is not taking a permanent back seat to your job.

2. DON'T LET YOUR STORIES ABOUT YOUR CAREER HOLD YOU BACK

Lawyers are trained in analysis and critical thinking, but following your best career path also requires the ability to look critically at how beliefs or stories about what is possible in our careers can limit us.

Dean is a junior partner with an Ivy League pedigree who has spent his career in an Am Law 200 firm. The firm's fortunes have sputtered over that time and many have left the practice group and firm. Dean has struggled to generate business or cross-referrals.

He hasn't tried to move because he has so many stories about why he is trapped. The stories range from his making a mistake at the start of his career to go with a multi-service firm rather than a specialty boutique to his lack of SEC experience to its being too late to make a move to a competitor with a more robust practice in his specialty.

These stories have kept him stuck in place, complaining about his situation but believing he has no alternative. These limiting beliefs have stopped him from pursuing other jobs, getting SEC experience, or retooling.

3. MANAGE YOUR CAREER—DON'T DELEGATE IT

Many lawyers mistakenly assume that hard work ensures a successful career. This is not true: I have personally outplaced many of those lawyers. Doing good work and depending on a paternalistic firm or employer with generous course offerings, coaches, and mentors to guarantee career satisfaction and longevity is a big mistake. No one has the same investment in your career that you do.

Lara was the protégé of a leading e-business's General Counsel. She was his right-hand person and he promised her a promotion to Chief Compliance Officer when he was promoted to COO.

Unfortunately, when he got that promotion, he kept her in her current position because "I need someone I can count on to keep things running smoothly." This is a painful reminder that your career objectives may be in direct conflict with those of the boss or the company.

Instead of being rewarded and promoted for her dedication, loyalty, and trust, Lara's career growth was blocked by her boss. He disappointed her personally and professionally, and undermined her self-confidence in her ability to move up. We can all learn from Lara's misplaced confidence.

4. CREATE A CAREER PLAN TO GUIDE CAREER MOVES AND CHOICES

A career plan is absolutely indispensable to finding your best career path. We all know people who fell into their dream jobs, but we remember them because they are so rare. A career plan can guide you to your path and help you make strategic decisions to make the most and the best of your career.

A career plan does not need to be elaborate to be effective: three lines on a piece of paper can provide important direction. Take 30 seconds to record answers to the three following questions:

1. What is my long-term career goal?
2. How do I plan to build my skills and employability in pursuit of that goal in the next year?
3. In the next three years?

A brief career plan makes a world of difference. Todd worked in the Office of the General Counsel at a major university. Numerous university budget cuts, along with the hiring of an autocratic new GC, reduced the scope of his job and his learning opportunities. Todd was bored and stifled.

Putting together a brief career plan made Todd realize that he needed business development skills and experience to become competitive for an in-house position in a Silicon Valley company, particularly for his long-term aim to take on more business (instead of legal) responsibilities.

The plan helped him identify courses to take and university task forces and special projects to volunteer for or design in order to build these skills. Less than two years later, he is working in-house.

5. BUILD YOUR EMPLOYABILITY

David Maister, the former Harvard Business School professor and long-time investigator of professional service firms, points out that a person's professional assets (skills, knowledge, experience) are the source of employability. These assets are always expanding or declining but are never static.

When you do something well, you are usually asked to do it again and again. Maister points out that this all-too-common situation of repeating successes actually means your professional assets are declining.

By defining where you want to enhance your employability, a career plan helps you seek or create opportunities to do new things that build skills and knowledge in new and desired areas. That often requires volunteering for additional assignments beyond your job, but it also provides a way to escape the trap of doing the same thing repeatedly, and experiencing career stasis instead of career growth.

6. BUILD YOUR BRAND

Most lawyers assume that having a brand is irrelevant for lawyers—at least, until and only if they decide to seek another job. However, a brand constitutes the unique and objective set of results and competencies that set you apart. This is an essential way to differentiate yourself from the competition for jobs, business development, assignments, promotions, and resources.

Two crucial aspects of your brand are (1) the accomplishments in your resume that depict the concrete array of measurable results or contributions (the micro version of your brand) and (2) the competitive advantages, which are a set of three to five global factual themes about your career that define what sets you apart from the competition (the macro version of your brand) and that answer the important question: Why hire or select you?

These branding and positioning career tools have many uses, including bidding for a promotion, raise, or new assignment; getting on a board; testing your worth in the marketplace; developing a contingency plan if the firm or you run into problems; boosting your self-confidence; and pursuing a new job or venture.

Josh was interested in taking on leadership roles at his firm, a very traditional firm dominated by old, straight, white men. As a young gay black man, he believed he could add a diverse perspective to the firm's policy decisions to help achieve a more competitive position.

Josh spoke to a couple of partners who had mentored him during his first year of practice, but not surprisingly, they still thought of him and his skills as they had been eight years earlier, since they'd had limited contact since then.

With the help of a career consultant, he put together a powerful accomplishment-based resume that showcased his measurable results in the practice and in firm administrative roles. He came up with competitive advantages that differentiated his career and showed how he could add value to leadership decisions, in factual and hard-hitting terms. Josh is now on the powerful Policy and Planning Committee at the firm.

Like Josh, having a brand is critical to increasing visibility and impact at your current place of employment and in the broader marketplace, and it is crucial to your career success, whether you stay where you are or decide to leave.

7. TAKE SMALL STEPS TO CREATE MOMENTUM

Small measurable steps provide a way to pursue long-term goals in a sustainable fashion. The small step strategy supports simultaneous pursuit of a demanding job *and* long-term career goals and desired career path. Use your calendar to provide timely and regular reminders of next steps to your goal.

Measurability is key. You must identify whether the designated steps are occurring, and if not, pinpoint why not and correct the impediment or problem. Examples of small steps are (1) conducting 15-minute interviews with members of your network to gather information on alternative positions and (2) scheduling an hour per week to work on resume accomplishments.

Another advantage of this incremental approach is that it provides the time for thoughtful reflection that is essential to wise and well-considered career decisions. Don't wait until you are desperately unhappy to invoke this small steps strategy.

Christine made this mistake. Long unhappy with her job in the city attorney's office, it wasn't until her firing as part of a major layoff that she began a belated consideration of what she wanted and how to get it. She hadn't been thinking about her career path or making small steps to find it, so when she suddenly found herself out of a job, she was panicked by financial pressures. She took the first job she could find—in another municipal government agency—and is still miserable about government bureaucracies and salaries.

8. KEEP YOUR BRAND UP TO DATE

Your brand changes as your professional assets increase, so periodic updates are important. One simple and important way to update is to keep an accomplishment log, a computer document you update daily or weekly with your tangible accomplishments.

This information will facilitate resume revisions and will also provide current information for performance reviews, compensation discussions, and negotiations for future assignments.

9. CULTIVATE EMOTIONAL INTELLIGENCE

Legal training and practice focus on the technical knowledge and skills needed to be a successful lawyer, but the empirical evidence clearly shows that emotional intelligence (social and interpersonal skills) is even more important to success in the law and at work generally. In fact, leadership success is almost entirely due to emotional intelligence rather than to cognitive intelligence and technical skills.

That finding has been replicated in my coaching practice: when called to help a valued partner or associate, it is due to challenges dealing with other people, not with the technical caliber of their work. Think about it: how many problem lawyers at your workplace are problems due to social skills rather than IQ or technical skills?

Scott is a formidable rainmaker as well as a brilliant lawyer and has built a big practice group at a major law firm but with a high body count to match. The group's success has been hampered by the high level of turnover among associates who complain about his abrasive style and his public humiliation of them if their work does not measure up to his high standards.

By focusing on how to communicate with others, understand their points of view, deliver useful feedback, and build trusting relationships, Scott was able to boost morale and productivity and drastically cut turnover.

The good thing about emotional intelligence skills is that they can be learned. After practicing for 25 years, Scott was able to acquire much stronger interpersonal and social skills, and so can and have many others. There are many ways to build emotional intelligence. You can seek regular feedback on interpersonal as well as technical performance at the conclusion of a deal or case. Remember that you can seek feedback from peers or subordinates, as well as people senior to you.

Another way to build EQ is to participate actively in your organization's performance review and any 360 performance feedback programs that solicit feedback from bosses, subordinates, peers, and sometimes clients. You can also seek out internal and external seminars on building interpersonal skills. Finally, you can work with a career coach to work on your EQ in a focused fashion.

Your own career will be much more rewarding the sooner you learn that emotional intelligence skills are not simply nice to have—they are essential to your success and satisfaction and to the success and satisfaction of those you manage.

Do not assume that women are naturally more emotionally intelligent than men. Aside from the issue of individual differences, the research shows that women tend to score higher, as a group, on empathy and social skills, but men tend to score higher on stress tolerance and self-confidence. All are important parts of interpersonal and social skills and deserve your attention.

10. CONDUCT PERIODIC REVIEWS TO ENSURE YOU ARE STILL ON THE RIGHT PATH

Even a "best career path" has detours and changes. A career path is a dynamic process that benefits from occasional re-examination and course correction.

Morgan made a move to a family law practice and firm after a painful divorce and unpleasant encounters with divorce lawyers gave her firsthand experience of where her litigation and counseling background could have a profound impact on individuals' lives.

She loved the work, but after a couple of years in a small firm, it took taking stock to realize that her greater satisfaction with this work masked her frustration with the autocratic management style of the founder. This realization instigated a process that ultimately led Morgan to relocate to another firm where she continues to enjoy the practice of family law in a more hospitable environment.

SUMMARY

The ten principles and steps enumerated in this chapter help the reader address crucial career issues, including the importance of identifying your passion; avoiding self-limiting beliefs about career possibilities; taking an active role in managing your career; creating a career plan to guide you; building and updating your brand; cultivating your social and interpersonal skills; and taking periodic stock of your career path to make course corrections and ensure you are still following your best career path. You can apply these principles in small steps and over time to create and build a career you love.

CHAPTER 11
Professional Success and Maintaining Personal Well-Being

Steven Meyers, Esq.

Editor's Note: Steve's firm, Meyers Nave, was a serial client over the years, but I only met Steve briefly. Don Oppenheim, former *ABA Journal* Associate Publisher and Meyers Nave Executive Director, and friend of my late wife Marty Africa, was my main contact. Don became a friend, and when I told him about this book he said Steve, who had just retired, would be a great contributor. I'm glad I listened. Steve's passionate conviction comes through loud and clear. His questions are sure to wake up many lawyers about the path they are traveling. As someone who cross-examined his way out of a healthy marriage, I understand his message. I hope you will too.

Our most precious commodity is time, yet it is both scarce and subject to intense competition. The service of our chosen profession is measured by increments of time, but our personal wellness and the happiness of our families are dependent on the allocation of a large measure of that time. What are the particular aspects of the law that determine the allocation of this precious resource, how can we recognize and deal with these competing demands, and what extrinsic and intrinsic forces of our profession bear on personal and domestic happiness?

Steven Meyers has practiced public agency law for more than 40 years. He is recognized for his expertise in municipal and special districts law, economic development, land use, environmental law, utility regulation, and public-private partnerships. Steven formed Meyers Nave in 1986 based on his vision of creating one law firm that could provide the complete range of legal and regulatory services that public agencies typically needed. His goal was to transform the traditional business model into one that was more effective and efficient for clients as well as providing alternative working styles and objectives for lawyers. Steven helped guide Meyers Nave's growth to more than 80 attorneys in offices throughout California.

Are these goals and aspirations reconcilable? Is there something about the practice of law that makes striving for professional excellence antithetical to domestic tranquility? What characteristics of the business of law cause us to sacrifice our well-being and that of our family for the demands of the profession? What can we do to productively manage our professional and personal lives to create the optimum life work balance?

It's manifest that the pursuit of personal happiness is a simple aspiration. The fact that this simple goal is so difficult to achieve is the raison d'etre for our uniquely American phalanx of psychotherapists, marriage and substance abuse counselors, and self-help seminars, as well as an entire pharmacological industry. If there is one thing that has the consequence of personal tragedy and distraction, financial upheaval, emotional loss, and destruction of self, it's the failure over time to apply sufficient attention and concerted consciousness to one's own well-being, family, and marriage. Like the proverbial frog in the slowly boiling water who doesn't realize he's cooked until it's too late, no one deliberately or overnight approaches the non-professional aspects of their life with the stated intention to have an unhealthy marriage or an unhappy family and otherwise unfulfilled personal existence, yet it is my personal opinion and professional experience in 40 years of practice that many, if not a majority, of my colleagues either fail to perceive the warning signs or, worse, acknowledge them but pay lip service to change. Many aspects of the business model that animates our profession contribute greatly to this condition.

The question posed in this chapter is whether it is our profession, the rigorous and particularized mental training we undertake, or the business of law itself that makes it more difficult to achieve a healthy and fulfilled life than perhaps another profession or occupation. To be a professional success, must we allow the practice of law to consume all our available time and emotional resources? What are the attributes of those who successfully meld devotion to the law, their profession, and their clients to the needs of the self, spouse, and children? As I was once asked as a young lawyer, "What would you chose for your epitaph, 'He billed the most hours' or 'Devoted husband and father'?"

The foremost culprit in this matter is blind devotion to the "billable hour" as a measure of success, profit, and competency. With apologies to Mark Twain, the reports of the death of the billable hour have been greatly exaggerated. The second aspect of our profession that bears responsibility for familial pressures described in this chapter is a growing marketing and sales culture voraciously consuming hours and hours of non-billable time in one-on-one business meetings and peer socialization, scholarly papers and presentations to trade groups.

It seems, too, that it is in the very nature of the analytical thought and deductive logic drummed into the young law student's head, the Socratic method, as well as the obsessive need to win, that causes otherwise normal social and family interactions to become a cross examination or interrogation with winners and losers. I recall a conversation with my wife about an important family issue. After listening attentively, I arrived at what seemed to be the solution. She then said, "Yes," as I smiled inwardly at my solicitous active listening and brilliant logic, "but we still have to talk about it."

THE BILLABLE HOUR: THE BANE OF OUR EXISTENCE

The young lawyer appears before Saint Peter at the Pearly Gates and asks plaintively, "Why have you taken me now? I'm 35 and in the prime of my young life and career." To which Saint Peter replies, "Well, according to your billing records, you're 85."

More has been written about the billable hour than perhaps any other subject in law practice management, and this is not intended to be an extended discourse on the subject. Simply stated, the revenue side of the business of law is determined by the number of "billable hours" of a lawyer times the rate for that hour less uncollectibles. Since the market may constrain the hourly billing rate, the *only* variable in this simple equation is the number of hours in a day. That's it. With few exceptions, this is the business model for a quarter of a trillion dollar industry. I believe therein lies the problem.

Some will argue that this is an institutional constraint we need to work around. Others say it's the fairest measure of value for professional services rendered. Unfortunately, that attitude justifies the inertia that has prevented real and creative changes. It's curious that in a profession where the first duty of loyalty is to the client, the very nature of the business model places the lawyer in an ethical dilemma with that very client: what are the billings if we go to trial versus settlement; is this deposition really necessary; is this an this an issue that requires research; is this document dump likely to lead to probative evidence; how many associates do we need to assign to this matter? The idea that these considerations never enter into the equation is risible. The profitability of many firms is also determined by the corollary of the billable hour called "leverage." Lower compensated associates billing two or three times their cost in billables translates into higher per partner profits. Law firm partners cannot earn their stratospheric salaries without leveraging the work product of lower cost lawyers into higher gross billings. Ever wonder why the big firms send four associates to a deposition? This is no secret to anyone and is the driving force behind the continued reverence of the billable hour.

Professional services ought not be measured in tenths of an hour but by the value imparted and success achieved; yet I have heard the words "alternative billing practices" for decades without a real or demonstrable move away from the billable hour standard. Lawyers, and managing partners in particular, exhibit fear and loathing at the prospect of a fixed fee for service or any commoditization of legal services. A similar Pavlovian response is elicited by the concept of billing to a fixed budget without so many contingencies as to make the budget worthless. How is it that a construction firm can bid on the construction of a skyscraper and itemize the costs of construction down to the last girder or brick? There are labor, material, weather, and other force majeure uncertainties in construction as complex as any legal matter. There is no good reason other than institutional bias why most legal work can't be itemized, budgeted, and cost segregated as long as there are realistic expectations, budget decision points, and enumerated contingent factors. It is common to criticize government as inefficient and bureaucratic but in my experience of representing public agencies large and small, being forced to prepare litigation budgets has become commonplace and expected. The exercise of budgeting forces critical thinking about resources, staffing, and strategy. On more than one occasion I have shown up with an associate in tow while the opposition represented by big firms will have four or five.

Some in our profession consider the rejection of the billable hour as heretical and simplistic, but as long as law firms predicate their evaluative system of lawyer performance, compensation, advancement, and the coveted "partner track" on the number of annual hours billed and collected, nothing will change. Despite hefty compensation plans wrought with consultant-speak bells and whistles to make it sound as if there is a new paradigm, the billable hour remains the touchstone as relatively objective, easily calculated, and directly related to the financial success of the firm.

Yet this system is potentially destructive to the quality of life for the practicing lawyer looking wistfully at the magic number of 2080 (52 weeks times 40 hours per week). A less than 100 percent realization rate, non-billable administrative time, practice management, professional and business development, sick time, and coffee breaks all chip away at that numerical goal. An annual two-week vacation (a standard which is low by standards of western democracies) takes 80 hours off the top of the remainder. Does your practice of law own Saturdays and Sundays? What about "date night," kids' t-ball, the school play, soccer, and parenting in general? We are told by Hollywood and our cultural arbiters that professionals—from the involved dad to the working mom—can "have it all" if they multi-task, actively listen, prioritize family needs, schedule quality time for kids, etc. This sounds attainable . . . on paper. Working "just a couple" of hours every day of your family vacation seems reasonable in the moment. Missing a swim meet to strategize the summary judgment motion seems necessary at the time. But these absences come at a cost, and the devotion to the billable hour places a thumb on the scale of professional advancement at the expense of marital or familial happiness.

For professionals without families, there is still a need for a healthy and well-rounded self. Have you taken the time to read a (non-legal) book, seen a movie or play, or recharged your batteries through travel? Often the best lawyers are those who are well-rounded, well-read, and well-traveled; perhaps it's the perspectives given or received that account for this. Non-billable "blue sky" thinking is often more valuable than hitting the books. "Life-work balance" may sound simplistic and hackneyed, but there is truth in this. Creativity and innovation are natural impulses and human qualities are suppressed by overwrought devotion to the billable hour.

So what are we to do about this? One choice is to be realistic and lower billable hour standards. It's said that a firm's lower billable hour expectation in order to be "family friendly" reflects management's choice to be a lifestyle firm. In this context, it's pejorative. Competency, aggressive representation, and creative problem solving are not a function of billing tons of hours. Instead of paying lip service to alternative billing systems, lawyers have to better commoditize professional services to create fixed fees and realistic budgets with multiple decision points to evaluate contingencies and the value of the services rendered to date, and to create pay for performance and success standards.

Even while continuing to use the billable hour standard, a parallel phantom budget should be prepared for comparison purposes. Over time, such an exercise will evolve into a new billing methodology. In a recent conversation with a senior partner at another firm, he lamented that the last time they did a fixed fee for service, they lost their shirt. Whose fault is that? Certainly it is not the client's. Clients hire lawyers for their expertise and experience in specific practice areas, which presumes that the lawyer has the ability to forecast with some certainty how a case or matter will progress. Law firms spend huge sums on various time and billing software and databases. Such data can be used to create models for budgeting and scheduling. We have the data and technology to create a realistic model of much of our work. We just need the incentives to use them in this way.

Law firm management should focus on the future costs, liabilities, burn-out rate and unintended consequences to the individual of the frenetic and heedless pursuit of billables. Family friendly practices will pay future dividends of loyalty and domestic peace and avoid future losses of time, productivity, and profit. A capable and promising young associate should not be expected or even permitted to bill in excess of 1800 hours per year. Vacations should not be at the discretion of the lawyer but should be mandatory. Sabbaticals for pro bono work, public services, or simply mental heath should be the rule and not the rare exception at firms. Firms should cover the costs of having family members attend business conventions or practice development conferences to create mini-vacations. Childcare incentives and flexible hours for the lawyer raising small children are keys for retention. Firm-paid counseling services should be a standard employee benefit. Bonuses tied to hours in excess of billable goals ought to be eliminated in favor of subjective performance and client satisfaction rewards. The small costs associated with "take your kid to work" days, firm sporting events, firm picnics, and brown bag lunches will reap rewards in retention and mental health. I once organized a firm retreat around competitive high performance driving at a racetrack—very revealing and still talked about 20 years later.

Finally, clients themselves need training and control. In 40 years of practice, I can recall only a few times that a matter was so consequential and existential that late evening or weekend calls were necessitated. A physician may need to be on call because life and death is in the mix. You can't say that about the practice of law no matter how important we think we are. I've had hard charging partners tell me that big clients really like the fact that they can have 24/7 access. If that is what a client demands, then the client should dearly pay for it with a retainer on top of an hourly rate. Access alone to a skilled lawyer used to be a component of overall compensation (what we used to call a true retainer); hourly rates were for the actual work itself. Unfortunately, all the technological advances in the past 40 years, which are now so integral to our profession and practice, are the major culprits in creating a 24/7 access expectation of the client. Technology is neither neutral nor particularly labor saving; it simply creates a different plane in which work is accomplished. Slavish devotion to the little screen outside the office is harmful to relationships and, frankly, bad manners.

For the senior partner worried about the profitability of the firm adopting such a family-friendly philosophy, consider the moral responsibility to your employees to create a healthy working environment. Law firms occupy premier office space with comfortable if not luxurious amenities; they provide medical, dental, and other insurance fringe benefits; they provide parking; they cater coffee and food for hungry hardworking lawyers; they spend prodigious amounts on hardware and software. Why is it strange or controversial to consider the long term marital, family, and self-health of the lawyer?

BUSINESS DEVELOPMENT

Would most law students today be able to identify the offense of "barratry"? A crime at common law as archaic as "criminal conversation," barratry is the institution or encouragement of groundless litigation for personal gain of the attorney. Clearly the term "groundless" is up for interpretation. Barratry is most often found with its fraternal twin, "solicitation," which is unlawfully seeking legal representation and is more colloquially known as ambulance chasing. Since the pronouncement of first amendment protected commercial speech permitting lawyer advertising, the profession has struggled uneasily with the distinction between the lawyer passing out business cards at the scene of the airline crash and passing out business cards at the ABC widget convention.

Like it or not, marketing, more politely referred to as business development, is here to stay, and a voracious consumer of professional time and energy and a source of considerable stress and angst among lawyers—particularly young lawyers. Preparing the slides for a presentation to a group of prospective clients is not billable and the hours spent are unrecoverable unless the actual client business eventuates. But in today's highly competitive and mercantile marketplace, a young lawyer trying to create a practice or become a partner must and is expected to publish, present, or perish. Law firms, by and large, do a poor job of reducing the stress of business development. Telling an associate to "become an expert on something" is unfair and insufficient. Practicing the "elevator speech" does not turn a wallflower into a sales dynamo. Actual training, real mentoring, and leadership by example are necessary.

In addition to the black hole marketing creates in billable hour expectations, there is a more pernicious aspect to marketing and business development, for the self and for gender equality in the workplace. Here I stray onto thin ice, but there is a significant difference in the landscape in which men and women market. Law firms and the senior partners of such do not understand or want to understand these differences. This distinction is not readily apparent when marketing consists primarily of publication and presentation of subject matters of interest to potential clients. Rather, it is in the lawyer-to-client social interactions, which represent such an appreciable share of marketing time, that these differences exist and are unrecognized. While the time-honored traditions of business development for men may consist of bars and steakhouses, golf, and sports games, the marketing game for women is less straightforward and potentially fraught. If firms were to acknowledge this fact and providing training and creative solutions, the benefit would be to male and female attorneys alike, particularly as the profession reaches parity between the sexes and the number of female clients increases.

Finally, it's critical to recognize the different strengths among professionals. Two equally capable and ambitious lawyers may have entirely different skill sets when it comes to marketing. One may be comfortable with social small talk and the other may be a wallflower. One may be a naturally gifted speaker and another may have stage fright. Law firms would do well to offer specific training. Speaking coaches, mock social events, well practiced elevator speeches, cross marketing information, and even a professional actor (I used this once to great effect on a poor communicator) are all investments in people which will pay dividends and reduce the stress of business development.

WINNING AT ALL COSTS

We are trained to objectively evaluate the facts, research, logically deduce, and then apply established principles of law to a situation or problem. We then advise a client of the legally correct course of action and the liabilities and uncertainties associated, craft a defense or prosecution from those facts and law, argue effectively in support of a client's position and, above all, win. To accomplish this, we work very hard, give and take orders, argue, delegate, take risks, and debate. The work can be stressful and emotional and rewarding at the same time. Stress is the physiological response to potentially harmful situations. Stress can be productive in sharpening the mind and focusing emotions, but it can have long term harmful effects like increased blood pressure, adrenaline highs and lows, and exhaustion. What is the effect of this stress on the lawyer and his or her family and spouse, and what is unique about this insofar as the legal profession is concerned? Police officers, teachers, doctors, and others have great stress in their respective employment. Can we isolate those aspects that are unique to the lawyer?

Lawyers are taught to win. Whether it's the acquittal of the innocent defendant, the conviction of the miscreant, the class action suit against a corporation, or the injunction against the government, winning is the ultimate high. Not only does winning define success for the lawyer, it's usually a team victory for colleagues, paralegals, and assistants. The client is vindicated, the judicial system works and the adversarial nature of our profession is ascendant. Of course, not winning has the opposite effect.

Living and working in such a culture of adversarial relationships and binary results of winning and losing has a direct and manifest bearing on our social and personal relationships. Your spouse is neither your secretary, associate, nor subordinate. A parent cannot deal with the vicissitudes of child rearing on the basis of winners and losers, deductive logical and argumentative persuasion. Rather, discussion, cajoling, empathizing, and compromising are the means to a conclusion and the actual end product of parent-child relationships. Treating a child (or spouse) as a hostile witness to be cross-examined is wrong, counterproductive, and insulting, and equally unlikely to carry the day on any family problem. When you are trained in this manner, however, you have to make a conscious choice to avoid falling into this trap.

Is it possible to leave your training, thought process, and professional abilities at the front door along with the stresses and problems of the day? How can you measure the relative importance of what you are doing at the office with the emotional needs of your children, spouse, or significant other? Is your son being teased at school about the color of his backpack as consequential as the legal minefield you navigated for your client that day? To your son it is. Can you empathize with your daughter's first pimple after losing a summary judgment motion for a big client? If your spouse wants your impression of his boss's latest sales goals, can you provide your full attention even as your star expert witness blundered at trial?

These conflicts are not particularly unique to lawyers; a brain surgeon may be similarly distracted by the life and death nature of his or her work and thus inattentive to the quotidian. But it is also true that physicians are taught bedside manners, which are, by their very nature, empathetic. There is no such training for lawyers. Doctors heal, cure, and rehabilitate; often the lawyer has to destroy to win, to tear down in order to succeed. It is the nature of what we do that implicates behaviors that create misunderstanding and antipathy in the family. The singular trait that the lawyer needs to hone in dealing with children, spouse, or partner is to listen, listen, and listen . . . and then listen some more. The recipe for a happy family is often as simple as shutting up and listening.

Many may resent this critique of the profession and the business of law, but it is the failure to be critical that leads to the continuation of practices that are often destructive of the individual practitioner. The profession of law is a noble calling, but to be successful we need not sacrifice our spouse and family or self. It takes conscious and concerted effort to change the business paradigm and to sublimate behaviors we are trained to use. Neither is an easy task. The billable hour may have been institutionalized for over a hundred years or more, but it needs to be discarded for a better, more predictive model. If the profession does not do so, clients will inevitably demand it.

Law firms ought to take a holistic approach to their lawyers; a keyboard and office alone will not create a viable and long-term success. Being family friendly is not a slight on the quality of the firm or its lawyers but a realization that this is a demanding profession with great benefits and fulfillment that need not be at the price of family and self.

Marketing is here to stay and recognizing the different approaches to business development is critical. Most successful marketers are trained and not born with those skills.

Finally, we often have to leave the lawyer in us at the office, or as my wife has said, on more than one occasion, "Leave it at the front door."

Of the accolades and praise I have received during my career, the thing that meant the most to me was when my son said at my retirement party, "My Dad never missed a game." Can you meet that standard?

CHAPTER 12
Financial Impacts on Health and Well-Being

Edward Poll, JD, MBA, CMC

Editor's Note: For as long as I have been involved in law practice management circles, Ed has been one of the go-to experts with experience on the ground in both law and business and as a writer and speaker. I knew this book had to have a chapter about financial success and Ed was the person who immediately came to mind. He delivers on the high points, the critical things a lawyer must address to be financially successful and to operate a successful business over the long haul.

The successful practice of law requires more than legal competence. Viewed from the client's eyes, "success" is whether his goal was achieved at a cost he is willing to pay; viewed from the lawyer's eyes, success is whether the fee is paid and the client refers others in the future. If the client's wants (client's perspective) and needs (lawyer's analysis) are different, they must be resolved for this to occur. These skills are not taught in law school. This chapter presents some critical aspects of running a business that lawyer well-being requires.

Edward Poll is a nationally recognized legal management expert whose advice has helped thousands of lawyers create more rewarding legal practices and directed hundreds of national, regional, and local law firms towards higher profitability. He is the author of 17 books and audio products. *The Attorney & Law Firm Guide to The Business of Law®* is in its third edition, and *Collecting Your Fee: Getting Paid from Intake to Invoice* are published by the American Bar Association. Ed practiced law and has been a CEO of manufacturing firms and a law firm management consultant.

You can help clients only if you are legally competent to address their issues and have sufficient financial resources to adequately prosecute their cause. Financial resources can be seen as finances a client needs to engage appropriate experts and pay related costs to move the matter forward along with what the lawyer needs to operate the law office and pay for family living expenses and related matters. As a lawyer, it is critical to know you have the cash and credit required in each category. This reduces stress in this area. You will then have the clear mind you need to focus your attention on your client's needs.

Firm and personal finances can be enormous sources of stress. When clients are late in the payment of their fees, when the lawyer is inefficient in delivering services, or when the law firm grows exponentially faster than current cash reserves can afford, there will be stress. Financial literacy and expertise help manage, reduce, or eliminate these sources of stress.

In one exchange with a client, I used a financial term. My client had a different interpretation of what I said. This created a great deal of stress as our conversation continued. I learned to be careful about making sure everyone was on the same page with a shared meaning. Everyone benefits from a basic knowledge of financial terms to better understand the playing field and reduce the stress of inadequate financial expertise. Following are some some important financial concepts essential for lawyers and clients to understand and essential for running the business operations of a law practice.

> **Cash basis accounting:** Items go on the financial statement only as cash is received or paid. Most small and mid-sized law firms use cash as the basis to express the financial position of the firm. Accrued debt, then, such as future lease obligations or vacation obligations that have not yet been paid, is not on these statements.
>
> **Accrual basis accounting:** Items go on the financial statement as the revenue is due or the expense/debt is incurred, even if paid at a later date. Larger law firms may have two statements, one on the accrual system and one on the cash system to describe their financial condition.

Professional service providers, such as attorneys, generally work on a cash basis. Recently, several legislators have floated the idea of converting lawyers' accounting systems to the accrual method. This would dramatically impact the tax basis of law firms and lawyers. In our current political climate, it is best to understand the impact of each system on lawyers.

> **Hourly billing:** Setting your fee per hour and tracking the amount of time worked on a given matter. One's gross revenue (total amount of fee income) rises either by increasing the hourly rate charged or the number of hours billed. There is a limit to the number of hours one can bill; there are 24 hours in a day and 7 days in a week. How you convert time expended into time billed has a direct impact on gross revenue. How many of your work hours get converted to billable time (utilization rate)? Of those hours billed, how many hours are converted to money (realization rate)? The higher the percentage in each category, the greater will be your gross revenue and the more financially successful you will be. The factor changing most is the hourly rate, increasing as the lawyer's expertise grows and is in greater demand.

Accounts receivable: Amount previously charged but not yet paid. This will appear in the first part of the balance sheet of the financial statement. It is a "liquid" asset and will be carefully reviewed by a lender of credit to the lawyer. This is an asset that can quickly disappear when the firm has financial problems and the clients perceive they will not be targeted for collection. This segment of a lawyer's assets must be monitored carefully and protected. If you bill at $200 per hour for a five-hour day but collect only $600 of the total $1,000 billed, you effectively have billed only for 3 hours of work at the $200 rate, lowering your rate to $120 per hour.

Because of these limiting factors and some client push-back, alternative billing approaches are sometimes sought to escape these limitations.

Contingency billing: Setting a percentage of recovery (e.g., 6 percent of a settlement) with nothing due if no settlement. Issues such as cost advances (filing fees, court reporters, etc.) and payment to the attorney only as and when money is received on the settlement versus when the verdict or settlement is made (through moneys received over time) need to be clarified in the engagement agreement.

Value billing: Determining the value of the service to be delivered, irrespective of the result obtained. Some law firms, even large firms, are now experimenting with value billing—that is, value to the client—as the basis of the lawyer's fee. This is more than merely a percentage of recovery. Value billing has the general impact of causing both the client and the attorney to behave more as partners in the matter. One result of this process is to enhance the communication process between the two. Self-esteem and confidence in one's value, and continuing communication with clients, are the keys to value billing, high realization, and success. The number currently using this approach is small but a growing segment of the lawyer population.

If the client does not adhere to the terms of the engagement agreement and you allow the client to ignore the terms of the engagement agreement's payment plan, you essentially tell the client that payment is not important to you.

Most standard engagement agreements provide for 30-day payment terms. Unfortunately, most clients do not pay in 30 days. It might be wise to review the terms of your engagement agreement. Would it be better to provide an incentive for early or timely payment, such as a 5 percent discount? Or a dis-incentive for later payment, such as a 5 percent add-on or termination of representation? These are topics that should be reviewed and discussed. Ignoring them increases your stress for client non-payment. One scenario to avoid is a client failing to pay, your wanting to resign from the representation, and the court requiring you to continue representation because of the critical juncture of the case. Now you will be working *pro bono* under court order or Bar supervision. Think about how you would feel. Would you be happy? Would you feel stressed? Because of the increased stress, would you be likely to miss a critical date or other important benchmark for the client? This did happen to a client of mine, resulting in a later suit against him for malpractice. Think about this: working *pro bono* instead of for a fee and then having to defend yourself in a subsequent lawsuit and incur an increased cost of malpractice insurance. That is very stressful!

Over the years, firms have become larger because they enforced payment terms with clients that made their cash flow management healthy, allowing them the resources to grow. Likewise, several large firms and a number of small firms have closed their doors for failing to monitor and enforce payment schedules.

Finley Kumble opened their doors in 1968 using assertive collection efforts that enabled them to use current billings and only limited borrowing to finance their exponential growth to become one of the first national law firms. Speaking with many larger firm lawyers, they uniformly talk about the push by their management committees to collect outstanding accounts toward the end of their fiscal year.

A client failed to take my advice on this matter. His rationale was that his client made payments periodically of significant sums of money that would reduce the total account receivable. He also believed this client would refer other clients to him. But over time the total owed kept growing and, in the end, the lawyer was forced to write off the entire account receivable. No other clients were referred. He continued to work for the client and, by the time the lawyer declared bankruptcy, he was owed $80,000, having been "sucked in" by the client with only dribs and drabs along the way. This was the first lawyer I knew who went into bankruptcy.

> **Collections policy:** Determining what efforts are to be made to collect the outstanding billing and when those efforts are to be instituted. This generally is one area ignored by lawyers for fear of offending a client and risking the loss of new business from that client. This is an area of concern and heightened stress for many lawyers. An old expression that "the first loss is the best loss" comes to mind. If you have a problem collecting from a client, it is better to know that sooner when the amount owed is smaller, than later when the amount is larger.

Create a weekly or monthly accounts receivable schedule and review it weekly. Refer to the client's payment commitment and the consequences of their failure to pay in accordance with their agreement. Decide when to cease work for this client if the payment schedule is not honored, and do so before a time of crisis for the client or critical juncture in the case where the court might conclude you are putting unfair pressure onto the client or it is difficult for you to withdraw representation.

Do not accept new work from clients who fail to honor their engagement agreement. You are merely inviting more trouble and increasing the likelihood of a claim of malpractice. Rather than work for clients who do not pay, or pay very slowly, continue your marketing efforts to seek honorable clients who observe their commitments. Look for clients who appreciate your skills and will honor their commitments.

> **Staff and/or attorney turnover:** The speed of personnel change. Both training new personnel and the time taken to become as efficient as the departed personnel result in increased costs. Clients become familiar with the personnel in your organization and the disruption of that closeness frequently increases financial costs to the organization. The "glue" between law firm personnel and clients frequently is strong enough to prevent poaching of clients by other lawyers.

> **Business plan:** A statement of objectives of the firm for a period of time, usually a year, by month, listing collections and expenses by category. With more law students having a business or business school background, thinking

about one's future in the law and creating a business plan is gaining traction. Having a plan allows you to track your financial success and reduces the negative stress of uncertainty. The size of firm you want, the number of attorneys in the same skill set and/or other areas—these and other factors impact the numbers in your business plan and *pro forma* financial statements.

Every business, including the practice of law, has three dimensions. Adlai Stevenson, former senator from Illinois, said that "law is a . . . business service station and repair shop." This recognizes that the client has an issue that can be addressed either as a preventive service or an ameliorative service. Sometimes, the problem can be patched; sometimes it can be prevented.

The first dimension is marketing, promoting your skills far and wide, to attract clients. After the initial marketing efforts, the second dimension is production and/or delivery of the service and documents—for example, the delivery of a will for signature, the settling or trial of a personal injury matter, the creation of a trust, etc. This is the area of substantive expertise on which most lawyers focus their energies. But it is only part of the package. Being the "best" lawyer, from a substantive perspective, is not enough. You must work not only in your business (delivering legal services) but also on your business to be successful!

The third dimension of business is pricing, billing, and collection for services delivered. Pricing, even after years of practicing law, is an art, not a science. Neither the lawyer nor the client handles this conversation well. Generally, it's not whether the client can "afford" it, but rather whether the client places sufficient priority on the issue confronting them and the confidence in your skill to perform and deliver a particular result.

Creating a pricing policy that works for you, your practice area, and your clients is essential. Too few lawyers discuss the total cost of representation. Hourly fees generally do not contain a "cap" and the client has no fix on what additional costs are and how much they will be. If experts or major photocopying costs are involved, these items need to be discussed. The metric that is most important to clients is the total cost for the needed services. That is what the client wants to know. If you cannot estimate this, then either a "cap" can be set forth or a schedule by time and number of hours on a monthly basis can be estimated. Have the client initial approval of the expected fee and set forth a procedure for going beyond expectation, or do so in chunks: a review of the facts for $X in the first month will occur, after which the parties, attorney and client, will come back to set the next stage and cost.

After marketing and delivering the legal service, billing and collecting are often afterthoughts to the lawyer. Billing is more than a piece of paper sent to a client monthly. It is a marketing opportunity, describing what was done, impressing the client with the effort expended and success achieved for their benefit. This is a grand opportunity to emphasize what was achieved and why the client made the right choice in selecting you as their attorney. Too few attorneys take full advantage of this opportunity.

With the advent of billing software programs, most attorneys merely set forth the time spent on a matter, a short description and a total at the bottom of the page. If you use this approach, you'd be well advised to use a cover letter to describe what was done in greater detail, what was accomplished, and what is yet to be done during the next segment of time.

To keep stress levels low, maintain continuous communication with clients, using progress reports that set forth the amount paid to date, current billings, and amount still owed. This is best done no less frequently than monthly. One benefit of progress reports is that it forces the lawyer to "touch" the file every month. Sometimes we get so busy that we forget to do things, such as setting depositions or filing motions that we intended. This is one way of staying current with your case strategic plan. It also allows you to remind the client of their payment commitment.

Monitor payments by clients and deposit receipts immediately, no less frequently than the day following receipt. Waiting longer invites negative possibilities, such as a client going out of business, their bank account being levied on, or a change of heart and stop payment on the check. Other ways of receiving payment are automatic bill pay, ACH payments, wire transfers, and credit card payments. Some have costs attributable to the method, either for the creditor or debtor.

The Business of Law® enables lawyers to analyze the economics of their practice and improve the delivery of services to clients. While there is more to the law firm business than expressed here, focusing on these concepts and how they impact your law firm business is important to you and your clients. When you don't talk about these things, stress levels rise. Your success depends on paying attention!

Remember the quip attributed to John Wooden, famous coach of UCLA basketball: "Failure to plan . . . is planning to fail." One can argue that law is a profession, which it is if you define profession as a practice that requires much skill, education, and a license indicating that certain skills have been attained. It's also a business, which it is if you define business as the transferring of personal services in exchange for money. Improved results will impact your financial performance, improve your well-being, and reduce your stress.

Create a financial plan or budget and monitor your progress. Match the budget with the financial capabilities of the client. Do not take a matter that the client cannot afford to pay for (unless it is intentionally *pro bono*). How might you know what the client can afford? Create a credit application to be completed by each client on their first visit and a fee agreement that also describes the consequences of failing to honor the payment schedule.

Make the client part of the team and manage client expectations. By doing so, the client will feel part of the team, will understand the process, and accept the result without directing blame or fault toward you. Following these practices reduces the normal stress of practicing law in a competitive and combative environment, produces positive results for your clients, and contributes to the health and well-being of both you and your clients!

CHAPTER 13
Using Stress to Your Advantage

Eva Selhub, MD

Editor's Note: I met Dr. Selhub when I was working on a project developing a television show whose purpose was to tell stories about collaborations between traditional physicians and alternative health practitioners. Given her experience on the Harvard Medical School faculty and her holistic orientation toward healthcare, I thought she would be a good person to talk about how important physical health is to overall well-being. I'm glad I asked.

You can be successful at your work, have meaningful relationships, and take better care of yourself, all the while using stress to motivate you and also warn you when you need to go and when you need to stop. You have the power to make choices that will support you to function at your best at all times, enabling you to be truly resilient. Resilient leaders have the ability to think clearly and find solutions to complex situations even under duress. They are able to maintain adaptability and flexibility in the midst of change, stay open to support and learning, cultivate optimism, have dedication to personal renewal, and, ultimately, thrive in the face of adversity. You can be this resilient leader by knowing the difference between adaptive coping and maladaptive coping; developing awareness; having a quiet mind, a meditation practice, and healthy behaviors and attitudes; and cultivating the ability to gauge when to stop and when to keep going.

Eva Selhub, MD, guides clients to the best version of themselves through her six pillars of health. She is author of *Your Health Destiny, The Love Response,* and *Your Brain on Nature*; Adjunct Scientist in the Neuroscience Laboratory at the Jean Mayer USDA Human Nutrition Center on Aging at Tufts University (HNRCA); a Corporate Wellness Consultant, Innovation and Resiliency Coach, and Stress & Mind-Body Medicine Specialist; a former Instructor in Medicine, Harvard Medical School; and Associate in Medicine at the Massachusetts General Hospital.

WHAT IS STRESS?

Stress is part of life. You can't get around it. If you did manage to get around it, you would likely be dead. You actually need stress to live.

Without stress you would not get up in the morning, get to work on time, put food on the table, or shift positions when you are uncomfortable.

Feeling hunger—that's a stress. Feeling cold—another stress. Worried about meeting a deadline? Stress. Changes in the weather, traumatizing world news, looming deadlines, pollution, blood pressure changes, feelings of fatigue, inflammation, sleep deprivation, ingested toxins or processed foods, emotional upset—stress comes in many forms. The list is endless. To the brain, anything that challenges the body's steady state or homeostasis qualifies as a stress.

And this is a good thing. Because without stress, no action would be taken and you would be dead. You wouldn't be alerted to eat when hungry, put on something warm when cold, or run when being chased by a bear. You wouldn't be motivated to do much of anything.

When stress is present, the brain will activate the stress response as well as a whole host of actions that kick the body into action to solve the problem so that the system can get back into its state of stability. The process of achieving stability through change or adaptation, a course of action that every living organism lives by to survive, is called allostasis. It is the reason we procreate, innovate, run marathons, or climb mountains. When something within us wants for change, we are driven to make it happen. That drive comes from the stress response.

THE STRESS RESPONSE

The stress response is a physiological response that invariably enables individuals to get out of bed in the morning, fight infections, maintain blood pressure, survive traumas, meet nutritional needs, and allow energy to be expended in response to a wide range of signals to heal wounds so that we can adapt to an ever-changing environment and survive.

Walter Cannon, a Harvard physiologist, coined the term "fight or flight" in the 1930s to describe our inborn defense response to threat or danger that ultimately ensures survival.[1] When faced with danger, we are catapulted into action by stress hormones like adrenalin and cortisol as our senses become hyper-alert, pupils dilate, peripheral vision is blocked, muscles tense, heart rate rises, breathing rate increases and becomes more shallow to economize on oxygen consumption, and the digestive system shuts down so that all energy is focused towards fighting like mad or running like the wind. The liver releases stored sugar into the blood stream while blood flow is diverted to the brain, heart, large muscles, and lungs. With a built-in turn off switch, the stress response will eventually extinguish itself once the threat is gone.

Hans Selye, in the 1950s, expanded on Cannon's work and explained that you do not have to be chased by a raging animal for the fight or flight response to be triggered and that this heightened reaction occurs regardless of whether the challenge

---

1. WALTER BRADFORD CANNON, THE WISDOM OF THE BODY (1939); WALTER BRADFORD CANNON, BODILY CHANGES IN PAIN, HUNGER, FEAR, AND RAGE (1929).

at hand is life threatening or not.[2] You could be late for work, preparing for public speaking, or worried about your mortgage getting paid. And each time stress is perceived, whether real or imagined, the stress response is evoked, setting off a myriad of physiological reactions.

THE REAL PROBLEM WITH STRESS

If the stress response is left unchecked, all the physiological responses that were activated that are meant to be beneficial in the short-term become harmful as they rage on. Heightened blood pressure can turn into heart disease, muscle tension into fibromyalgia, negative mood into depression, and heightened inflammation to a wide variety of immune disorders. In other words, stress itself is not necessarily always the problem, but rather, the hyper-activation of the stress response that prevents the system from resuming homeostatic stability.

Whether it is a result of the stress itself (highly traumatic or chronic), a genetic predisposition to an over-active stress response, or how an individual perceives themselves and their resources, the result is taxation on the system, which can eventually lead to physical, mental, emotional or psychological pathology.

The point here is that stress itself is not always or necessarily bad. It is the perception, real or imagined, that stress isn't manageable that leads to an over-activation of the stress response, a burdening on the mind-body system, and pathological outcomes—physical, psychological, or emotional.

THE KEY TO RESILIENCE: MANAGING STRESS

The key, then, to a resilient mind-body system is to manage stress more often than not. Though this task might sound impossible as many stressors are out of our control, it is often not necessary to manage a particular stress, but to believe that you can if you need to, both consciously and unconsciously.

The more an individual believes in their own abilities and resources, the more likely they are to perceive stress as manageable, resulting in less worry, more confidence, and positive expectation, which translate into a shorter-lived stress response and a more resilient mind and body.

The glitch is that you have to be aware that the body is in stress and doing something about it to uphold this belief, at least sub- or unconsciously. If you are not taking care of your body, for instance, the body will not have the tools or resources to handle challenges.

For instance, if your body experiences a drop in blood sugar, you eat and the problem is solved. You have coped adaptively. But let's take another scenario. This time you are anxious or worried about something. To soothe your nerves you eat, even though the body is not in need of more fuel. By eating, the sensation of feeling anxious is temporarily resolved, but the problem you are worrying about isn't resolved. Additionally, you have likely added stress to your system by putting in energy when it is not needed, so now it has to be put into your fat stores. If you are

2. Hans Selye, Science; Stress and Disease, October 1955, 122: 625–631. Z. Fadel, S. K. Johnson, B. J. Diamon, D. Zhanna, & P. Goolkasian, *Mindfulness Meditation Improves Cognition: Evidence of Brief Mental Training*, 19 Consciousness and Cognition, 2: 597–605 (2010).

like most other Americans, you have also chosen to comfort yourself with "comfort" foods, containing high fructose corn syrup or trans-fats, which add to the stress by enhancing inflammation and putting toxins in the body, wreaking havoc on the gut-brain connection, heightening anxiety, worsening your mood, causing stomach irritability or headaches. The heightened stress response and resultant stress hormones then shut your mind down, destroy your memory and slow down your cognitive processing and ability for higher reasoning. Though you have enabled yourself to cope temporarily by eating, you have actually harmed yourself in the long run. This is known as maladaptive coping.

Through discomfort of one kind or another—physical, mental, emotional or psychological—the body lets you know that there is an underlying problem it would like you to address. If you listen close enough, you will understand what your body or brain is trying to tell you and make better choices. The better choices you make, the more both the mind and body develop a surety the future stress will be manageable, as you learn to use stress as a signal for change rather than letting it get the best of you.

Here's an example: You have a big case coming up which entails a lot of research and late nights. You have little time to exercise, sleep, or eat healthy, though somewhere in the recesses of your mind, you know that you could probably allow some time for self-care, but choose to repress the knowledge. You are being driven by deadlines and something that you deem far more important. Unfortunately, it is that time of the year that the flu is traveling through the office. You notice that you feel more fatigued and a bit achy, but you chalk it up to your hectic schedule. You drink more coffee, grab a bagel loaded with cream cheese to boost your energy, and keep going. Next thing you know, the minute the case is done, you find yourself unable to get out of bed with a raging fever, cold sweats, chills, and a deep cough. You feel like you are dying. You aren't dying. You have the flu and you have little to no immune system right now to fight it. Whether you want to be in bed or not, you are stuck there for the duration of the illness.

Could you have avoided getting so sick? The answer is most likely, yes. By ignoring the body's whispers, the stress happening in your body went unchecked, leaving your immune system weaker and less capable of fighting off the flu virus as it passed through the office. Better sleep, nutrition, and self-care would either have warded off the virus completely or at least kept it at bay so that it didn't completely knock you out.

OLD HABITS DIE HARD

Though adaptive coping is enticing, it is not easily done. Most of us are wired to automatically fall back to old coping patterns that have been working for us since childhood, especially when negative emotions or beliefs are triggered. Trying to stop a bad habit that helps you cope is like trying to stop a shiver when it's cold outside because the stress response is being driven by memory.

Emotions and emotional memory are directly connected to physiological responses, both positive and negative. When faced with challenges, the brain searches its memory bank for details to see how such challenges have been handled previously, what resources were used, and what the outcome may have been. It will match the current emotion to the data bank of emotional memories, igniting the associated assumptions, beliefs, behaviors, physiological reactions, and physical behaviors.

The result is that situations that arise today can trigger a positive or negative physiological response and subsequent belief and behavior, based on a past memory. For instance, perhaps a colleague is disrespecting you or not taking your advice. If in your past you were often criticized and put down, this type of situation may trigger you to get extremely upset and angry, more so than someone else might, whereby your rational brain is bypassed and your subsequent actions are harmful to others or yourself (e.g., you drink alcohol to calm your nerves). But since this is what you have always done to relieve your stress, it is challenging to behave differently, even though it is maladaptive.

Let's take another scenario, common to legal practice. Part of your job as an attorney is to be able to see clearly and objectively predict and plan for likely consequences based on advantages and disadvantages of taking various actions. When you have no emotional stake in the outcome, attaining this objectivity is more possible. The same is true when you are well rested, fed, and feel calm yet alert. But what if you are sleep deprived, coming down with the flu, and having problems at home with your spouse? Feeling a tremendous amount of stress, is objective decision making as possible, not to mention being completely thorough in your work? How beneficial for your client are you now?

STOPPING THE CYCLE AND USING STRESS TO YOUR ADVANTAGE

Always remember that the environment is constantly changing and so are you. This means you have the ability to influence any change in a positive or a negative direction by the choices you make. You have the power to transform your mind and improve the functioning of your body, if you choose.

As attorneys, you will invariably experience negative emotions, be stressed by time or the need for information that is yet unavailable, and be vexed by decisions that are hard to make. You will also be stressed by family concerns, lack of self-care habits, relationship issues, and so forth. You can choose to employ these six action steps and master your ability to use stress, rather than let it use you.

1. Pause, Breathe, Listen

So you feel stressed. You are tired. You are trying to find information that will help your case but keep reaching a dead end. You feel frustrated and like a headache is coming on. What to do?

This is when and where you want to learn to quiet your mind and your stress response. You may wish to take a moment and ask yourself these questions (rather than pushing forward with your task at hand): Why am I anxious? Why am I tired? What is my body really telling me?

Then simply breathe in and out slowly while witnessing your body's signals and your thoughts without judgment. Witnessing your physiology involves listening and observing your body and how it speaks to you. You observe with an open mind without judgment. Nothing is good or bad; nothing is right or wrong. Witnessing has its roots in the Buddhist meditation practice called mindfulness, which is now a widespread secular practice. Mindfulness involves being in a moment-by-moment awareness of your thoughts, sensations, and feelings, as well as of the surrounding environment, and has the added benefit of turning down the stress response, which then improves your mood and ability to cope more effectively.[3]

How to do it:

Stop. Take a pause. Take a deep breath in, counting to four, and let the breath out, counting from four down to zero. Do this five times. Allow your thoughts and tension to be released with your breath. As you quiet down, ask your body what it needs. Observe and listen. Keep focusing on the in and out of your breath, continuing to count. Release the thoughts from your mind and the tension from your body. Listen and observe.

2. Redirect the Focus to Positive Expectation

Once you have taken this pause, you can begin to recognize the negative stance you are in, what the cause might be, and that you need to take a time out to take care of yourself a bit more. At this point, you can also recognize that you have the ability to gain more balance simply by choosing to redirect your focus away from your task or negative thoughts and towards a memory or thought that is light, joyful, or loving.

It is possible to disassociate from negative emotions and beliefs and from unhappy memories, and reprogram the brain with positive emotions and expectations of trust. Positive perception is directly correlated to inner surety or trust in success or manageability of a particular endeavor or challenge. This positivity, according to current research, confers better health in mind and body.[4]

How to do it:

Take a pause, breathe, listen, and then redirect your focus to something that will activate your brain's positive expectation centers (reward centers). You can focus on your favorite place in nature, someone you love, something funny, or any situation that elicits the feeling of awe or love. Focus on this image as well as your feelings of appreciation for having this experience or person in your life for at least ten breaths. For the best results in reducing stress response reactivity overall and over time, aim to extend this practice to 20 minutes a day.

3. Move Your Body

The term "survival of the fittest" means your ancestors had to be fit to survive. Not only did the strongest and fastest person get to the food first, but research also tells us that regular exercise not only helps your cardiovascular functioning but also reduces your stress response activity.[5]

---

3. Z. Fadel, S. K. Johnson, B. J. Diamon, D. Zhanna, & P. Goolkasian, *Mindfulness Meditation Improves Cognition: Evidence of Brief Mental Training*, 19 CONSCIOUSNESS AND COGNITION, 2: 597–605 (2010).

4. Heather N. Rasmussen, Michael F. Scheier & Joel B. Greenhouse, *Optimism and Physical Health: A Meta-analytic Review*, 37 ANNALS OF BEHAVIORAL MEDICINE 239–256 (2009).

5. D. E. R. Warburton, G. W. Nicol, & S. S. D. Bredin, *Health Benefits of Physical Activity: The Evidence*, 174 CANADIAN MEDICAL ASSOCIATION JOURNAL 6, 801–9.

How to do it:

It doesn't matter what kind of exercise you do, as long as you do it. I personally recommend alternating days of vigorous exercise (can't hold a conversation) with days of moderate exercise (holding a conversation) with active rest days (strolling with the dog, or someone else's dog).

4. Food Is Your Fuel

It is important to keep in mind that food is not your enemy, nor is it your savior when you are anxious. Rather, food is fuel, your source of energy; it does not have to be a source of inflammation. If you slow down and eat mindfully and take the time to listen to how your body reacts to different foods, you discover that certain foods leave you feeling more achy, tired, or irritable, even though in the short term, they enable you to feel better as your cravings are tempered. Indeed, studies now show that sugar intake, particularly in the form of glucose, is likely more of a risk factor for developing high blood pressure and cardiovascular disease than high salt intake.[6]

How to do it:

Choose food that is grown naturally in your environment. Choose grass-fed foods. If it doesn't grow in the earth or natural bodies of water, don't eat it regularly. How do you feel, not only immediately after eating your food, but the next day? Aim for an 80/20 healthy eating plan (20 percent of the not-so-good stuff, if you can tolerate it and you still really want it).

5. Make Time for Rest and Recovery

We live in a society that encourages us to push ourselves, go faster, work harder, sleep less. High-level athletes know that their best performance happens when they take the time to allow their body to rest and recover. Even modest sleep deprivation of one or two hours negatively affects your physiology, especially stress physiology.[7]

How to do it:

You may wish to ask yourself why you might be tired, if you are. Are you rested when you awaken in the morning? Examine your food intake. Examine the stimulants you may be taking (caffeine, sugar, etc.). Examine the quality of your sleep—how comfortable is your bed? Do you have physical pain disturbing your sleep? When does your energy dive during the day? When do you lose your focus? Perhaps this is a time to take regular naps or practice a ten to 20 minute meditation.

6. Play Has a Pay-Off

I am sure you have heard of the saying, "All work and no play makes Jack a dull boy." According to how the stress response works, if stress accumulates without periods of rest, recovery, and fun, your mind does dull. Play, socialization, or finding ways to ignite your creative nature all enable stress response reduction and can

---

6. J. J. DiNocolantonio,& S. C. Lucan, *The Wrong White Crystal: Not Salt But Sugar As Aetiological in Hypertension and Cardiometabolic Disease.* 3 OPEN HEART 1 (2014).

7. Michael R. Irwin, *Sleep Deprivation and Activation of Morning Levels of Cellular and Genomic Markers of Inflammation,* 166 ARCHIVES OF INTERNAL MEDICINE 1756 (2006).

empower your sense of well-being. Several studies, for example, have reported that social support facilitates coping and improves psychological and physical health.[8]

How to do it:

Think about who or what ignites your fire. What gets you excited or passionate? Who or what causes you to feel like you belong to something greater? Who or what supports you to feel and act at your best? Whatever and whomever this may be, choose it and do it.

JACK'S TURN-AROUND

One of my clients came to me to help him with rising anxiety, insomnia, headaches, and, ultimately, marital problems. As one of the partners in his firm, he told me, he had to keep up appearances and worked hard at hiding his symptoms and never spoke about his flailing marriage. It was all taking a toll on his health, life, and productivity. He could not find the motivation to work as hard and bring in clients. He was worried the other partners were going to pull him aside or ask him to resign. He was worried he was going to lose his wife. His worry was affecting everything.

After listening to Jack's worries as well as hearing about his childhood and young adult history, we started working on Jack's abilities to control the stress response through breathing and meditation techniques. He took out sugar, dairy, processed foods, most grains, and alcohol for three weeks (and reduced caffeine) to clear the body of stimulants that might be worsening symptoms of anxiety, headaches, and sleep deprivation. He added exercise three to four times a week (a 30-minute brisk walk outside) and we worked on ways to improve his sleep hygiene and calm the mind with meditation prior to sleep.

Within this three-week period, Jack started feeling better; he found his headaches were gone, sleep improved, and anxiety reduced. As we continued forward, I had Jack expand his meditation practice to include connecting with feelings of compassion and love, which helped his anxiety even more. At work, he was instructed to take breaks every hour, for a minute to five minutes, to breathe deeply, practice mindfulness, or do a meditation. Over the next three months, Jack continued to see positive changes not only with his health and mood, but in his perspective on life, work, and his marriage, and he found himself communicating better with his wife.

I am happy to say that one year later, Jack was back to being a high-earning partner and had renewed his vows with his wife.

USE STRESS SO IT DOESN'T USE YOU

You see, it is possible to have it all. You can be successful at your work, have meaningful relationships, and take better care of yourself, all the while using stress to motivate you and also warn you when you need to go and when you need to stop.

---

8. B. N. Uchino, *Social Support and Health: A Review of Physiological Processes Potentially Underlying Links to Disease Outcomes*, 29 Journal of Behavioral Medicine 4 (2006) 377–87.

You have the power to make choices that will support you to function at your best at all times, enabling you to be truly resilient.

Always keep in mind that resilient leaders have the ability to think clearly and find solutions to complex situations even under duress. They are able to maintain adaptability and flexibility in the midst of change, stay open to support and learning, cultivate optimism, have dedication to personal renewal, and, ultimately, thrive in the face of adversity.

You can be this resilient leader. Understand and observe the differences between adaptive coping and maladaptive coping and the importance of developing awareness. Cultivate a quiet mind through a meditation practice and foster healthy behaviors and attitudes. Gradually, you'll develop the ability to know when to stop and when to keep going.

CHAPTER 14
What You Need to Know to Nourish Yourself

Felicia D. Stoler, DCN, MS, RDN, FACSM, FAND

Editor's Note: I met Dr. Stoler when I was working on a project developing a television show whose purpose was to tell stories about collaborations between traditional physicians and alternative health practitioners. Given her education, experience, and teaching, I knew she had a contribution to make about how important nutrition can be to overall health and well-being.

What we know about nutrition and exercise is that it can be the least expensive, least invasive, and most effective way to prevent, treat, and delay the onset of many diseases. The question is whether we can all prevent or delay the onset of these diseases. Your health is in your hands and your food choices may play an important role in your overall health. Prevention is the best medicine.

Being well nourished helps the immune system to function properly. When humans are malnourished, they are at risk for diseases and illnesses. Dietary intake habits that are rich in plant-based foods—fruits, vegetables, beans, legumes, whole grains—and low in fat—especially saturated fat—are better for health promotion and the planet.

Dr. Felicia Stoler, America's Health & Wellness Expert™, is a registered dietitian nutritionist, exercise physiologist, and expert consultant in disease prevention, wellness, and healthful living. She has a bachelor's degree from Tulane University, a master's degree in applied physiology and nutrition from Columbia University, and a doctorate in clinical nutrition from Rutgers University. She is a Fellow of the American College of Sports Medicine, a Fellow of the Academy of Nutrition and Dietetics, and a Council member of the True Health Initiative. Felicia recently became a diplomate of the ABLM/ACLM—the inaugural class of Lifestyle Medicine Board Certified professionals. Dr. Stoler hosted the second season of TLC's groundbreaking series *Honey, We're Killing the Kids!* and is the author of *Living Skinny in Fat Genes*™: *The Healthy Way to Lose Weight and Feel Great* (Pegasus). She has been a contributor for FoxNews.com, the Patch.com, and Active.com, and written several book chapters. She authored ACSM's Sports Medicine Basics on Childhood Obesity.

Everyone eats, right? What do you think you know about nutrition? You are a bright, resourceful professional, but perhaps your analytical mind is not sure how to sort out fact from fiction when it comes to feeding your body (and mind) in order to be healthy.

There is a very good chance that beyond the most basic and probably minimal required amount of nutrition education, you do not know what you need to eat to be healthy. Humans do not intuitively eat the right combinations of nutrients—carbohydrates, protein, fat, vitamins, minerals, and water. When a person has a "craving" for a food, it does not mean that they have a deficiency of the nutrient(s) that may be contained in the food they have a burning urge to eat.

Keep in mind: this is just one chapter. There are many books and online resources you can get more in-depth information from or engage the services of a professional. The Internet can be a wonderful thing, but as you must know by now, there's plenty of fake news and websites that appear credible but are not. This chapter will provide you with a foundation for healthy eating choices plus some reliable sources that can keep you up to date as nutrition science changes.

Let's establish some important definitions before proceeding.

Food is any substance that the body can take in and assimilate that will enable it to function.

Nutrition is the study of the nutrients in foods and in the body; also the study of human behaviors related to food.

The word *diet* represents all foods that one consumes (usually by mouth).

Essential nutrients are those that one must take in through diet, and cannot be created in sufficient amounts by the body. Examples of essential nutrients are carbohydrates, essential fatty acids, essential amino acids, vitamins, minerals, and water.

DISEASE PREVENTION

Nutrition is a relatively new science. Science is always changing. Epidemiologists are scientists who study the relationship between disease and lifestyle behaviors to try to find a link. An important truth in science is that correlation does not mean causation. For example, it is well established that smoking can cause lung cancer. It does not mean that every person who has lung cancer was a smoker or that every person who ever smoked will develop lung cancer. Dietary intake habits and physical activity can affect the following diseases/conditions:

- Cancer
- Cardiovascular disease
- Depression
- Diabetes (Type 2)
- Gallstones
- High cholesterol
- Hypertension
- Joint and orthopedic problems
- Obesity
- Osteoporosis
- Sleep apnea

The American Cancer Society reminds us that more than 60 percent of all cancer deaths could be prevented if people ate healthier foods, exercised more, discontinued smoking, and did the recommended cancer screenings. Heart disease is still the number one cause of death in the United States and worldwide, and many of its triggers can be reduced or minimized by lifestyle choices. Lifestyle is referring to food/beverage intake, physical activity, sleep, and stress management.

What we do know about nutrition and exercise is that it can be the least expensive, least invasive, and most effective way to prevent, treat, and delay the onset of many diseases. The question is whether we can all prevent or delay the onset of these diseases. Your health is in your hands, and your food choices may play an important role in your overall health. Prevention is the best medicine.

Being well nourished helps the immune system to function properly. When humans are malnourished, they are at risk for diseases and illnesses. Dietary intake habits that are rich in plant-based foods—fruits, vegetables, beans, legumes, whole grains—and low in fat (especially saturated fat) are better for health promotion and the planet.

THE DIETARY GUIDELINES FOR AMERICANS

It may seem rather confusing that every few years, the federal government comes out with new recommendations about nutrient intake and physical activity guidelines. However, science changes every day, and as information from research is collected, the US Department of Agriculture (USDA) and the Department of Health & Human Services (DHHS) gathers groups of scientists (social, academic, research, etc.) together to discuss the latest and greatest ways to improve your health.

The Dietary Guidelines for Americans are recommendations about nutrient intake and physical activity behaviors. They are a collaborative effort of the USDA and the DHHS. They are science-based guidelines, as the name would imply, for generally healthy Americans over the age of two. Key components include:

- Consume nutrients and other essential compounds from whole foods and beverages.
- Consume fiber-rich whole grains, fruits, vegetables, fat-free dairy, and lean meats, and control portion sizes.
- Reduce fat intake, especially saturated fat and trans fats.
- Reduce sodium intake.
- Alcohol consumption should be moderate, if at all.
- Maintain appropriate body weight, balancing calorie intake with calorie expenditure.
- Engage in regular physical activity for 30–60 minutes each day, and reduce sedentary activities to promote health, psychological well-being, and a healthy body weight.
- Engage in cardiovascular (aerobic), flexibility, strength, and endurance exercise.
- Avoid microbial food borne illness (food safety).

GETTING YOUR NUTRIENTS FROM THE FOOD SUPPLY

Are all calories created equal? The answer is no. Here's the quick Nutrition 101 lesson. What is a calorie? A calorie is the amount of heat that is generated to raise the temperature of one kilogram of water by one degree. Nutritionists use this as a way of measuring the energy intake of food (measured in calories or kilocalories). People consume calories (energy) to be used to fuel body functions. The process of metabolism is the utilization of energy, from carbohydrates, protein, and fat, along with oxygen, to yield energy (defined as ATP), carbon dioxide, and water. We basically do the opposite of what plants do in photosynthesis.

Nutrients are the components of food that are indispensable to the body's functioning. They provide energy, serve as building material, help maintain or repair body parts, and support growth. The nutrients include water, carbohydrates, fat, protein, vitamins, and minerals. We often hear these terms and forget they are components of whole foods!

Carbohydrates are those foods that are of plant origin (the only exception is dairy products). They have 4 calories per gram. Carbohydrates are also referred to by many as "sugars." While the simple building blocks of all carbohydrates are sugar "molecules," the form used in the body is called glucose. Essentially, regardless of food origin, once carbohydrates are absorbed through the lining of the small intestine, it goes directly to the liver. It cannot leave the liver to be used in the body as anything except glucose. Which of the food groups have carbohydrates? They are found in breads, rice, cereal, pasta, whole grains, fruits, vegetables, and dairy. It is the preferred fuel for most body functions and we have a very limited capacity to store carbohydrates in the body (only six to seven hours' worth). Our brains rely exclusively on carbohydrates for fuel!

Protein is made up of molecules called amino acids (the building blocks of protein). Amino acids are found in most foods except fruits. They are found in grains, vegetables, dairy, meat, poultry, fish, eggs, nuts, seeds, beans, legumes, and soy products. Protein has the same 4 calories per gram as carbohydrates. However, protein takes longer to be digested and absorbed than carbohydrates, and many people have greater satiety (feelings of fullness) after eating protein-rich foods. Protein is frequently found with fat in its food of origin (or in the cooking process). Protein is considered an "expensive" form of energy (hint: we don't really use much for fuel). We have a limited capacity to store protein. Contrary to popular belief, eating more protein does not increase muscle mass in the body.

Fat is a controversial nutrient (unless you're on Atkins). Fat has 9 calories per gram and it has subclassifications based upon saturation of the molecule (chemistry stuff): monounsaturated, polyunsaturated, and saturated. Some other terms you may be familiar with now are "trans" or "hydrogenated" oils. This is the process of taking a fat that is liquid at room temperature (oil) and making it solid (like margarine). The problem with trans fats is that they act somewhat like a saturated fat in the body, and the difference is that our bodies cannot clear (or fully break down) trans fats the way we break down other fats. This can have a direct impact on increasing blood cholesterol levels (total cholesterol and triglycerides). Science has shown us that consuming trans fats on a regular basis is more dangerous to our health than the consumption of cholesterol. Cholesterol is not considered an essential nutrient because the body can create it. Cholesterol is the starting material for other substances in the body like bile, steroid hormones, and much more!

There are essential fatty acids that we need as well. You may have heard of omega-3 and omega-6 fatty acids. The "good" fats can be found in fish, nuts, seeds (chia, flax, Ahiflower), soy, olive oil, and avocados. Fats are found in the fat food group: dairy; meat; and two fruits, avocados and coconuts.

As the Academy of Nutrition and Dietetics has led the charge, "All foods can fit—in moderation."

In terms of the amount of nutrients that one needs to consume, carbohydrates should make up 50 to 60 percent of the diet, with protein at 15 to 20 percent and fat being no more than 30 percent each day.

FAMILY MATTERS

As a dietitian and a mother, I am able to put into practice everything that I learned in my many years of graduate school. The most important message is that nutrition is a family matter. Everything that we do in this country involves food: family life cycle occasions (births, birthdays, deaths, weddings), holidays, religious rites of passage, movies, sporting events, etc. Parents should be role models for their children. It is not enough to tell children to eat fruits and vegetables; if parents do not eat them, the children will copy that behavior.

It is also important to think about your "work family" and the dietary habits they have. Given that practicing law is not a 9-to-5 experience, we often eat with colleagues or eat at our organization's facility. What choices do we make as individuals about what we consume and what institutional decisions can we impact?

Good behaviors should start at birth; however, there is always time to make changes towards more healthful eating behaviors. Remember, by the time a family of four goes out to eat, it could be just as quick and usually less expensive to make a meal at home—it just takes good planning.

PLANNING/SHOPPING

There are few people who plan an entire week's menu every Sunday. The best thing one can do is to have good ingredients on hand—whether they be canned, frozen, dried, refrigerated, ready-prep, or quick-prep. If foods in your crisper drawer are never used, don't buy them—or remember to dig into that part of your refrigerator next time.

In most cases, fresh is best; however, frozen and canned products can be just as good. Using dried herbs in place of fats can add a lot of flavor to foods without adding unwanted fats. Food manufacturers are trying to meet the demands of consumers—many products are ready-prepped and can be cooked in the package they come in. Even purchasing dried foods that need to be reconstituted with boiling water can be tasty, nutritious, and fast.

The best strategies for grocery shopping are:

- Go to the supermarket with a shopping list and try to stick to it.
- Leave the kids home (if you can or have proper supervision for them)—they will throw all that junk food into the cart!
- Spend an extra 20 minutes perusing the shelves for new products—especially to find the quick and ready-prep items.
- Shop the outer perimeter of the market—that is where the less-processed foods are found.
- Do not go to the store hungry!

JUST DO IT!

Did you have a home economics or cooking class in middle or high school? Unsure of how to cook? Thank goodness for cooking shows, YouTube videos, and Instagram—all great ways to find recipes and learn how to cut an avocado or seed a pomegranate. Have fun with it! Consider one of the many meal delivery services that send you ingredients that you simply have to assemble! Many adults do not know how to cook and refrain from cooking because of insecurity in cooking skills. Kitchen time can be a source of great pleasure, fun, and stress-free time alone or shared with others.

If you like to snack, make sure you have access to healthy and nutritious snacks. You are more likely to consume fruits when they are washed and left out (as in a fruit bowl). Melons that are cut and stored in the refrigerator will be consumed sooner when ready to eat. Get a melon baller or cookie cutters to make foods into fun shapes.

Are you a picky eater? Know that it can take up to ten exposures to a food before you like it. Keep stressful topics out of the kitchen and away from the table while eating. Do not watch television while eating; it only creates a mindless eating environment.

SPORTS NUTRITION: BEFORE, DURING, AND AFTER

This is a big topic for someone in my field. The best professional recommendation is that just as practice makes perfect for the physical sport—eating before, when appropriate, and afterwards takes practice. The general dietary recommendations in terms of nutrient percentages are the same. What is critical is timing of food intake in relation to exercise/sport performance. The person who eats dinner at 6 pm and wakes up at 6 am the next day to run for 30 minutes is running on an "empty" fuel tank. Would you go 12 hours during the day without eating?

Think of the body as a car—we put gas into a car to make it go. Carbohydrates are the "fuel" that our body needs for vital functions and for voluntary activity—especially sports. Generally, full meals can be consumed three to four hours prior to exercise or sports. As the time gets closer to the activity, the texture of the foods would go from solid foods, to gelatinous foods, to liquids.

Not everyone who exercises needs a protein shake (or bar)! After the sport or exercise is done, make sure to consume plenty of fluids (discussed next), carbohydrates, protein, and fats.

HYDRATION

Experts have not been able to agree on the quantity of fluids that we each need. However, they have been able to agree that fluid intake should replace losses. Nobody walks around measuring their fluid output, so there is one easy way to do this: the pee test. Urination that is pale and plentiful means you are well hydrated. If it is dark or scant, then you need to consume more water! If it's fluorescent yellow, there's a good chance you recently had a multivitamin supplement.

Water is best for meeting hydration needs. However, electrolytes—especially sodium—followed by carbohydrates are very important for exercise that lasts more than one hour or exercise that is done in extremely hot and humid conditions.

Remember, sodas and other flavored "drinks" can add extra calories with very few other nutritional benefits. Many people are naïve about how many calories they consume from beverages each day!

MAGIC PILLS, POTIONS, AND BARS

When asked about quick fixes, ergogenic aids, and performance enhancement products, a graduate professor once said, "There is no such thing in life as a free lunch." What that means is that one should assess the risk versus the reward. Is it really worth it? There are no magic substances that are legal that can increase muscle mass, melt fat away, or enhance sports performance that don't have a potential harm. The supplement industry is not regulated by the US Food & Drug Administration (FDA). Contrary to what the manufacturers would want you to know, just because something is "natural" does not mean that it is safe. No matter how "impressive" their research may appear, to the trained eye, often the "research" is contrived and manipulated advertising.

Save your money for buying good quality, whole foods!

FAD DIETS

The US Federal Trade Commission estimates that over $30 billion is spent each year on weight loss. Many of the programs, books, and products can be expensive; they offer unrealistic weight loss goals; and most people do not succeed. Those who attain their weight loss goal often are plagued by gaining back most, if not all, of their weight, and sometimes even more than what they lost! Remember to be a savvy shopper of nutrition information. Just because someone has the letters "Dr" in front of his name does not make him credible to dispense nutrition information. Celebrities are not credible resources for nutrition, diet, or weight loss information. A program that worked for your co-worker won't necessarily work for you. Could you imagine what would happen if we tried to self-treat all of our medical conditions through books and websites and hiring unskilled professionals for assistance? Surely we would have a bigger medical crisis on our hands. Perhaps that would mean more work for lawyers!

To find a nutrition professional in your community, check the website of American Dietetic Association (www.eatright.org).

ONLINE RESOURCES

We've covered the basics of healthful eating in this chapter. For more details and up-to-the-minute research, see the following websites:

The American Cancer Society: www.cancer.org
The American College of Sports Medicine: www.acsm.org
The American Diabetic Association: www.diabetes.org
The American Dietetic Association: www.eatright.org
The American Heart Association: www.americanheart.org
The US Department of Agriculture: www.nutrition.gov (this is for all nutrition
    information, including the Dietary Guidelines)

CHAPTER 15
Well-Being and Physical Exercise

John Mitchell, Esq., MBA

Editor's Note: I exercise for about 40 minutes every day, unless I'm really ill, 365 days a year. I remember seeing John for the first time in Puerto Rico, very early in the pool. He was making waves with vigor! Watching and listening to him talk about physical activity and observing the way he carries himself in the world you can't help but draw the connection. John's infectious energy, confident posture, exuberance, and clarity are easy to feel. Sharing this chapter was a stretch he took on like an exercise. I know he took value from the experience and I know you will take value from his powerful personal story.

Physical exercise seems like a no-brainer when it comes to being healthy. On closer examination, it becomes clear that physical exercise does much more than create a strong healthy physical platform from which we pursue our goals. Physical activity directly and positively impacts our emotional, mental, and spiritual health. If you are ready to learn more and experiment, please try the practice pointers in this chapter. You will be on your way to using physical activity to stimulate a healthier you in all dimensions.

John Mitchell is a former chair of the ABA Law Practice Division. He is committed to helping lawyers discover their leadership potential. Mitchell specializes in working with lawyers in formal roles like general counsel, managing partner, and practice group leader and those in informal leadership roles. Helping leaders successfully transition to new leadership roles is one area of John's expertise. He has extensive experience assisting women and attorneys of color in successfully applying their talents to new roles and new environments. Mitchell's 20-plus years of business experience ranges from working as a professional in a social service agency, to practicing law in a large international law firm, to leading a large urban affiliate of an internationally known not-for-profit. John received his JD and MBA from Northwestern University.

I have been participating in athletic endeavors for more than 50 years. I first learned the value of being physically active when I was just over four years old. Fortunately for me, my first exposure to the benefits of physical activity was *not* about changing my body, increasing my physical health, or doing something faster or better. As a small child I learned that physical activity can be the path to freedom and independence.

When I was four years old my family moved to the Panama Canal Zone. My father was a military officer assigned to a post in Panama. My mother had a small child (me) and a toddler (my brother) in an environment that was physically beautiful yet lacking in most of the resources that families typically want to manage a couple of young children. The Air Force base pool became a haven for my mother and me. She wanted me to be able to go to the pool by myself so I could hang out with the lifeguards and have fun while she tended to my younger brother back at our house or the other places she needed to be.

The lifeguards made my Mom a deal. If I could swim a length of the pool (50 meters), without touching the side walls or the bottom, and jump off the diving platform (10 meters high) and make it back to the ladder, they would let me swim at the pool without a parent present. I was a scrawny little boy. The likelihood of making these requirements was slim to none. My Mom and the lifeguards decided to work with me to see if they could get me there. Guess what? The lifeguards took me under their wing and in a matter of months they built my endurance and my confidence so that I was able to swim 50 meters without touching a wall or the bottom. Jumping off the platform tower scared me silly (and it still does) but I realized it was the last step to having the lifeguards adopt me, so I made it work. I cried crawling up the ladder that was more than 30 feet high and I shrieked like the child I was as I jumped off the edge and hit the calm cool water and swam to the ladder. Mission accomplished. I could now be at the pool without my Mom (this would never work today, but this was the late 60s!) and I took my first steps toward becoming independent.

THE PHYSICAL BENEFITS OF EXERCISE

Fast forward just over 15 years and I started to learn my next series of lessons about physical activity. I knew that being active, fit, and confident were a key to being independent. Now I started to learn how physical activity could help me in all aspects of my life.

My next lesson was about the physical benefits of exercise. While this may seem like a no-brainer, my experience was profound. As I left college and moved into adulthood I started to realize that physical activity made a difference in how I felt each day and how I performed, even if it meant sitting at a desk or walking casually with others. By this point in life I was swimming, cycling, and running on a regular basis. Between a lack of talent and a lack of training, I was doing none of these activities enough to become competitive, but that did not matter.

At the same time, I was doing enough workouts that I was becoming stronger, faster, and more confident in everything that I was doing in my life. My commitment to exercise covered all sorts of sins. Too much of this and not enough of that could be easily overcome by staying focused and making sure I hit enough workouts to compensate for all of the things I sometimes or even frequently put off.

This was also the period I began to relate science to what I was learning about exercise. I knew that exercise was the key to my freedom as a small child. I didn't understand the mechanism that exercise played to create that freedom. As I aged I explored my physical capacity and my humanity and learned a lot.

I was a sickly child growing up. Allergic to everything; prone to ear, sinus, and throat infections; scrawny until puberty and constantly forced to move from one location to another as a member of a military family, I never quite made it to a completely stable place until I made it to college. Thankfully, that experience taught me more lasting lessons about being active.

I discovered that pushing myself a little gave me a lot of confidence and increased my abilities. I also discovered a counterintuitive truth—the harder you work, the stronger you get. I also learned the corollary that growth was not based simply on how much work you did, it was based on how much recovery you took. That blew my mind, so I started to do some research. I learned that the "work" we do is part of the "breaking us down" process and the "rest" we take is the "building and growing" process. By this time, science had caught up with much of the exercise world and determined that significant activity boosted one's immune system while too much activity diminished the immune system.

Science also reminded me of an essential truth: all living organisms are part of a cycle of life. We use energy and then we replenish that energy. Often people have thought that this simple truth is only about physical energy. Over time, we have come to learn that all forms of energy are finite and that as we use energy (emotional, mental, spiritual, etc.) we need to replenish it if we are to continue to grow and thrive.

The cycle of breakdown, then building back up, repeats itself in almost everything we do. Understanding this allows us to build in time for recovery—whether sleep after a hard workout, relaxing after a strenuous exam, or relieving stress after an emotionally charged hearing. Though we like to think that we're superior machines, the reality is we are often frail organisms that only succeed when we allow ourselves to be replenished on a regular basis.

Practice Tips

For those starting a new program:

- Check with your primary care physician before starting an exercise program.
- Find a friend or colleague who is also interested in starting to exercise so you can keep each other motivated and on track.
- Pick something that you like to do (walking, swimming, tennis, etc.) to get started.
- Don't worry about duration of the activity—just try to repeat it three times a week and build from there.

For those with years of experience:

- Ask family or friends for feedback on your exercise routine (listen for hints you are over-doing it or losing sight of other things in life).
- Try new cross training activities to avoid boredom and use different muscles.
- Focus on regular activity frequency even if the duration needs to be shorter to accommodate other things in your life.
- Set new athletic goals.
- Start (or stop) racing for a few months and explore how that feels mentally and emotionally.

THE IMPACT OF PHYSICAL FITNESS ON OUR MENTAL STATE

My journey through health via physical exercise took on another level of intensity during the beginning of my legal career. Law school was a lot of fun. It played to my preferred learning style, I was at a great school that was collegial, and I met the person who would become my life partner. Life was good! My "big law" job during my second summer, however, foreshadowed the intensity of the world I was about to enter.

The increasing level of responsibility, the rapidly increasing level of challenges, and the predominance of the written word over the spoken word (yes, writing this chapter is killing me) created incredible levels of cognitive dissonance and stress on a daily basis. My mind was constantly working, problem solving, attempting to manage, organize, and process multiple and often conflicting inputs. Nothing I had done in my life prepared me for this experience.

Entering the legal profession coincided with a shift to including a lot of running in my exercise routine. Running didn't require a lot of equipment or time and it was something over which I had a great deal of control. I quickly discovered that running allowed me to relieve my mental stress. On my worse days, focusing on the physical allowed me to forget my mental state for a while.

Running for exercise turned into running races to push myself to higher levels of achievement. A dubious pursuit for someone not born into a typical runner's body and lacking significant fast twitch muscles (to run fast) or significant slow twitch muscles (to run long), I was determined to give it a serious shot, and I am glad I did. Racing was an entirely different world from "going to work" and the lessons learned are in use to this day.

One of the first things I learned was that racing required an incredible amount of focus. I needed to be able to endure pain, manage frustration, and overcome challenges in the moment as my mental, emotional, and physical states all constantly shifted in the intensity of a 5K sprint. I learned the power of negative versus positive self talk as the former made me frustrated with myself and the latter enabled me to get over whatever hurdle I faced with a positive attitude, allowing me to perform at a higher level the next time.

I try to use the focus I learned from racing in my daily life, especially at work, where I am easily distracted. Knowing I can choose to shut out distractions doesn't mean I always do it. It does, however, take away one of the countless excuses I make for myself when I am not performing well. The lessons racing taught me about self-talk are applied during every stressful conversation and experience I face. I also use positive self-talk before every presentation I do. As someone who gets paid to speak, people often seem surprised when I admit that I am always nervous before a presentation. I've learned to manage that nervous energy and convert it to something that is much more positive and useful.

Moving beyond short races produced an unexpected benefit. When I stepped up to the half marathon and marathon distances, my training time increased dramatically. A creature of habit, I typically ran a particular distance on the exact same route. Over time I became so used to the routes that I probably could have run many of them with my eyes closed. This familiarity coupled with few people other than runners on my route enabled me to relax my focus from running. I began to increasingly experience what I called "moving meditations," where my mind would wander far away from the task of running. I began to tackle problems and challenges that I was facing at work. I found that I frequently approached things in a non-linear fashion and often came up with some of my most creative solutions and ideas while engaged in these "moving meditations." I continue to use this technique while running more than ten miles and while swimming distances over a mile.

Practice Tips

- Try taking your movement to another level—for example, from training to racing—and set a BHAG (big hairy audacious goal).
- Learn something new that requires physical dexterity (a musical instrument, cooking, teaching something, etc.).
- Create a list of your most powerful tools and achievements in the physical world. Translate each tool or achievement into at least two applications to other parts of your life.
- Explore your daily activities and examine what helps replenish your cognitive abilities. Add more of those activities back into your day.

THE CONNECTION BETWEEN PHYSICAL FITNESS AND OUR EMOTIONAL STATE

Scientists studying the human brain discovered something that athletes have talked about for decades—high intensity cardio or load bearing exercise can makes us feel good during, and especially when we complete, the workout. We now know that this is because endorphins are produced in our body and they create this positive feeling. While many internal and external stimuli cause the production of endorphins in our body, exercise is one of the easiest (and healthiest) ones for us to control.

This one piece of scientific data has a lot of consequences for pursuing a healthier life. It is incredibly easy in our society to find coping mechanisms and tools that soften the pain (physical and emotional) that we feel in daily life. Exercise, like all such tools, when taken to an extreme, may cause a great deal of harm. When used judiciously, exercise can be a great tool to help us manage our emotional state.

High Intensity Interval Training (HIIT) is not just a great way to build physical fitness; it is a great way to exorcise demons that seem to creep into our days at work, at home, and, especially for those who travel, out on the road. A HIIT workout can be done using cardio or resistance exercises. The key is to do sets of an exercise for a short interval (20–90 seconds) at an exertion level that is close to your all-out maximum. Take an extended recovery period and perform another set of intervals. A cardio example is to use a stationary bike to do six 30-second all-out efforts with 15 seconds between each effort. At the end of that set, spin easy to rest for two minutes and repeat the set. A simple resistance example is to do 45 seconds of burpees (dropping from standing into a squat then thrusting your legs into a plank or pushup position, then back to the squat position before returning to standing) followed by 15 seconds of rest for a total of four minutes. Rest for two minutes and repeat the set. Weights can also be used for those with experience and excellent form.

Choosing to intentionally pursue a HIIT workout can be a first step toward managing those negative and hurtful emotions. Then the physical act of engaging in the workout releases the endorphins that block pain and can make you feel happy or euphoric.

There are times when we cannot engage in a HIIT workout (recovering from an injury, dressed inappropriately, no safe environment or equipment available for your favorite workout) and get the benefits described above. A simple alternative for many people is to engage in light aerobic activity with a great musical playlist. This can be a solo ride on a stationary bike in your gym, a short run on a video equipped treadmill, or a simple walk wherever you happen to be. Grab your favorite portable device loaded with your favorite music and you have the makings of an instant, mood-altering experience.

The most powerful use of exercise to manage emotions is a technique I have honed since law school. Like the "moving meditation" discussed in the mental state section of this chapter, I have found that long cardio at an endurance pace often puts me into an autonomous state. I can get there easily when I am running on a path I've been on hundreds of time before. The easiest way for me to get to this state is when I am swimming laps with no time interval or distance in mind. During this physical exertion, when my mind is not focused on my technique or time, I often find myself in a deep contemplative state.

Like any meditation, the more I pursue this state, the easier it is for me to move into it. Significantly, I also find that the more I pursue and enter this state, the more quickly I admit and examine emotional pain I am experiencing in my life.

This emotional state of exploring my feelings without judging and labeling them has been very powerful for me. I find that I can more readily identify what is hurting me. I can more readily forgive those who I feel have harmed me, especially when I perceive that harm to be intentional.

Most important, this emotional state allows me to more readily forgive myself for the things that I do to hurt myself and those around me.

Practice Tips

- Slowly build your physical activity so that you are able to maintain a high aerobic level for 45 minutes or more.
- Hire a coach or personal trainer and experiment with High Intensity Interval Training. Explore how it affects you during and after the workouts.
- Create a list of your coping mechanisms and experiment with substituting appropriate physical activity for each mechanism that relies on external stimuli.
- Create your ultimate musical playlist and keep it on all of your devices. Use it when your mood, attitude, and feelings do not support you well enough.
- Find a place where it is physically safe to "tune out" from your environment and "tune in" to your deepest thoughts. Gradually push the time limits in this place to a half hour or more.

FINDING SPIRITUAL ANSWERS THROUGH PHYSICAL ACTIVITY

Spiritual exploration is different for every person who embarks on this journey. As a child, I was raised as a "generic protestant." I had very small expectations about developing a spiritual point of view. Once again, my physical journey as an athlete led me to a new experience and a new level of learning.

When I was a young teenager, I had an opportunity to attend the Boy Scouts' famed Philmont Scout Ranch in Cimarron, New Mexico. By this time, I had lived in four states, two countries, and eight houses. I had seen and done a lot at an early age. Yet somehow that bus trip from Northern Virginia to New Mexico and back changed my spiritual outlook on life. I discovered that the known and observable world were just a small percentage of my experience. I also learned that there were things much larger and more significant in the world than me.

At thirteen I had not yet hit puberty. I was still a scrawny little kid struggling not to get stepped on by the bigger kids. As I traveled across the country with a band of other kids and adult volunteers, I began to get a sense of the connectedness and interdependence of all living things. While I did not yet have the words to give meaningful expression to this discovery, I was profoundly moved by the experience. My ability to walk (or hike, as the Scouts called it) became my ticket to experience all sorts of experiences many 13 year olds never even fantasize about.

That experience changed my life forever. Hiking in brown bear country, where I realized that man is not the alpha predator, shaped my world-view. Seeing natural rock formations that cannot be explained by logic created a curiosity and wonder that continues to this day. Later in my life, hiking the lava fields of Kilauea, paddling with humpback whales in Resurrection Bay, rappelling through the jungles of Costa Rica, scaling the Sagrada Familia in Barcelona, crawling through the Cu Chi tunnels in Viet Nam, and gazing at the Milky Way in a remote campsite in Colorado gave me both a sense of great understanding and profound confusion.

Ultimately, it was an extreme exercise activity that presented one of my greatest spiritual experiences. In the late 90s my various forms of physical activity had become very focused on triathlon. As I completed longer and longer races, I become convinced that Ironman was in my future. In 2002, Ironman came to Wisconsin for the first time, and I was lucky enough to make the registration cut-off (2000 total entrants) and was signed up for the initial event.

As a fan of Ironman I had spectated in Kona for the World Championships and watched numerous Ironman races around the world. Training for this event was a whole new experience for me. First of all, you are doing three events, each for much longer than most people do any one of them. Second, you are doing all three on the same day. Third, you have to complete all three of them in 17 hours or less. Finally, you have to deal with whatever comes your way: bad weather, bad equipment, bad food, and whatever else shows up. And if you don't finish in 17 hours or less, you are not considered an Ironman. Your time just doesn't count!

Foolishly, I decided all the learning I had though 40 years of life was the perfect platform to prepare for an Ironman race, so I decided to train on my own without a coach or any formal support. This was one of my more reckless decisions in many years of athletic competition. As I prepared, one thing became very clear to me. The athletes competing were very different and they all relied on different forms of energy. The pro athletes and the top age group athletes performed based on physical prowess. The next tier of athletes finished the race based on their mental toughness. The third tier of athletes was special. Physical and mental toughness were not enough to get them through the race; they had an emotional edge that helped them power through this insane event.

The fourth group of athletes was the most significant to me—because I was part of this group. These were the people who desperately wanted to complete this race. They would give anything they had to finish in 17 hours or less. They were going to finish the race somewhere north of 14+ hours. They didn't have the physical ability, the mental toughness, or the emotional strength to get through a 2.4 mile swim, a 112 mile bike ride, and a 26.2 mile run. They didn't have any business being out there on the course, and yet they were determined to make it to the end. These were the people who had only one hope of completing this race. It was going to take some sort of miracle, some supernatural power to get them to the end, and ideally in less than 17 hours.

In the 15 years since I finished that Ironman race (in under 17 hours), I have come to realize that we all have challenges and we all have gifts. Sometimes our challenges so overwhelm us that our gifts do not seem up to the task. This is when connectedness to fellow humans can make a difference and get us wherever we need to go. Our humanity is not based on our strengths and weaknesses. Rather, it is based on our ability to connect with each other and with all of the life that is around us each day. None of us have the innate ability to do some of the miraculous things we do each day. Embracing that void and filling it with the faith that we will find a way is part of what makes us human.

Practice Tips

- Exercise with no purpose or goal in mind.
- Physically explore a finite space very, very slowly and deeply (hiking, snorkeling, laying in a bed of wild flowers and observing nature, etc.).
- Pursue a goal that is impossible for you—it doesn't matter if you complete it or not, the journey will take you places spiritually.
- Use your body to take you to an experience you've never had before (hike to Everest base camp, parasail off a cliff in Brazil, hike a portion of the Appalachian Trial, etc.).
- Take on a challenge that scares the heck out of you.

A WORD OF CAUTION

For most of us, exercise is a tool that facilitates better physical health. In addition, I hope my stories show how exercise can be a tool that facilitates stronger mental, emotional, and spiritual health.

That said, exercise, like all tools, can be incredibly damaging when overused or used improperly. Science has shown us that pushing our efforts too far, and not taking enough time to rest and replenish the body, will weaken our immune system and make it harder for us to grow stronger. Every tool and strength we possess as humans can ultimately lead to our destruction if we are overly reliant on that tool.

One way to utilize exercise as part of your healthy regime is to periodically incorporate it into social activity so that other people are experiencing what we are experiencing and giving us feedback on what we are doing. This will let you know if you are taking your exercise routine too far. You can still do periodic solo, steady state exercise; just incorporate some group activity to give yourself regular feedback.

CONCLUSION

Focusing on physical fitness can pay huge benefits in living a longer and healthier life. It can also help you have a happier and more fulfilling life as you experience mental, emotional, and spiritual benefits. It has for me!

CHAPTER 16
Psychological Capital and Lawyer Success

Martha Knudson, JD, MAPP

Editor's Note: PsyCap is another important tool for lawyers as it can contribute to higher performance, lower stress levels, and increased well-being. Made up of four positive mental capacities that can be increased with training, PsyCap is a resource important for lawyers' mental health and mental strength.

Scientific evidence from the fields of positive psychology and positive organizational behavior shows that Psychological Capital (PsyCap), consisting of the resources of hope, optimism, self-efficacy, and resilience, shapes the underlying attitudes and behaviors associated with increased performance. They may even buffer lawyers against the occupational hazards of the profession that cut against long-term success—hazards that include stress, mental health issues, and substance abuse. This chapter advocates for traditional new lawyer training programs to be enhanced to include the development of PsyCap. I discuss how policies that promote lawyer strengths and well-being are good for the lawyer, law firm, and business.

Martha Knudson brings her unique combination of expertise in law, business, and applied positive psychology to her work as a consultant, speaker, and educator. Previously, she worked as a lawyer for nearly 18 years. Ten of those years were as a law-firm litigator, where she rose to the rank of shareholder. The remainder of her practice was spent working as General Counsel of a nationally ranked real estate management company. In 2015, while still practicing law, Martha earned a Master of Applied Positive Psychology from The University of Pennsylvania. Since that time, and in addition to her consulting work, Martha has served on this graduate program's teaching staff.

PSYCAP: MENTAL STRENGTH AND FLEXIBILITY FOR NEW LAWYERS

Every year a new group of lawyers enters the practice of law. Eager to test their skills, they join law firms, government or corporate legal departments, or set out on their own. They find much about their new job rewarding and interesting. They also find that lawyering comes with a generous helping of stress that can wear on the performance, mental health, and continued job satisfaction of the best of their colleagues. How can these lawyers ready themselves for challenges inherent in their new jobs? What will make the difference in whether they have a successful and sustainable career?

Traditionally, the legal profession's answer to these questions has been for law firms, legal departments, and bar associations to invest time and money in developing new lawyers' skill sets. This approach makes sense. Law is a people-based business and organizations rise and fall based on the strengths of their legal talent. But this approach is also incomplete as it fails to prepare new lawyers to weather the realities of their chosen profession. Law firms, legal departments, and bar associations should also take an active role in developing new lawyers' Psychological Capital, the positive mental capacities that can help lawyers not only to survive but to thrive.

Psychological Capital (PsyCap) is a well-researched positive mental capacity that may be thought of as positive mental strength and flexibility. It is made up of four critical resources that can be developed.

1. **Self-Efficacy:** Having the confidence to successfully take on and put in the necessary effort to succeed at challenging tasks.
2. **Optimism:** Having a positive expectation about one's ability to meet challenges and succeed now and in the future.
3. **Hope:** Having the ability to persevere toward goals and, when necessary, to redirect goal pathways to succeed.
4. **Resilience:** Having the capacity to cope, sustain, and bounce back when problems and adversity strike.

When combined and used together, these four PsyCap resources have a synergistic quality. This means that, while each resource individually contributes to lawyers' positive mental strength and flexibility, when combined, they become stronger than the sum of their parts.

A large and growing body of research shows PsyCap as strongly linked with increased job performance—even over that which is related to skill and intelligence alone. Those high in PsyCap have stronger beliefs in their ability to handle obstacles on the job, which in turn drives their motivation to perform well. Heightened PsyCap also raises well-being, another factor strongly linked to many aspects of performance.

Performance alone provides a compelling reason for law firms and legal departments to pay attention to PsyCap. But PsyCap is also associated with many other things organizations care about: higher commitment, job satisfaction, and lower absenteeism and attrition rates. It can also be preventative, shielding valuable employees from burnout, stress, anxiety, and depression. PsyCap can even help facilitate perceptions of work-life balance. These positive outcomes represent more than just interesting research findings. They are very real factors that can have a direct impact on a legal organization's bottom-line profitability.

BUILDING LAWYER PSYCAP

Lawyers are the key assets of law firms and legal departments. It makes good sense to invest in PsyCap. Like the traditional investment in skill building, developing lawyers' PsyCap supports the continued success, performance, and competitive advantage of the organization. Doing so need not be costly in terms of either time or money. PsyCap can be effectively and sustainably developed through brief workplace training interactions. Here are a few ideas for how PsyCap development can be integrated into the legal workplace.

1. Improve Self-Efficacy

Self-efficacy is the belief that we have the capability to accomplish goals we set out to achieve. At its core, our self-efficacy is not based on our objective skills. Instead it is based on our judgments about what we can and can't do with the skills we have. It is a product of the intersection of past experiences, perception of the degree of difficulty of the chosen task, and belief about whether our skills are adequate.

Developing lawyers' self-efficacy makes sense as it plays a major role in the difficulty of the goals we choose, how much effort we use, how long we persevere, and our resilience if faced with setbacks. Research ties self-efficacy with job performance and satisfaction, as well as with lower rates of burnout, depression, anxiety, and turnover.

Consider two new lawyers fresh out of law school. Both are entering the practice of law with very similar skills. Both face a steep learning curve with tons of new challenges. One lawyer, however, has a strong sense of self-efficacy that her skills and abilities are up to snuff. The other does not. The lawyer with the high sense of self-efficacy is more likely to (1) approach problems as challenges to be mastered; (2) develop a deeper interest in and commitment to her tasks; and (3) sustain her efforts in the face of failure and recover quickly from setbacks and disappointments.

On the other hand, the lawyer with a weak sense of self-efficacy is more likely to (1) avoid or withdraw from challenging tasks; (2) believe that difficult tasks and situations are beyond her capabilities; and (3) quickly lose confidence in her abilities and focus on personal failings when setbacks happen.

Which of these two lawyers will perform better and be more satisfied with her job? Research tells us it's most likely to be the one with a high sense of self-efficacy. This is because self-efficacy lays the foundation for how we interact with our work and what we're capable of achieving. The relationship is cyclical in nature. Performance affects self-efficacy, which in turn affects performance. This cycle can either be positive or negative.

Lest you are tempted to believe that lawyers are immune from having doubts about their self-efficacy, recent research found lawyers in larger law firms to have lower self-efficacy compared to lawyers in other contexts.[1] This finding isn't thought to be because these lawyers were objectively less capable, but because they were less likely to believe in their capabilities.

Several approaches are highly successful in building self-efficacy, including (1) mastery experiences, (2) vicarious learning, and (3) receiving feedback from respected advisors.

---

1. Lawrence S. Krieger & Kennon M. Sheldon, *What Makes Lawyers Happy? Transcending the Anecdotes with Data from 6200 Lawyers*, THE GEORGE WASHINGTON UNIVERSITY LAW REVIEW, 83, 554–627.

a. Provide Mastery Experiences

The most reliable way to develop self-efficacy is to learn by doing, so give new lawyers ample opportunities to practice new skills and get feedback. Remember, no one goes from "zero to hero" in an instant. Set goals that are specific, close in time for completion, and at the upper edge of a lawyer's skill set. More experienced lawyers can help new lawyers accurately assess the demands of the chosen goal and suggest how they can best prepare for and perform these tasks as they become increasingly difficult over time.

Helping new lawyers achieve task mastery will require an initial time commitment by more senior lawyers, activities that may not be billable to clients. This investment, however, should reap financial benefits over time. Once new lawyers find some success, their self-efficacy for taking on new and more difficult challenges will likely improve. The result of this is increased confidence to more quickly become self-sufficient practitioners and to persist when inevitable obstacles arise.

b. Allow for Vicarious Learning

Another way new lawyers can shape self-efficacy beliefs is through vicarious learning. This could involve watching other lawyers successfully perform job-related tasks like arguing in court or conducting witness interviews. Another effective approach would be for more senior lawyers to take a few minutes to explain how they prepare for a task, highlighting the rationale behind any strategy choice. This kind of learning works best when new lawyers can observe someone they identify with and view to be similar.

c. Provide Constructive Feedback

Self-efficacy beliefs can also be built through constructive feedback from other lawyers that the new lawyer respects. This is because we are easily influenced by what others tell us we can or cannot accomplish. Lawyers who work in a firm or legal department are, hopefully, provided with feedback on their work and performance. But the range of feedback can be wide, ranging from almost non-existent to that which is so overbearing and abusive as to be equally unhelpful. When giving feedback, a good rule to remember is that while not all feedback needs to be positive, it should be actionable. It is balanced, specific, and genuine, with praise only following deserving work.

The benefits of taking time to develop the self-efficacy of new lawyers are many. In addition to those we have already discussed, research shows that high-efficacy people are more likely to approach time pressures, responsibility, and a heavier workload with energy and engagement rather than with avoidance and a sense of depletion.[2] These are factors that more quickly lead new lawyers to independence and financial profitability. Yet we often sideline providing opportunities for mastery experiences, vicarious learning, or constructive feedback in favor of attention to the billable hour and organizational cost containment—a focus that may be short-sighted.

2. Cultivate Hope

The PsyCap resource of hope is about building targeted goal-setting and planning skills. Don't let the word throw you into images of dreamers and fluffy clouds.

---

2. Ventura, M., Salanova, M., & Llorens, S., *Professional Self-efficacy as a Predictor of Burnout and Engagement: The Role of Challenge and Hindrance Demands,* 149 THE JOURNAL OF PSYCHOLOGY: INTERDISCIPLINARY AND APPLIED 3: 277–302.

Instead, hope can best be understood as a dynamic cognitive motivational system. You could have the most talented new lawyers in your organization, but if they didn't also have hope, the will and determination to set and achieve goals, their talent won't take them (or your firm) very far. A recent study of law students backs this up, showing that hope predicted grades in law school over and beyond LSAT scores and undergraduate grades.[3]

Developing hope involves teaching new lawyers to establish clear goals, imagine multiple workable pathways toward those goals, and to persevere even when obstacles get in their way.

a. Set Clear Goals

Encourage new lawyers to set goals valuable to their learning and career development. Goals should be challenging but also achievable, and have clear beginning and end points. If the goal is a large one, divide it up into smaller sub-goals that are "steps" to be tackled along the way to the larger goal's achievement. For a new lawyer, goal setting could involve a bunch of things, including learning to take a deposition, to argue a legal motion before the court, or to successfully navigate working with challenging clients. Generally, goal setting is more effective when someone senior provides guidance on goal selection, gives encouragement and constructive feedback, and adds a level of accountability.

b. Generate Multiple Pathways toward Goal Accomplishment

Without having the means to reach them, goals are just wishful thinking. New lawyers should be taught to approach goals by identifying multiple plausible routes to achievement and anticipating possible obstacles. As the practice of law fundamentally involves anticipating and overcoming obstacles, this skill is vital to a new lawyer's success. For example, trial work often involves opposing parties actively throwing obstacles in the path of a desired goal. By helping new lawyers to anticipate these roadblocks while also generating several ways around them, they will be better able to persevere toward success without getting derailed.

Hope is a powerhouse. Hopeful thinkers achieve more and are physically and psychologically healthier than less hopeful people. Also, a bulk of research strongly associates hope with positive work-related outcomes, including higher performance, satisfaction, profitability, and commitment.[4]

3. Develop Resilience

Resilience is the capacity to bounce back from problems, failures, or even from the stress of increased responsibility. Having a sustainable legal career and successfully navigating the stresses and challenges inherent in the practice arguably depend on the practitioner's level of resilience. Research tells us that because resilient people "are open to new experiences, are flexible to changing demands, and show more emotional stability when faced with adversity"; they are better equipped to deal with

---

3. Kevin L. Rand, Allison D. Martin & Amanda M. Shea, *Hope, But Not Optimism, Predicts Academic Performance of Law Students Beyond Previous Academic Achievement*, 45 JOURNAL OF RESEARCH IN PERSONALITY 683–686 (2011).

4. Suzanne J. Peterson & Kristin Byron, *Exploring the Role of Hope in Job Performance: Results from Four Studies*, 29 JOURNAL OF ORGANIZATIONAL BEHAVIOR 785–803 (2008); Youssef, C. M., & Luthans, F., *Positive Organizational Behavior in the Workplace: The Impact of Hope, Optimism, and Resilience*. JOURNAL OF MANAGEMENT, 33(5), 774–800.

workplace stress.[5] Job performance, satisfaction, and happiness are also strongly linked with high resilience levels.[6]

The primary focus of resilience development should be on instructing new lawyers how to best cope with common job stressors. Key competencies here are learning to realistically assess setbacks and to cognitively reframe how we think about adversity.

a. Realistically Assess Setbacks

Encountering, assessing, and coping with setbacks are normal in the practice of law. New lawyers should be taught to expect them and, when they inevitably arrive, realistically assess their impact. Doing so includes identifying those factors that we can and cannot control and then finding realistic options for action. Pinpointing associated risks and any assets at our disposal are also important parts of this skill development.

This training should ideally involve modeling by senior colleagues. For example, another lawyer could identify a difficulty he has faced—perhaps a tough loss or a sticky interaction with a client or colleague. Then he could explain in detail how he assessed the setback, including the associated risks. Did the loss fundamentally change the trajectory of his case or did it block only one avenue forward? Was he working with a client who was savvy about the ups and downs of litigation or one ready to blame the lawyer for any setback? Next, the senior lawyer could discuss all the assets at his disposal and how he used them to cope. Assets might include having the help and support of competent co-workers, the ability to draw from his own experience in similar situations, a recently released appellate decision that could change the game, or a large litigation budget that could be put to strategic use.

This process should be infused with resilient optimism, the fourth PsyCap resource. Realistic optimism isn't an unchecked process of figuring that everything will just somehow "work out." It's being able to accurately evaluate a setback while also believing in your ability to be successful in any given situation. This capacity is highly correlated with heightened performance, job satisfaction, and work happiness.

b. Reframe Thinking

The ability to adjust how we think about adversity is key to resilience. We can do so by learning cognitive reframing, an extensively studied skill based on cognitive behavioral therapy. The goal is to learn that it is our thoughts and not external events that really drive how we react to setbacks, and to then be able to identify and control the thoughts and beliefs that trigger our strong reactions. If we can change how we think about a trigger event, we can adjust our resulting reactions so they stay at a level in line with the setback. Mastering this skill does take effort, and it may require hiring a qualified consultant or coach or purchasing training materials.[7] But doing so is worth it. Cognitive reframing has been found to be more effective than alternatives for reducing perceptions of stress.

---

5. James B. Avey, Fred Luthans & Susan M. Jensen, *Psychological Capital: A Positive Resource for Combating Employee Stress and Turnover*, 48 HUMAN RESOURCE MANAGEMENT 677–693 (2009).

6. *Id.*

7. A helpful primer on cognitive reframing can be found in the book *The Resilience Factor: Seven Essential Skills for Overcoming Life's Inevitable Obstacles*, by Reivich and Shatte.

Law firms and legal departments don't have to choose between developing high performing new lawyers capable of boosting the organization's bottom line or cultivating their mental strengths, well-being, and ability to handle the realities of the profession. Science tells us that these things go hand in hand. PsyCap training can shape the underlying attitudes and behaviors known to increase and sustain performance while also keeping the firm's most important assets healthy and able to successfully navigate the stresses of the profession. Ultimately, an investment in PsyCap is good for the lawyer, good for the organization, and good for business.

CHAPTER 17
Leveraging Coaching for Greater Well-Being

Anne Collier, MPP, JD, PCC

Editor's Note: About 18 months ago at an ABA meeting I sat next to Anne at an outdoor restaurtant on St. Thomas. It was interesting to hear her story of making the transition from Washington, DC, tax attorney to lawyer coach. At first thought, these two disciplines seem diametrically opposed. Reflecting a bit more, they are not. You might think that tax law is all about working with objective numbers while coaching is about the "black box" known as human beings. I hope that by now you can see that we've covered many people-oriented tools that have objectivity and systems in mind to help reduce what at first blush seems uncertainty. In meticulous tax attorney fashion, Anne introduces the gems of MBTI and coaching.

Two law firm partners discuss how a coach helped one of them, Chris, go from burned out to happy. Chris explains how a coach can help any lawyer create a fulfilling career and life. Chris' coach focused on five themes: (1) to manage oneself better through greater self-awareness; (2) to use strengths to follow one's passion; (3) to shift in perspective to have more compassion for self and others; (4) to look for and create the support necessary to not just get the job done, but to get it done well while building the practice; and (5) to communicate and delegate more effectively.

Anne Collier is dedicated to improving culture, collaboration, and communication. She believes that everyone deserves to have a fulfilling life and career and that every organization can be a great place to work. Anne founded Arudia and began coaching in 2004 after practicing law for 11 years. Her clients include lawyers and other professional service providers as well as corporate and not-for-profit executives. Drawing on years of personal and client experiences, Anne is both unconventional and practical in approach; she coaches individual clients to manage stress to make them more effective and develops organization-wide initiatives for scaled results.

Lawyers are highly autonomous. They prefer to work alone, creating their own silos within law firms and chafing at being managed and receiving feedback on performance. Lawyers are also more skeptical and less optimistic than most, which generally makes them better lawyers. This, along with their hardwired preferences for autonomy, means that lawyers epitomize the DIY ("do it yourself") mindset about most anything. This mindset is limiting when it comes to making behavioral changes, which is why the support of a professional coach and the structure that coaching offers can be very helpful.

Meet Pat. Pat is a newly minted partner at a mid-sized litigation firm located in the Midwest. Pat works hard, loves the work, and is starting to feel that the pace of life isn't sustainable. Pat is married and has two kids. Every time Pat sees the sports equipment gathering dust in the basement, a slight melancholy feeling surfaces and the stress, lack of time with family, pudgy middle, and burnout become ever more apparent.

One day, over a lunch with a slightly more senior partner—Chris—Pat divulged these concerns. Chris understood, having been in the same place a couple of years ago. Chris gives Pat this advice: "You need a coach! I felt the same way, and if it weren't for my coach I wouldn't be as happy as I am with my life and career. I never would have figured out how to better self-manage while using my strengths to follow my passion. My coach also helped me shift my perspective so that I have compassion for myself and others; I now look for and create the support necessary to not just get the job done, but to get it done well and to build my practice. My coach also helped me focus on how to leverage the support I have through more effective communication and delegation.

"The real value of coaching," Chris continued, "is in the focus on you. How much time do you spend thinking about yourself, your career trajectory, and what you really want out of your career and life?"

"None," Pat answered.

"Exactly!" Chris continued, explaining that the best coach knows and understands lawyers and their struggles and pressures, and has the ability to tailor the process to each client. "My coach made productive use of my time. I was hesitant to use a coach because of the time commitment—like any of us need one more thing on our plates! But my coach promised that I'd feel less, not more, stressed. The truth is that I grew to look forward to our 30-minute calls. And, in just a few months, I went from verging on burnout to being excited about work and my personal life. I'm exercising again, and that's helping me in so many ways. Dealing with the stress while improving fitness is obvious, and I am mentally sharper and more creative after I work out. Additionally, I've grown the business and am enjoying speaking at conferences and getting out to meet people more often."

KNOW YOURSELF IN ORDER TO BETTER SELF-MANAGE

Chris explained the coach's methodology. First, perhaps most important, is knowing yourself in order to better self-manage. This is the foundation of all the work. It means truly knowing how to maximize your strengths and minimize the effects of your blind spots.

The coach began by giving Chris a couple of personality assessments and a questionnaire to complete. "You wouldn't believe how helpful the questionnaire was. I identified things like my long and short-term goals, my frustrations, and what was important to me. There were even some seemingly random questions like, 'Who do I admire in history?' and 'What I would do if money weren't an issue?' It may sound crazy, but these questions made me think and gave me a clearer vision of my priorities. I was able to make changes in my life that stuck. I exercise regularly now and our family actually takes vacations. I still work hard, but life works better, and I enjoy it more."

Chris continued, explaining that learning about Myers-Briggs Type (referred to as "Type") was not just interesting, but extremely useful. Understanding Type helped focus on using natural strengths while mitigating the effect of blind spots. "We all have blind spots, meaning that we all encounter certain tasks that are difficult and require a lot of focus. Rather than getting frustrated and blaming myself, I've embraced the blind spots as merely another fact of life—another problem to solve. Now I intentionally look to partner with colleagues who are good at what is difficult for me, and vice versa. I've also made opportunities for myself by noticing which tasks others struggle with, and offering to help. That's why our team is so effective, and I believe we're all happier."

Type is a theory of preferences for one of each of the four dichotomies; each person prefers one of each of the following pairs.

- **The Energy Flow Attitude**, which describes the **Extraverted** world of people and activity and the **Introverted** world of reflection;

- **The Perception Functions**, which describe how people perceive information via **Sensing** (details, specifics, and here and now) and **iNtuition** (patterns, generalities, and future focus);

- **The Judging Functions**, which describe how people analyze and make decisions about the Sensing and iNtuitive information that they have perceived. **Thinking** describes decision making that is based on logical standards, and **Feeling** is based on subjective standards and person-based values; and

- **The Outer-World Attitude**, which describes the use of either one's preferred **Judging** function or **Perception** function in the outer world. Behaviorally, Judgers look scheduled, decided, and systematic as compared with Perceivers, who look more open-ended and go-with-the-flow, and who delay decisions as they wait for more information.

A person's Type doesn't change over time, so what feels like change is actually a person's skills improving to compensate for blind spots. Chris' coach helped Chris get better at using non-preferences, which led to greater effectiveness. Chris says, "Just knowing my Type, ISTJ (Introversion, Sensing, Thinking, Judging), helped me appreciate my strengths and develop strategies for areas in which I struggled. I was then able to adjust the use of my time, focus, and energy to accomplish goals that otherwise presented real challenges for me."

Chris continued, "I used to think my partners' ideas were off the wall. I learned to appreciate that some of Sydney's ideas are absolutely brilliant, so I intentionally seek out Syd's advice when I am stuck. The point is that my coach helped me see the value in people who are quite different from me. Instead of being annoyed, I appreciate the differing perspectives and am enjoying working with my partners more."

Pat asked, "I want to go back to something you mentioned earlier; this notion of 'better self-management.' It seems strange. Can you tell me more about it?"

Chris replied, "Well, like I said, I learned about Type and work style. What became clear is that I need a lot of structure—more than most—to be effective. So now I don't feel guilty or stupid taking the time to create structure. That, and you know how I need my time alone? Well, I definitely have a preference for Introversion, which means that I plan time to be alone, so I can think through problems. I used to feel embarrassed, almost like there was something wrong with me, but now, with the help of my coach, I figure out how to make that time. When I attend conferences, I think about when I have to be on and when I can recharge. The point is that you can manage yourself to be more effective *and* less stressed."

USE YOUR STRENGTHS TO FOLLOW YOUR PASSION

Chris continued, "Through Type, my coach helped me shift to an empowering mind-set about myself and what I now refer to as 'blind spots.' My coach also taught me to stay away from characterizing 'blind spots' as 'weaknesses' because doing so is defeatist. It's more productive to describe challenging tasks as falling in a 'blind spot.' This subtle wordsmithing is more empowering, because blind spots can be overcome simply by knowing they are there; weaknesses feel more difficult to overcome because a weakness is a limitation. Let's face it, everyone has these blindspots—even the very successful people who appear to have it all together. It is not that they do not have them, they just do a better job at recognizing and managing around them."

A coach can help a client identify concrete strategies to ensure that blind spots don't derail success. Strategies include working with colleagues who are very different, and identifying steps that become part of a routine; to ensure that blind spots don't stay blind. As people mature, they tend to get better at applying these strategies. So much so that the older a person is, the more difficult it can be for an observer to distinguish between when the person is employing hard-wired preferences, and what the person is doing to compensate for their blind spots in order to be effective.

As Chris says, "My coach helped me to figure out that I am passionate about helping entrepreneurs succeed and build something. The way I follow this passion is by seeking out entrepreneurs as clients and by helping them with anything needed to start or grow their business. It wasn't until I began working with my coach that I realized how much I love the entrepreneur space and being part of creating something great."

A coach can not only help a lawyer identify the kind of work for which there is a passion, but can also help him or her use strengths in following that passion. Passion and strengths are typically intertwined, and lawyers who use the latter to achieve the former are typically quite happy and fulfilled.

COMPASSION FOR YOURSELF AND OTHERS

"What did you mean about the importance of having compassion for yourself and others?" Pat asked.

Chris responded, "It sounds obvious, but you know how I said I had to learn that many of the tasks that are easy for me are difficult for others?" Pat nodded in agreement. "Just knowing this helped me be less frustrated with others—especially associates, which makes me a better mentor and a more effective lawyer. My coach encouraged me to think about my colleagues as a team that I could rely on for insight and tasks that fall within my blind spots. What's most interesting is that valuing my colleagues' differences has led to better working and personal relationships. So, like everything I do, the compassion is very practical. I say practical because the focus is on understanding and accepting oneself and others. This means recognizing that everyone has struggles and, as long as they're trying, I am here to help."

Coaches understand that people are very hard on themselves for being challenged by any aspect of their work or life. They're hard on others, too, and this perpetuates a defeatist attitude and impedes effective teamwork. The upshot is that if the lawyer being coached moves from annoyance to acceptance of struggles, whether his or her own or a team member's, he or she can focus on finding the solution. Sometimes lawyers will share their own struggles and ask for support from the team. Sometimes the lawyer will deal with it alone. Here Chris shares an example.

"Remember how I used to get so annoyed with Taylor speaking in run-on sentences? Discussions took so long, and I, of course, had work to do. Once my coach helped me realize that Taylor is different than I am, and needs to talk out issues to get to the best strategy, I actually felt a little guilty about being so hard on Taylor. As a consequence of my newfound understanding and my willingness to share it, I am more patient and know when I need to either listen or let Taylor and others know that I don't have time. And, now Taylor knows to ask if I have time to 'talk it out' or to ask if we need to schedule a time to talk later. I have learned that it doesn't help anyone to sit there trying to listen but just steaming while thinking about all the work that I could be getting done."

Understanding that others have different strengths fosters compassion. Remember that what one person finds easy or "no big deal" may be quite difficult for others. Appreciate your own unique strengths and be patient and supportive when colleagues struggle. An important key to success and well-being is to have compassion all the way around—for yourself and others.

A COACH CAN HELP YOU CREATE THE SUPPORT YOU NEED

Through coaching, Chris appreciated the importance of building support. Chris said, "I used to try to do everything myself. I was terrible at delegating, and this meant my ability to take on new clients was extremely limited. My coach helped me to appreciate that it's ok to delegate when done so effectively.

"Now I'm able to spend the time I need with clients and build the business. It's not that I don't get into the nitty-gritty of law practice, but I am more effective if I have a fresher eye when I review the work of others. As a consequence, I am able to take on more clients and use delegation as a means of mentoring associates." All in all, Chris is delighted with the happy turn the practice has taken.

Pat considered this, then stated, "That all sounds great; and clearly I need to do the same thing. I'm overwhelmed by all the work. I feel like I'm still doing associate work along with my work. I need to get out of the office more, but whenever I think about it my blood pressure skyrockets."

Chris responded, "I know. Believe me, I know. One of the most significant benefits of working with a coach is the shift in perspective. I thought I had to work harder and spend my weekends in the office. My coach focused me on building my team, by clearly and strategically identifying who could help me. In all seriousness, it's changed my life."

Chris explained that to build support, a lawyer must first assess his or her needs. Once the lawyer has done so, then he or she must find the lawyers, paralegals, and other staff members who have the right skills or can be efficiently trained in the necessary skills. This may require hiring someone. The process will take some time and reasonable expectations are a must. Every work relationship needs to develop, so be patient. Focus on communication and debrief after every project, identifying and discussing, "What went well?" and "What would have made it even better?" As Chris' coach said, "Effective delegation and collaboration require you to eschew blame and embrace the challenge of solving the problem at hand, even if it's a problem that one of your colleagues caused."

A COACH CAN HELP YOU IMPROVE COMMUNICATION

Most of what any person—lawyers included—needs to accomplish requires communication. A lawyer can't lead, can't build a team, and can't ask for what needs to be done if he or she doesn't communicate effectively. To be effective, communication must be clear without triggering defensiveness or being perceived as aggressive.

Chris continued explaining, "I already had a lot of responsibility for managing projects before I became a partner. What I didn't get was that I also had to learn to manage *people*. My coach helped me understand my hard-wired communication style, when to use it, and when to use a different style. It made all the difference in the world, and now associates seek work from me! My coach also helped me develop a process for delegation and management without micromanagement. I now give assignments with more clarity, I check for understanding, and schedule time to check-in with associates to ensure that they are on the right track. As I mentioned, I debrief all projects, even the ones that go exceptionally well. You know, I tended to hibernate when I was really into a project. Well, it was getting in the way of effectively managing my team, so I have created a system that allows me sufficient time to work and support my team members."

The coach taught Chris how to deliver constructive feedback in a manner that conveyed caring and fostered learning. Chris embraced being a mentor and made sure that associates knew that the feedback was to help them learn. Importantly, Chris made sure each associate knew that Chris believed in his or her ability to learn and deliver excellent quality work. Chris learned how to deliver "criticism" by using collaborative language, avoiding loaded language, such as "you should have . . ." and giving ongoing feedback, rather than waiting for periodic evaluations. Chris became a master at turning every discussion about work into a learning experience for associates.

Chris also learned to listen more effectively, staying open to options and not always being the "no" person. This helped with partners, associates, and especially with clients. In fact, working with a coach helped Chris have more positive interactions, which led to more business. Chris also asked for feedback from colleagues and clients, even the associates. This fostered trust and led to even more effective communications and work relationships.

Pat sat back and reflected, "It sounds like your coach helped you to be more effective, productive, and happy while reducing your stress. What's your coach's number?"

Part III
Engagement

CHAPTER 18
Providing Exceptional Client Service

Micah Solomon

Editor's Note: Micah was an easy find. Not knowing anyone in my personal network who worked with professional service firms, I searched online and up came Micah. Given his stellar credentials and how easy he was to work with, I understand why he's considered the "guru" by the *Financial Post*.

In learning to provide exceptional client service and a superior customer experience, you'll be building a strategic advantage that will sustain your law firm in good times and bad. The resulting loyal clients will be less fee-sensitive, more willing to forgive your small foibles, and largely immune to competitive entreaties from the legal practice across the street or across the continent.

Exceptional client service is about more than ensuring your success financially. Providing great client service is an emotional comfort and pick-me-up, a true spirit lifter, once you get the hang of it. Knowing that your entire firm is committed to, and succeeding at, providing exceptional service to every one of your clients, you will have

Micah Solomon is a customer service, client service, and customer experience consultant, serving law firms and other professional, commercial, governmental, and not-for-profit organizations. He is one of America's most popular keynote speakers on building bottom line growth through customer service. A bestselling author, Micah specializes in building stellar, profitable customer experiences, company culture, 21st-century marketing, and social (and anti-social!) media. Micah was recently named the "new guru of customer service excellence" by the *Financial Post*. His latest bestseller, *High-Tech, High-Touch Customer Service* (AMACOM, 2012), as well as his perennial bestseller, *Exceptional Service, Exceptional Profit* (AMACOM, 2010, a collaboration with the creators of the modern-day Ritz-Carlton) have won multiple awards. His expertise has been featured in *Inc. Magazine, Bloomberg BusinessWeek, CNBC, Forbes,* and the *Harvard Business Review*. He can be reached at micah@micahsolomon.com or (484)343-5881.

better days in the office, and more restful nights at home. And the principles and practices involved in providing faultless service to clients will inevitably spill over to change how you treat everyone around you, over time. You'll find yourself "serving" your family, friends, and acquaintances in personal and social situations that have nothing to do with work, in a way that will reduce stress from these experiences, and bring comfort to your heart and soul.

Here are seven principles that will guide you toward providing exceptional client service and an exemplary customer experience. These are derived from my consulting and customer service initiatives for law firms and other professional service organizations. They have been battle-tested in the real world of practice management.

1. CLIENTS JUDGE YOU BASED ON WHAT THEY KNOW

Even your most experienced legal clients are unlikely to understand the law on a technical level. Even in a litigation practice, where the scorecard would seem to be the most cut and dried, it's hard for a layman to determine what represents a good result for any particular client. By contrast, it's easy for clients to judge you on factors such as whether your office is warm, welcoming, and seems to be well run in a business sense. In other words, client loyalty is often based on factors that may seem more trivial, or soft, than pure, easy-to-misconstrue legal outcomes.

2. DON'T BENCHMARK OTHER LAW FIRMS' CLIENT SERVICE

It's time to raise your game: Benchmark yourself against the best performers in service-intensive industries, because that's what your clients will do. All clients judge every interaction with you based on expectations set by the best players in hospitality, financial services, and other industry sectors in which experts have made a science of customer service.

3. SHELVE YOUR LEGAL SKILLS WHEN IT COMES TO RESOLVING CLIENT PROBLEMS

When an upset customer confronts you with a perceived service gaffe, avoid taking a legalistic, "let's sort out the facts here and allocate responsibility" approach. Instead, strive to see your client's side, immediately and with empathy, regardless of what you think the "rational" allocation of "blame" should be. And be prepared to apologize, even if this goes against your nature and professional training.

4. FASTER SERVICE WINS THE DAY

Today's customers expect speedier service than did clients of any preceding generation. Happily, there is a trick to controlling customer expectations for speed, as follows: If drafting a legal opinion will take you four days, *first* immediately contact the client to explain how much time you're going to need; *then* dig in to do the actual work. Clients don't know what is involved in you completing a matter for them; unless you let them know otherwise, they're going to assume you can fulfill their requests as automatically and quickly as if they had placed an order for socks from Amazon.

5. FEES MUST BE APPROPRIATE AND APPROPRIATELY PRESENTED

Clients will notice if your fee for proofreading documents is some astonishing figure like $350 an hour; if it is, it's essential to find a way to reduce it. (You'll make up the difference easily in retained clients and referrals.) And don't bill for large amounts of unexplained copying or other generic-sounding charges, or for incidentals such as a Starbucks latte that you would have bought anyway while traveling.

6. EVERY HELLO AND GOODBYE MUST BE PERFECT

Psychology studies demonstrate that people remember the first and last minutes of a service encounter much more vividly—and for much longer—than what comes between. So, make sure that the initial and final elements of your client interactions are particularly well engineered, because they are going to stick in your client's memory. Do you or your employees sound as though you've been interrupted—even for that telltale split second—when a client calls, or do you and they project genuine pleasure in hearing from the client? Do you screen calls unnecessarily? Do you "cold-transfer" people? If so, it's time to stop. At the end of a project, is the last communication to your client an impersonal, mailed statement? Or do you offer a proper farewell, including thanks, and an invitation to return if anything else is needed?

7. RECOGNITION IS THE MASTER STROKE OF EXCEPTIONAL CLIENT SERVICE

If I were to put the secret of client service into one word, that word might be "recognition." While clients certainly come to you for results, they also expect, or at least hope for, recognition. They want to know that you're "their" lawyer, which is an effect that is only possible to pull off if you make it clear that you're aware and appreciative of them as a client and a human being; that both the book of business they bring to you, and their actual (or virtual) human presence—in person, on the phone, or via email or videoconference—is appreciated and worth acknowledging.

PUTTING PRINCIPLES INTO ACTION

When I'm consulting with a law firm on a client service initiative, I start with a review of the firm's current client service practices. Often this turns up unintentional incidents of disregard and non-recognition. Here's a simple example:

> Client calling in: "Good morning, this is Mark Somberg."
> Receptionist: "Yes?"

Maybe this exchange sounds fine to you. But, believe me: it isn't. The client invested emotionally by volunteering his name ("Mark Somberg") to the reception-ist, to which she responded by implying that Mr. Somberg's name has no meaning to her or to her firm.

Let's try that again.

> Client calling in: "Good morning, this is Mark Somberg."
> Receptionist: "Oh, good morning, Mark. How are things in Tulsa?"

That just required eight additional words (and getting rid of an insensitive one: "Yes?"), but those words can make all the difference to a client, emotionally, by providing recognition.

Dedicate your firm's systems and practices to remembering and acknowledging each client in a way that is personal to the client. Loyalty *isn't* built by besieging clients with pro forma mailings about additional services your firm can provide; it's built by treating every client as unique, and uniquely of interest to you.

THE RED BENCH PRINCIPLE

This final point, the importance of providing client recognition, is one I'd like to expand on, by sharing what I call "The Red Bench Principle." The Red Bench Prin-ciple is an essential secret, a meta-master stroke, of great client service. If you remem-ber nothing else from this chapter, get this red bench into your mind, your memory, your consciousness, and teach it to every employee of your practice as well.

Years ago, my wife and I took our daughter to her first half day of nursery school. On that fine New England morning, the young teacher collected our daugh-ter from us outside the classroom, where we were sitting together on a red park bench. When the teacher brought our daughter back to us at noon, my wife and I were again sitting on that same red bench. It wasn't until two or three weeks later, as the routine continued, that we figured out that our daughter believed her parents were sitting on that red bench each day throughout the entire morning, awaiting her return. She didn't think this in a vague or metaphorical sense. She didn't *kind of* believe this. She *really* believed it.

I find this a good reminder of the nature of the relationship of a law practice to its clients. Adult clients nonetheless exhibit this dependent-child quality; they're unaware of (and uninterested in) the other obligations, interests, and activities of their lawyer and law firm. Clients assume, until you prove them wrong (which would be a mistake) that your world revolves around them, 24 hours a day. The thing is: you *benefit* from encouraging this impression rather than allowing yourself to become resentful that a client is presumptuous enough to be thinking this way. It's a credit to your level of client service, if your law firm successfully sustains the impression in every individual client that you're all about them—and only them—all of the time.

So, I'm going to suggest you throw out the clichéd image of "rolling out the red carpet" and replace it with "red bench service" as the ultimate in client care. In other words, what's most important isn't so much that you put on an all-star show for your clients as it is that you create and maintain the illusion that you are always there awaiting your client, attending to them as if you had nothing else on your agenda that could possibly interfere. Pull this off and you're well on your way to guaranteeing yourself clients for life.

CONCLUSION

Achieving exceptional client service depends on aligning your employees and your systems to anticipate what your clients want before they ask for it. It depends on providing recognition: letting clients know that you see them, appreciate them, and remember them. And great service requires custom fitting; rather than trying to get away with treating every client the same, adjust your service specifically to the clients in front of you, in every interaction that you have with them. The results will build your business, and be personally gratifying as well, providing a deep sense of doing the right thing, in the right way, for the right reasons.

CHAPTER 19
Smart Collaboration for Greater Well-Being

Dr. Heidi K. Gardner

Editor's Note: I know something about the benefits of collaboration. I've reframed much of my own work from managing conflict to developing collaboration, which is why we manage conflict. I've also experienced the extraordinary value of being part of a high-performance team during my time at AT&T. When I discovered the extraordinary work Gardner has done with Law Firm collaboration, it was no surprise to me that her work validates what Larry Krieger's research revealed about lawyer happiness. The partners in Gardner's research explain why when they say, "A problem shared is a problem halved—it is reassuring to have the right expertise on hand. I feel more supported and less anxious about the responsibility I carry," and "I'm more engaged as part of a team."

Smart collaboration—the integration of specialized expertise to solve complex problems that no single lawyer could tackle alone—produces quantifiable benefits in terms of revenues, profits, client longevity, and talent retention. But beyond its financial rewards and strategic impact, smart collaboration also promotes a strong sense of well-being for lawyers—at all levels—and fosters their creativity, productivity, and fulfillment at work. Our research reveals that collaboration produces three key outcomes: commitment and belonging, goal alignment, and what is often called "meaning and mastery." In a legal arena characterized by intense competition for talent, these human-related outcomes translate into significant competitive advantage.

Professor Heidi K. Gardner, PhD, is a Distinguished Fellow at Harvard Law School's Center on the Legal Profession, and author of the book *Smart Collaboration: How Professionals and Their Firms Succeed by Breaking Down Silos* (Harvard Business Press). Previously she was a professor at Harvard Business School. Her research, teaching, speaking and consulting focus on leadership and collaboration in professional service firms. Dr. Gardner earned a Master's degree from the London School of Economics and a PhD from London Business School. Previously, with McKinsey & Company and as a Fulbright Scholar, she has lived and worked on four continents.

INTRODUCTION

Today's complex problems demand that specialists across practices work together to integrate their specialized knowledge bases and skill sets to forge coherent, unified solutions. Client problems are so sophisticated that only *teams* of experts, working across traditional silos, can tackle them. Lawyers have to collaborate, in efficient and effective ways. I call it *smart collaboration*.

For more than a decade, I've have examined smart collaboration among partners in professional service firms while on the faculty at Harvard Business School and now at Harvard Law School. My latest book, *Smart Collaboration: How Professionals and Their Firms Succeed by Breaking Down Silos,* is based on millions of data records collected across multiple firms, statistical analyses, case studies, survey results, and in-depth interviews. Both quantitative and qualitative findings reveal that smart collaboration makes firms more productive and more profitable.

Simply put, firms that foster smart collaboration earn higher margins, inspire greater client loyalty, attract and retain the best talent, and gain a competitive edge. Revenues and profits skyrocket. But aside from the financial rewards and strategic impact, collaboration promotes a strong sense of well-being for lawyers—at all levels—and fosters their creativity, productivity, and fulfillment at work. Our research reveals that collaboration produces three key outcomes: commitment and belonging, goal alignment, and what is often called "meaning and mastery."

As seasoned collaborators advance in their careers, they become motivated to collaborate by less tangible rewards in order to derive purpose and meaning from their work. While these "softer" aspects of collaboration are often underplayed, a thriving, collaborative culture is critical to a firm's success on many fronts, and I'll offer suggestions on exactly how to achieve it.

Our analyses include data from firms that span from truly global to completely domestic, giant associations to fairly small boutiques, lockstep to eat-what-you-kill compensation systems, and those headquartered in North America, Europe, and Asia. The findings we report below generally apply across these firms: human nature holds despite the size, location, or focus of the law firm. I've had the privilege of presenting and discussing these ideas with more than 15,000 practicing lawyers, not only in private practice, but also in in-house legal departments, national government agencies, and non-governmental organizations. Again, we consistently find that smart collaboration is a path toward lawyers' greater well-being.

COMMITMENT AND BELONGING

Decades of psychology and sociology research show that the higher the number of formal or informal connections between individuals and their colleagues, the more those individuals are committed to both their job and their employer. The point is worth emphasizing: Employees who work more in teams develop a stronger psychological attachment to the organization, with the result that they tend to see the firm as an important part of themselves.

Have you noticed how some of your colleagues tend to say things like, "We are looking to grow in the X market," or, "We take it seriously when a partner says Y"? In organizational behavior research, those sorts of "we" statements are a strong predictor of not only a person's desire to stay employed in an organization, but also his or her willingness to engage in critical firm-building activities like mentoring, recruiting, and management tasks.

My own survey and archival research confirms that many knowledge professionals' motivation, sense of belonging, and ultimately retention rates increase as a result of their collaborative experiences. Many partners who had participated in collaborative client engagements reported that the most important benefit for them was the opportunity to meet new colleagues or deepen existing relationships. For example, one respondent wrote about "the camaraderie that comes with working as a group." Conversely, another welcomed collaboration because otherwise "being a partner can feel quite lonely sometimes."

Partners also mentioned how collaboration helped them feel supported in their work. For example, one wrote, "A problem shared is a problem halved—it is reassuring to have the right expertise on hand. I feel more supported and less anxious about the responsibility I carry." Still another answered, "I'm more engaged as part of a team."

That respondent was speaking to specific circumstances, but our empirical analyses show that it's fair to extrapolate a bigger picture. We have compelling statistical evidence across firms that people who collaborate more—that is, participate in substantive client work with a greater number of colleagues—not only stay longer at their firms, but are more financially productive while they're there. Productivity and job security can lower stress, enhance one's sense of worth, and promote both physical and mental health.

Committed, collaborative partners almost certainly generate positive trickle-down effects, too. When partners are better at collaboration, they are more likely to involve more junior partners and senior associates in substantive client work. Not just delegation of the "do this discrete task and return it when you're done" variety, but rather engaging smart minds to help solve complex problems. Not just taking their ideas as background for top-to-top discussions, but exposing those juniors directly to real-life clients. Juniors on those sorts of teams not only get increased opportunity to learn and demonstrate new capabilities, but also greater mentoring. Each of these aspects, in turn, enhances the retention of both high-performing associates and young partners.

GOAL ALIGNMENT

The more contacts a person has within an organization—such as the kinds of relationships that emerge from working on deal teams or joint pitches—the more strongly that person will believe in and accept the organization's values and goals. Senior leaders often bemoan their partners, referring to "my" clients instead of "our" clients. Collaboration could be the remedy: collaborative experiences motivate people to move beyond seeing themselves as a "franchise," and instead view themselves as part of an interdependent team.

Knowledge-firm partners often volunteer this perspective when responding to my survey questions about their personal experiences of collaboration. One wrote, for example, that he valued teamwork with fellow partners because it produced "the feeling that colleagues and I are working towards a common goal, namely the success and prosperity of the firm as a whole."

Another observed that by "working together as a team, your sense of pride and accomplishment is much higher." Collaboration across internal boundaries—such as practice groups, business units, or offices—breaks down the oft-decried (but too rarely countered) "silo mentality."

Collaborative teamwork doesn't just involve the solo lawyers, but includes their business support teams, such as marketing and business development professionals, as well as legal support staff, such as law clerks, paralegals, legal assistants, and investigators—to name a few. Promoting collaboration among all employees—no matter how client-facing their role is—has ripple effects on employee productiveness and their willingness to put in extra time. With support staff involved in the collaborative process, goals are aligned, culture is unified, and a "team" mentality is formed. Together this acts as powerful unifing force in a highly competitive arena.

MEANING AND MASTERY

Another way that collaboration among partners can increase motivation and productivity is by giving people a broader perspective on clients' problems and a deeper understanding of how their specialty contributes to a bigger solution. Psychological research has convincingly demonstrated that when a person feels like his or her work has meaning and is important to their organization—and by extension, to clients— then he or she exerts more effort and becomes more committed, both to the team and to the organization.

In response to my surveys, partners frequently mentioned their ability to learn from their peers during collaborative work. Broadly, the type of learning people talk about falls into two categories: content and process. Respondents reported gaining "knowledge about what other parts of the firm are up to, as well as market opportunities," a "broader understanding of what our client's business is, and which individuals to target for a particular business proposition," and "learning more about nuances of other colleagues' business lines." Beyond content knowledge, partners also mentioned developing their professional capabilities through collaboration, such as enhanced skills in processes such as problem solving, preparing for client pitches, and communication.

LESS TANGIBLE REWARDS FOR THE SEASONED COLLABORATOR

Highly experienced partners—or "seasoned collaborators," as I call them—are often motivated by four less tangible rewards during the advanced stage of their careers: the intellectual challenge of complex work, power, "staying young," and legacy. Yes, money still talks. And the competitive juices that helped them succeed in the first place are still flowing. (That's a good thing, because in most professional fields today, not even the most successful rainmaker can afford to be complacent.) But, most professionals conform to models of normal adult development: the older and richer they get, the more likely they are to seek meaning.

The first is the **intellectual challenge of complex work**. Most professionals crave intellectual challenge; it's part of the reason they spent years in graduate school preparing for a knowledge-based career. Collaborating across disciplinary boundaries gives them that challenge in a very potent form. It allows them to move up the food chain in their clients, advising people whose challenges are increasingly complex and interesting.

As one partner said, "If I'm doing work just in my specialty, then I'm almost certainly talking to clients with a narrow scope and more limited responsibility. Once I move into more sophisticated work, I move up toward the c-suite, and that's when the conversations get interesting."

A second intangible benefit is **power.** When a CEO is in crisis and picks up the phone to seek your advice, it's a heady experience. Whether it's advising the world's business elite, winning a huge grant as the principal investigator in a research lab, or directing hundreds of professionals in a worldwide account team—all are sources of heightened power and prestige, and in most cases, they are the result of a collaborative effort.

The third on my list of intangibles might be summarized as **"staying young."** Rainmaking sets you apart—in both a good sense and a bad one. The firm greatly appreciates your financial and reputational contributions, and justifiably celebrates you for them. Your very success distinguishes you, and sets you apart. At the same time, the more rarefied the air you breathe, the less likely you are to get your nose rubbed in new (and sometimes rude) realities. You are "set apart," in the sense of being isolated.

In the 1990s, when GE's CEO Jack Welch was already a celebrated business statesman, he made a surprising move: He found a 25-year-old computer whiz within the company to serve as his technology mentor. (He also insisted that his c-level colleagues do the same.) When people later wondered aloud how this relatively senior executive could make a powerful case for widespread digitization at GE—which he did—he had a ready answer: A young colleague had showed him the ropes. Of course, youth is only one of the broadening dimensions that one can encounter on a collaborative team; I use it here as a stand-in for team diversity. By building smart junior people into his or her network, the seasoned collaborator "stays young" in the sense of keeping diverse ears on weak-signal client problems.

Not surprisingly, perhaps, this list of intangibles ends with the concept of **legacy.** As the leader of one major law firm told me, "Some lawyers are more partner-like than others. Just as entrepreneurs want to leave a solid business behind for their children, these partners are motivated to pass on a strong client relationship to the next generation."

Social science research has determined that for many successful people, building a legacy—that is, leveraging your achievements and values in a way that helps others succeed after you're gone—is a prime source of enduring happiness. By helping to institutionalize the client relationship across multiple partners, seasoned collaborators build their legacy.

HOW TO FOSTER EMPLOYEE PRODUCTIVITY AND LOYALTY

The key outcomes and motivators of collaboration outlined in the previous section may have implied that collaboration automatically generated these benefits, but in fact, it's only *excellent collaboration* that ensures them. If partners simply call together a team and divvy up the work in a "the sum equals the total of the parts" way, the benefits are far from assured. Worse, ineffective and uncoordinated group work wastes time and demotivates people.

You can increase the odds that your partners are equipped and willing to lead their collaborative efforts in ways that generate the maximum returns. How?

- **Create a firm-wide approach for effective project launches.** McKinsey, for example, has a format in which a leader is expected to kick off every new project by briefing the team on the client and the project objectives, and then clearly discussing how each person's piece fits into the bigger picture. Teams also spend some time getting to know each other's work styles, strengths, and development areas. This step—which can take as little as a half hour or even less if the members of the team are already familiar with each other—is essential for aligning members' goals, helping them know where to turn with questions (which avoids the leader becoming the sole-source bottleneck), and allowing them to see how their specialty contributes to a bigger solution. Develop a template, train partners and senior managers how to use it, then give the system teeth: Withhold their expense code until they actually conduct the project launch. This is a powerful tool that even small firms can implement with relatively little investment.

- **Facilitate personal within-team interactions.** People won't build relationships or feel the benefit of peer support unless they have the opportunity to interact during collaboration. Provide a travel budget that allows members some face-to-face time together—ideally, early in the project, when they need to establish trust. Throughout and at the end of the project, a modest celebration fund will encourage teams to focus on their wins. These interactions enhance members' sense of pride and accomplishment, boost firm morale, and build the "glue" that is the essence of a collaborative culture. Smaller law firms might take for granted that their lawyers already have those bonds, but our research shows that enhancing cohesion pays off for enhancing collaboration even when a firm has as few as a dozen partners.

- **Embed explicit learning processes:** Taking a cue from elite military units, the best team leaders use the time right before the celebration event to conduct a short after-action-review (AAR) to boost team members' learning from both mistakes and successes. AAR is a form of group reflection; participants review what was intended, what actually happened, why it happened, and what was learned. Critically, the intent is to learn rather than blame, and to prompt the sort of reflection that makes learning possible. As a firm leader, you should model this behavior, and hold your partners accountable for doing it, too.

- **Provide a technology platform** that makes it easy for collaborators to see each other's work-in-progress, and to share knowledge about the project. This transparency helps foster a sense of common purpose by giving participants a deeper understanding of the issue and how various pieces intersect; it also aids learning as participants get exposure to others' ways of thinking—not simply their end results. Although technology does require a capital investment, many platforms can be purchased based on the number of licences needed, making it more affordable for smaller firms.

For boutique firms with smaller budgets and smaller arsenal of lawyers, don't be discouraged. Many of these suggestions to improve collaboration and well-being among your firms' lawyers can be done by being more strategic with your current resources and by breaking down these suggestions into small, more manageable steps.

- If your firm lacks the resources to implement firm-wide initiatives, then create a pilot program with a minimum of two lawyers with different specialties to work out the kinks before installing a massive overhaul of the current

MO. That way, firm leadership is better able to forecast costs, determine necessary institutional changes, and allocate time required for complete execution.

- Do a little detective work before selecting collaboration leaders to ensure that they're on board with the necessary changes and willing to put in the extra effort.
- Consider the suggestions and cater them to your firm. You know your firm better than any outside consultant, so be choosy when considering what change(s) to implement.

In many ways, smaller firms possess a distinct advantage. With fewer seniors, those embracing their role as a seasoned collaborator are more visible to their peers and juniors. With fewer offices, leadership tends to have better control over firm culture, making change implementation easier and less cumbersome. Larger, global firms do have more resources but have to overcome geographical and cultural barriers that can make collaboration trickier to implement.

The many specifics in this chapter—the how-tos—may lead the reader to believe that embracing collaboration is little more than a thinly disguised strategy for getting more work out of people. Far from it! Collaboration can be inspirational, motivational, and even joyful. A management consultant recently told me about his experience pitching new business. He had teamed up with a fellow partner, and the two of them made it their mission to go after some very high-profile potential clients in faraway parts of Australia. He said that he only had the courage and fortitude to do this because he had teamed up with somebody—and together they felt braver, and had a much higher risk tolerance. "It certainly didn't always work," he said, smiling at the recollection, "but when it didn't, she and I always ended up at the pub, laughing it off over a couple of beers. Whereas if I had suffered that same rejection on my own, I *for sure* wouldn't have gone to the next pitch."

CONCLUSION

A commitment to collaboration is a commitment to a collaborative culture. Firms that actively foster and celebrate smart collaboration better retain, motivate, and inspire their employees to perform at their best—a benefit with powerful financial implications. Collaboration doesn't just make people *feel* as if they are in the right place. In fact, it's a self-fulfilling prophecy: collaboration makes the "fit" better, makes the hard work more efficient and effective, and thereby makes the firm more successful. Of course, doing it "right" requires strong leadership, sustained efforts, and strong commitment from your partners at all levels to collaborate with colleagues. The money and energy your firm puts into fostering smart collaboration will almost certainly pay you back many times over.

CHAPTER 20
The Importance of Diversity and Inclusion for Attorney Wellness

Dean Joan R. M. Bullock

Editor's Note: I have been walking on this path with Joan for many years. We worked together on the ABA Law Practice Division Diversity Committee. We noodled with programs and initiatives. We dug deep, reflected, and, I think, learned something about what we were trying to approach in a positive, meaningful way. I am so pleased to be able to share Joan's current thinking. We are surely more alike than different in our aspirations and common humanity. Joan does an exceptional job of expressing how self-knowledge and self-awareness enable us to get the best of what everyone has to offer and how that contributes to better service and higher levels of well-being.

Broadly, diversity is about difference and how that difference shapes, enlightens, and enriches our life experiences. Inclusion relates to how welcoming and open we are in allowing our differences and the differences of others to impact our individual and collective life experiences in beneficial and meaningful ways. The acknowledgment of diversity from the vantage of inclusion empowers everyone in the professional environment to focus on how to harness and leverage difference in creating synergies that benefit both the individual and the firm. This focus acknowledges that each person has some measure of control in being able to meaningfully participate in matters that impact his or her personal and professional well-being. This level of control is positively correlated to attorney wellness.

Joan R. M. Bullock, J.D., MBA, CPA is the Dean and President of Thomas Jefferson School of Law in San Diego, California. Joan is a Michigan lawyer and CPA who has practiced before the United States Tax Court and assisted start-up enterprises with outsourced general counsel and CFO services and law firms with business advisory services. Joan is the 2012–13 chair of the American Bar Association's Law Practice Division. She currently holds a position of leadership in the ABA Section of Science and Technology Law, is a member of the ABA Council for Racial and Ethnic Diversity in the Educational Pipeline, and is a fellow of the American Bar Foundation. Joan is the author of *How to Achieve Success after the Bar: A Step-by-Step Action Plan*, published by the ABA Law Practice Division.

What do diversity and inclusion have to do with attorney wellness? Diversity is more than race, ethnicity, gender, age, class, sexual identity, and sexual orientation. Broadly, diversity is about difference and how that difference shapes, enlightens, and enriches our life experiences. Difference is not bad or wrong; it is merely a fact. Your unique set of differences is part of your identity and helps shape who you are and how you perceive the world. Inclusion relates to how welcoming and open we are in allowing our differences and the differences of others to impact our individual and collective life experiences in beneficial and meaningful ways for all concerned.

With this definition of diversity, everyone can be viewed as diverse because everyone is different. No two individuals are exactly alike. We each "broke the mold" when we were born. Unfortunately, this is not how diversity is generally viewed. Instead, there is first usually a normative reference. This reference becomes the standard by which the "ideal" is identified. Implicit in the normative reference is that any characteristic that does not align with the normative is considered divergent and "other than." Therefore, the more the divergent characteristic deviates from the normative reference, the more the diversity is perceived as not the ideal. This is a common perception, shared both by those in the normative and in the divergent groups. Consequently, many persons diverse from the normative seek to pattern themselves as much as possible after this reference so as to increase the probability of their being a partaker of the benefits ascribed to the normative, i.e., ideal enclave.

This view of diversity in which there is a common point from which all else diverges is fraught with bias. With the acknowledgment of difference comes the ascribing of judgment: other than the normative and not the ideal. So prevalent is the ascription of judgment that some in the normative group would rather dismiss the difference so as not to ascribe the judgment that comes with that acknowledgment. For example, many persons of color have been told, "I don't see color. I treat everyone the same." Those who say this may have meant well, but what they are implicitly saying is that if they acknowledge the color of the individual to whom they are speaking, they would have to also ascribe certain biases to that acknowledgment and they would rather not be perceived as doing so. Notwithstanding, the fact that the sentiment of not seeing color is expressed is an indication that color is perceived as an offense—a deviation from the ideal that is not positive. The difficulty for the person of color is that skin color cannot be shed like an item of clothing. This is part of that person's DNA—his or her identity, heritage, and culture. To dismiss that person's color is to dismiss the person and the unique challenges that person may have confronted as a person of color. To dismiss that person's color means that person's identity, culture, and perspective are devalued. Dismissing that person's color thus becomes his or her consolation for not being or fitting in as a member of the normative group. What is being said implicitly, therefore, is that the person of color should not see color either. If the person of color is willing to dismiss or diminish a part of his or her identity, he or she can partake of some of the benefits of the normative group. Inclusion is acceptable as long as the person of color does not "act too Black" or "act too ethnic," for example. The same applies to others who have been considered diverse. Inclusion is palatable as long as she does not "act too ladylike" or "play like a girl, " or he does not "act too gay."

There can be acceptance into the ideal enclave through dismissal or denial of diversity by both the normative and diverse groups. Frequently, this preclusion of offense to the normative group by dismissal or denial of diversity is regarded as a preferred methodology for creating and maintaining a professional environment. There may be perceived unity in such preclusion, but there is limited synergy because differences are not fully acknowledged nor their value leveraged. Indeed, synergy does not diminish the presence or power of unity. Instead, the synergy amassed by the harnessing of collective diversity towards common goals enhances the power of unity.

The view that every person is diverse, having a unique set of differences, removes much of the judgmental bias that comes with acknowledging difference. Without the normative reference, there is no one standard by which everyone else is compared or evaluated. Focus can then be placed on finding the synergies that come with diversity such that positive outcomes for the firm and the affected individuals are realized. This is important because people are not monolithic. They are fluid, for example, with thoughts and emotions that can change or remain rigid as it suits them.

The reality is that within legal circles in 2018, white males are considered the normative reference and the system and culture that have been developed support the characteristics and qualities associated with this reference as the standard by which everyone else is considered diverse. Often diversity is viewed as a negative in the workplace because it may be perceived as a threat to the group norm, the social order, and the political construct. Diversity may be perceived as upsetting the status quo of appropriated perks and benefits for those who are a part of the established order.

This being said, the importance of all concerned as viewing diversity as the unique set of differences that each person brings to the professional environment must be underscored. From this view, each person has the liberty to consider his or her differences and is empowered in determining how those differences can best be utilized to produce the optimal prospects for the individual and for the firm. Differences do not have to be minimized in order to conform to the normative culture. Instead, consideration can be given to how those differences can enrich the normative culture and make the professional environment better—not just for those who are diverse from the normative, but for everyone.

It is important that everyone take responsibility for attorney wellness and professional well-being. Viewed broadly, diversity and inclusion provides the vision of everyone contributing to the whole in a manner that adds value to the professional environment of the firm, allowing everyone to thrive. This includes white males. White males as the universal reference point, however, is not the ideal. The ideal changes with the issue and corresponding solution. A hammer is not always what is needed and neither is a nail. Too much of any one thing is not good, as the adage goes, and this applies to homogeneity as well. Pure strategists, for example, do not execute and pure tacticians cannot strategize; rules-focused individuals have difficulty thinking out of the box and free spirits have difficulty thriving in a formalized, ordered workplace. Balance is required as well as an acknowledgment of the diversity and value of what each individual is able to contribute to the whole.

People want to be valued and appreciated for what they do and for who they are. They want opportunities to shine and prove their mettle—to themselves and to others. The inclusion of individuals with diverse characteristics permits this and aids attorney well-being. Individuals are empowered to identify their own as well as others' unique set of differences from the vantage of inclusion and not exception. Inclusion becomes an organizational collaboration of intentional thought in identifying individual strengths and an active engagement in determining how those strengths can enrich the firm, enhance professional development, and provide an environment conducive for professional wellness. Inclusion also provides segues for discussions regarding the unique challenges associated with specific diversity characteristics and facilitates the identification of the means of approach by which those challenges can be addressed and overcome in the workplace.

The dynamic of diversity and inclusion efforts is about developing among a firm's stakeholders a shared understanding with collaborative effort and reciprocal trust in the direction and goals of the firm. The upshot is on how each stakeholder is able to meaningfully contribute to the direction and execution of those goals. Attorney wellness is influenced by the ease in which the specific needs of a person are addressed in the professional workplace.

THE VALUE OF DIFFERENCE

Attorney wellness begins with you. Your personal and professional development starts with your knowledge of self. You should be the expert when it comes to knowing what is personally best for you. This knowledge would be deficient without an understanding of your unique set of differences and what you need in order to present your best professional self. Knowing who you are at the core, along with your strengths and weaknesses, enables you to start an informed conversation with those in the workplace regarding your professional development and its alignment with the advancement of firm goals and objectives. Additionally, your acknowledgment and appreciation of your diversity increases your ability to discern, acknowledge, and appreciate the diversity of others. This inclusion seeks to draw out the best of each person for the betterment of the whole. If "two heads are better than one," it is because the two heads are not the same. This is an acknowledgment that difference adds value and perspective in a manner that sameness and similarity do not.

Your diversity is a source of empowerment and plays a role in your well-being. Your cognizance of your unique value provides you with insight on your purpose, allowing you to align what you do with who you are. The more alignment you have in what you do and your perception of who you are, the more purposeful and fulfilled you will be. You are a person with purpose and the efficacy of that purpose is facilitated by your unique set of differences. Do you know what they are vis-à-vis your professional environment? What is the strength of your diversity? How are you unique and how can you leverage that uniqueness for your, as well as the firm's, benefit?

In answering the above questions, consider how you connect generally with your environment.

- How do you connect as a person who happens to have this unique set of differences?
- What is important to you?
- What are your values?

Consider your work environment.

- What do you know or perceive to be the firm's values? These values coincide with how it generates business.
- List three ways in which the firm demonstrates these values in its operations.

Brainstorm how you, as a person who happens to have this unique set of differences, can advance some or all of the noted values of the firm.

- Avoid having your diversity viewed as an adversity.
- For example, you work for a firm that is seeking to grow and values the accumulation of billable hours. You are a recent parent and want to experience some semblance of family life. You notice that the firm's quest for billable

hours is not accompanied by strategic thought on the development of an ideal client base. As a rule-oriented, forward planning person, you offer to work with leadership to develop a client-seeking strategy that will align with the firm's brand and revenue goals and limit malpractice exposure. Working with leadership, you develop a rubric that all attorneys can use in seeking the firm's ideal client and vetting prospective clients for the firm.

Comprehending your unique value potential to your firm is the first step in understanding what you need for your professional development. It is important that you take the second step of promoting yourself, especially to decision makers who can provide you with opportunities to demonstrate your value to the firm. This promotion of yourself is best presented from a "This is how I can help you" approach rather than from a "Please let me in" approach. People respond more readily to those who want to give more than to those who want to get.

From an inclusive perspective, how does the diversity of others assist you in advancing the firm's goals? How can you encourage a professional environment that values the differences of others? What responsibility do you have in ensuring that not only you, but others as well, are appreciated, with opportunities to shine and make meaningful contributions to the firm?

- Continuing the previous example, you note that three other attorneys are also parents of young children and a fourth has recently become the main caretaker for his elderly parent. The firm espouses a progressive environment and claims that work completed and not face time in the office is valued. After meeting with the four attorneys and working out a draft arrangement, you lead the group in a discussion with management regarding the implementation of a formal flextime policy. You and your group submit a proposed flex schedule that assures management that all work will be completed on time. All works well—firm leadership is appreciative that work is completed on time and is able to tout their progressive culture in marketing materials. The four attorneys experience less stress and no longer have to use their personal and sick time for caretaking responsibilities.

THE VALUE OF STAYING TRUE TO YOUR SELF-IDENTITY

There is a saying, "Perception is reality." While reality is an existent fact, one person's perception of a fact may differ from another's. When it comes to matters of diversity and inclusion, perceptions do indeed matter. Unfortunately, diversity is often seen as a differentiator for the purpose of exclusion. It is a difference from the normative reference and is frequently considered replete with negative bias regarding the divergence. These perceptions, whether expressed or not, are difficult for the diverse individual to counter. The perceptions are viewed as reality—existent facts and thus unassailable.

As a consequence, those who differ from the normative reference often pattern certain behaviors and aspects of themselves after those of the dominant group. Kenji Yoshino, Chief Justice Earl Warren Professor of Constitutional Law at New York University School of Law, noted that individuals with stigmatized identities "cover" to downplay the stigma of their difference. This tactic of covering can be based on appearance, affiliation, advocacy, and association. For example, a Black female partner engages in appearance-based covering when she refuses to wear her hair naturally in the workplace for fear of being perceived as not professional. Affiliation-based covering occurs when a female associate refuses to have pictures of her children in her office for fear of others associating her being a parent as justification for being placed on the "mommy-track." An example of advocacy-based covering can occur when an person does not comment on the offensiveness of a remark about gays and lesbians for fear of either being seen as a homosexual or too liberal. An example of association-based covering can occur when the gay male associate refuses to bring his husband to the holiday party because of concern that his manager may stop sending him good assignments. While covering is an assimilation tactic resorted to frequently by those who are diverse, it is also a tactic of those in the dominant group in order to maintain the benefits of privilege. For example, a white male lawyer working in a conservative firm covers the fact that he is an atheist by doing pro bono work for a religious organization that is favored by one of the partners.

This curtailing of the true self can result in depression or fearfulness. It can demotivate, hindering initiative, creativity, and innovation because the focus is on assimilation and amenability. The diverse individual does not want to be treated akin to the single blade of grass mowed down because it was sticking up higher than the rest. So similarity and sameness become the desired outcomes. An environment supportive of the status quo is continued rather than an environment seeking to draw out and develop the best talents of each individual.

For the purpose of personal and professional well-being, it is important "to thine own self be true." People want to be valued not just for what they do. They want to be valued for who they are. So it is critical to be true to your self-identity and not take on characteristics inconsistent with your core for the purpose of being perceived as more acceptable to those in the workplace. What are your beliefs and values? Do they push you to reach your potential or do they limit you in order to conform to your firm's values?

In all things, strive to maintain your authentic self. If you are young and just starting out in your career, you may still be determining what is your authentic self. While you are figuring this out, you will have influencers in your life who are impacting how you think and what you do more so than in your later years. Your parents, mentors, spouse or significant other, and friends are able to influence how you think and act on matters.

Even in your later years these influencers can hold sway on what you value and how you prioritize what is important to you. If you are not intentional in articulating to yourself and others your values, you may find that you have ordered your life to the values that others convey to you. Get to know your authentic self and understand what you value. Otherwise, acting in conformity to the expectations of others may cause you to experience internal conflict with your unexpressed values.

THE IMPORTANCE OF FIT

Every firm has a culture—a certain landscape, inclusive of policies, procedures, and protocols. What do you know about your firm's culture? What are the assumptions underlying the firm's culture? Do you have a sense of the expressed as well as unspoken collective thinking, decision making, and motivational drivers by which the firm operates?

How well do you fit within this culture? If you do not know the culture, you cannot be intentional in influencing it. Your ability to accomplish purposed work—where your contributions result in tangible and meaningful outcomes to you and the firm, and your ability to develop your potential—is impacted by the culture of the firm. Culture drives performance. It can motivate as well as demotivate. The more you understand your firm's culture, the more confidence you will have in your ability to navigate the landscape to ensure your unique gifts and talent are recognized and rewarded.

THE IMPORTANCE OF RELATIONSHIPS

Attorney wellness requires the cultivation of diverse relationships. In this regard, diversity relates to a network system comprised of a personal network, a referral network, a tactical network, and a strategic network.

- The **personal network** is made up of relatives, friends, and those you trust to show sides of you outside the business context. They are your foundation and are there when bad things happen and things fall apart.
- The **referral network** is your "client-seeking" network. It is made up of people you know who could provide you with leads.
- The **tactical network** could be likened to a peer network, the purpose of which is to provide you with support in being able to do your job and deliver your services accurately, effectively, and efficiently. This tactical network includes those in your firm as well as those in the profession who are competent and experienced in the relevant practice areas and are willing to help you.
- The **strategic network** includes those individuals who can assist you in formulating a plan and process of getting to your "next levels." They will tend to be in leadership or high enough up in authority so as to have a good vantage point of the path you need to take and the obstacles that you need to prepare yourself to confront, tackle, or avoid. This network, while it may be considered the most important because of its ability to move you into places of promotion, can only be effective if the other networks (referral and tactical) have provided you with a foundation of substance and visibility. Those in the strategic sphere must have confidence in your ability to engage, follow through, and perform at the level of promotion to which they direct you. Their reputation as leaders and being able to discern good talent hinges on you being conscientious, capable, and competent in functioning at these higher levels.

Most likely the networks will overlap, with you having some persons included in more than one of your networks. With these networks, you are able to safely reveal different aspects of yourself for the benefit of your personal and professional development. As you are the expert regarding what you need for your well-being, wisely choose people who can give you the wisdom of their experiences and assist your upward advancement. You will be empowered and gain confidence by drawing from this customized knowledge base and diversity of perspectives that you created through these four networks.

In summary, the perception of value in diversity and inclusion is an individual and collective responsibility. The acknowledgment of diversity (i.e., each person's unique set of differences) from the vantage of inclusion rather than exception empowers everyone in the professional environment to focus on how to harness and leverage those differences in creating synergies that benefit both the individual and the firm. Everyone is responsible for inclusion. It cannot be left to those in the dominant group to create this environment.

Finding ways to be inclusive with your unique set of differences can be empowering. It acknowledges that you have some measure of control in your ability to meaningfully participate in matters that impact your personal and professional well-being. The level of control you possess over your professional destiny is positively correlated to your well-being and wellness.

CHAPTER 21
Transferring Wisdom with the Dual-Centric Millennial Mindset
Cross-Generational Conversation for Success, Sanity, and Satisfaction

Phyllis Weiss Haserot

Editor's Note: I have known Phyllis for almost 20 years. I had always thought of her expertise as being in the marketing of professional service firms. At least ten years ago, before anyone became focused on it, she told me she was shifting her professional focus to what she saw beckoning on the horizon—the reality that workplaces were becoming both more multi-generational while at the same time more cross-functional. Given the generational differences in values and communication styles, it was going to be essential to learn how to "get along." Phyllis was one of the few who was way out on the edge. I remember wondering what she was talking about. Now I know. I knew this chapter needed to be included and I knew the person best qualified to write it.

I encourage people of all generations to look at their career lives as an adventure with some risks and opportunities to try new things. Get to know new people and cultivate a predisposition for offering what you have to share, at age 20 or 75 or anywhere in between. In addition to individual benefits, it will make for economically stronger firms and happier places to work.

Phyllis Weiss Haserot is president of Practice Development Counsel, a trailblazing marketing/business development and organizational effectiveness consulting and coaching firm she founded over 30 years ago. She helps firms solve intergenerational challenges to boost client attraction and retention, productivity, succession planning, and knowledge transfer. Phyllis is a mentor to Law Without Walls, frequent contributor to the law and business media, and the author of *The Rainmaking Machine: Marketing Planning, Strategy and Management for Law Firms* (Thomson Reuters, latest edition 2017). Find her at http://www.linkedin.com/in/pwhaserot and @phylliswhaserot.

Then you can thrive and take pride that your firm gets visible recognition for being selected as one of "the best places to work" and "employer of choice," attracting the very best lawyers to work with.

Lawyers who are trained to be adversarial and competitive and see that behavior displayed in the media may look to the role models of abrasive, arrogant, and independent lawyers as modeling the behavior it takes to be "successful." There are many more lawyers, however, who excel through treating colleagues, opponents, and others civilly and respectfully. They reach out to help younger colleagues succeed in their professional and life journeys. They are rewarded and happier for it. That's the model most young lawyers want to follow and that will motivate them to help change law firm and legal industry cultures to people-centric (client and colleague), relationship-focused environments.

Law is about relationships, and relationships are built around conversations. Boldly stated: the keys to a lawyer's success, sanity, and satisfaction at any age are the relationships and conversations that guide the individual's work and life. They are the core elements of learning, teaching, advocating, and negotiating. Conversations bring mutual understanding with colleagues, clients, adversaries, influencers, supporters and other stakeholders as well as collaboration inside and outside a firm or other organization.

Increasingly those relationships and conversations are more multi-generationally complex in ways they never were decades ago, often leading to considerable stress from frustration, resentment, confusion, and emotional wounds. (There isn't room in this chapter to take you through the influences and worldviews that have and are changing the generationally related attitudes, behaviors, and structures of simpler times. I provide some sources at the end.) In this chapter, I provide some valuable strategies, approaches, and tips to help lawyers stay grounded and thrive in a multi-generational workplace and world.

Mentoring and its variations across the generations is one approach that quickly comes to mind. Before I focus on that, I touch on a number of issues that color the landscape of the legal employment environment.

UNDERSTANDING WHAT YOUNG PROFESSIONAL TALENT WANTS

Workplace culture is changing as younger generations gather strength in numbers. The ten items plus one below are what surveys and private conversations tell us young lawyers/professionals want and need to develop to their potential for their own success and satisfaction and that of their employers and clients. In truth, the three are inexorably tied. A workplace culture imbued with these ten attributes will benefit everybody.

1. Defined values and culture they can relate to
2. Career and professional development and ongoing training/mentoring
3. Career fulfillment—intellectual challenge, recognition, growth
4. A feeling they add value and make a difference
5. Active management of the talent—providing leadership, feedback

6. Team spirit, collaboration, appreciation, praise
7. Opportunities to contribute to the community or other pro bono activities
8. Fun—camaraderie
9. Relaxed atmosphere
10. Great facilities—comfortable, attractive, stimulating environment
11. And of course, the most tangible reward, compensation, which ranks higher for some than others, who would trade some dollars for more of the other items in this list

This list attests to the desired quality of work and its impact on personal lives. The younger generations are "dual-centric."

All of the generations also want most of these things, and they should be sought collectively at all levels and functions. It is not necessary to have been doing something for 25 or more years for attorneys to get an opportunity for a significant or leadership role. Standard "paying your dues" if it's "just because" is self-defeating for firms as well as frustrating and off-putting for talented individuals.

Much of the legal profession still encourages competitive cultures rather than collaborative ones and continues to resist fresh approaches that would be increasingly efficient and personally satisfying if more open minds gave them a chance. For example, de-stigmatizing work/life flexibility for all genders and generations would provide real choice for all to manage their pressured lives and lead to more camaraderie and respect. The prevalent culture, however, frequently is the opposite of motivating to young lawyers, particularly Gen Y/Millennials.

In fact, many firms' cultures and policies are so reputed to cause serious stress that young professionals anticipate in advance the difficulties posed by law firm life. My non-law colleagues and I have come up with a new term for the questions that come our way from students and young professionals—"pre-worrying." This refers to the angst about how they will handle work/life balance when they don't even know what they will have to balance yet. This is a big concern for men as well as women now, and for older generations who may have elderly parents to care for as well as children and are also seeking sane lives. It should be addressed early in law careers and firm life as an "everyone's issue" with sensitivity by management and mentors so that talented young lawyers will not be planning their exit and next career step the month after the gloss rubs off of their job offer and they start working.

CROSS-GENERATIONAL SOLUTIONS

How Mutual Mentoring and Circles Help All Generations

Generation Y/Millennials and the younger end of Gen Xers clamor for mentoring, and some Baby Boomers who came late to the game as mentees regret what they missed. If you fall into the latter category, make up for it by being generous as a mentor to individuals and teams. You will benefit more than you know in a myriad of ways.

You've likely heard the expression "what goes around comes around." If you are a giver, you will also receive. Reciprocity is the secret sauce of both networking and mentoring and is one of the six principles of persuasion defined by renown psychologist Dr. Robert Cialdini of Arizona State University. Whether older or younger, thinking in terms of giving first eliminates the stress of "owing" a mentor or referral source. It is easier asking if you have already offered. And it's not a formal, obligatory transaction. Mentoring should work in two directions, not just one, and it's not necessarily a matter of formal pairings. Formal mentorships can be fantastic if they happen organically, the chemistry works, and the parties are committed to making it work.

However, I prefer to champion **reciprocal or mutual mentoring**. The younger generations now believe they have a lot to offer the older generations, and they do. Mutual mentoring is excellent for women, men, and mixed gender mentoring too. But let's take it further. I advocate for and set up **mentoring circles** so people have several people to draw on, since no one person is equipped to supply all the advice any one person of any age/generation needs. Circles allow the chemistry factor to develop and take the time burden off one-on-one mentoring only. People within the circles are free to pair off as well.

When participants get comfortable with each other and serve as both mentor and mentee, it's somewhat like a jazz ensemble that improvises, riffing off from the contribution of the other players.

Mutual Mentoring across the Generations

A few definitions to clarify the differences:

Reverse mentoring is a process by which a person seeks out an "expert" who has less job experience than he/she does, but who holds a wealth of knowledge/skill on a topic that is continually changing and growing. This concept has been used in particular when older workers who were not accustomed to the computer-related technology that is now commonplace were slow to adopt new methods or lacked knowledge of the software and its uses. The mentoring usually comes from their younger colleagues.

Mutual mentoring occurs when each person brings to the table knowledge to teach and a different topic to learn, and they agree to exchange mentor and mentee roles as appropriate. This is a two-way process in which each party gives and gains.

Can you see the potential in the workplace, for example, between the tech super-savvy Gen Y/Millennials who may be challenged in some of their in-person and formal written communication skills and the Boomers who are working to become more technologically adept and have developed, through education and practice, more effective communication skills? The possibilities are endless, based on the skills and behavior desired and needed for career/life achievement and fulfillment.

How do we implement mutual mentoring in today's work context where age and experience has historically dictated and still colors the role behavior? Without wanting to play therapist here, I throw out the possibility that parent-child type hot buttons may surface in workplace relationships. This magnifies the impact of issues such as an older professional reporting to a younger one (increasingly common in many industries, even law), "paying your dues" versus solely merit-based recognition, or appropriateness of dress as well as informality of environment. Such challenges need to be addressed through meaningful, often facilitated, conversations among the generations.

Implementing Alternate Styles of Mentoring

The first step to better relationships is awareness of the emotions and the sometimes knee-jerk reactions and remarks they produce. Old-style law firm mentoring relationships—which took place primarily in all-male workplaces—often benefited from a dose of the parent-child devotion. It is likely the latter would work better between Boomers and Millennials than either with Gen X because Millennials tend to be close to their Boomer parents and have more similarities in general outlook. In these relationships, it is important to develop the attributes of self-sufficiency and independence that many Millennials (to generalize) are lacking.

As a formal process, mutual mentoring is most likely to take root if:

- It is put in the context of, and plays upon, professionals' natural desire to keep learning.
- It is open to and encouraged for everyone—rather than viewed as remedial.
- Expectations are set, self-evaluations are done, results are publicized, and mentors are recognized in meaningful ways appropriate to each generation.
- People are rewarded for their mentoring roles.
- A mentoring coordinator "gets" the process and has respect and influence with leadership. That will encourage accountability and sustainability of the initiative.

Here are some steps that can get your firm or organization started setting up and running a mentoring circle, whether internal to a legal employer, a professional or trade organization, or an alumni group.

- Determine that there are 6–12 people interested in participating of various generations and levels of experience.
- Designate co-chairs to administer the logistics.
- Decide how often to meet and where—in person, Zoom, by phone, video-conference, etc.
- Decide on basic ground rules and expectations.
- Select an outside facilitator, at least for the launch. After that, one or more internal facilitators in rotation can lead the way.

Once set up, mentoring circles must be monitored and nurtured to keep them going strong and producing powerful results.

With or without a firm mentoring program or individually initiated mentoring, here are several other ways to benefit from multi-generational conversations.

SEVEN SELF- AND CAREER-DEVELOPMENT TACTICS FOR CROSS-GENERATIONAL CONVERSATION

Here are some useful tips for both junior and more experienced lawyers:

1. Find someone in the firm, even if there is no formal mentoring program, whom you can be comfortable asking "how things work here" and about "unwritten rules."
2. Learn about your personal (behavioral) style and how to use your style strengths in relationship building both inside the office and outside with clients and possible referral sources.
3. Learn to "read" other people's styles so that you can build better and quicker intergenerational rapport.

4. Ask, relating to each assignment as well as big picture career development, what expectations are. Senior lawyers often are not accustomed to spelling out expectations unless asked. Explain how knowing expectations makes you more efficient and productive.
5. Ask—nicely—for feedback periodically and when you need it. Don't expect senior lawyers to automatically give frequent feedback. You may need to ask for it and explain how feedback will make you more productive than the "sink or swim" method of training.
6. Learn to see each situation from other people's perspective. Think about how you can make senior lawyers more successful and your clients more successful, and make that your purpose. Then they will find you valuable to keep around.
7. Ask for training—and make sure you attend. Focus on your professional development and keep learning.

A good coach or mentor, whether internal or external, who understands your organization and the intergenerational dynamics can help with all of the above.

I encourage people of all generations to look at their career lives as an adventure with some risks and opportunities to try new things. Get to know new people and develop a pre-disposition for offering what you have to share, at age 20 or age 75 or anywhere in between. In addition to offering individual benefits, it will make for economically stronger firms and happier places to work. Then you can thrive and take pride that your firm gets visible recognition for being selected as one of "the best places to work" and being an "employer of choice," attracting the very best lawyers to work with.

FURTHER RESOURCES

Learn about generational attributes, formative influences, and their implications:

- Request Phyllis Weiss Haserot's monthly newsletter on Intergenerational Relations and Cross-Generational Conversation (at www.crossgenerational conversation.com, www.pdcounsel.com, or pwhaserot@pdcounsel.com).
- Check the Practice Development Counsel website (www.pdcounsel.com), a web site chock full of relevant articles, videos, and more.
- Read *You Can't Google It! The Compelling Case for Cross-Generational Conversation at Work* (Phyllis Weiss Haserot, Morgan James Publishing, paper edition March 2018; eBook, fall 2017).
- Request the "Generational Wisdom" white paper from pwhaserot@ pdcounsel.com.

CHAPTER 22
Happiness and Pro Bono Legal Service

Julie LaEace, Esq.

Editor's Note: At first, I was surprised to find a large law firm with someone responsible for coordinating pro bono efforts. On second thought, it was not so surprising. It stands to reason that economies of scale would enable a large law firm to have such a position. My intuition led me to believe that pro bono work contributes to happiness. What follows is the documentary evidence that proves my point. Thank you, Julie, for going the extra mile.

Numerous studies have confirmed that those who volunteer tend to have higher levels of self-esteem and happiness. This connection between volunteerism and satisfaction also bears out in the law firm context: doing pro bono legal work can make you feel good about being a lawyer.

"Those who are happiest are those who do the most for others."
—Booker T. Washington

No book on lawyer happiness would be complete without a discussion of pro bono legal service. Every lawyer has a professional responsibility to provide pro bono legal services to those unable to pay. ABA Model Rule of Professional Conduct 6.1, which many states have adopted some variation of, encourages lawyers to contribute

---

Julie LaEace is Pro Bono Counsel and Firmwide Director of Pro Bono at Kirkland & Ellis. After graduating from Notre Dame Law School in 1998, LaEace specialized in employment litigation and employee benefits at two large Chicago law firms before transitioning to law firm management. Julie joined Kirkland in January 2007 and became the firm's first pro bono professional in August 2008, working with the firm's newly created Pro Bono Management Committee to create and build the firm's pro bono program. She is a member of the Association of Pro Bono Counsel and the Chicago Bar Foundation's Advisory Committee on Training and Professional Development in Legal Aid.

at least 50 hours of pro bono service a year.[1] But there are many other reasons, in addition to ethical responsibilities, to incorporate pro bono legal work into regular commercial practice, chief among them the professional and personal satisfaction doing pro bono work can bring.

First, what do we mean by pro bono legal service? The Pro Bono Institute, a national nonprofit that is mandated to explore and identify new approaches to pro bono legal assistance for the poor and disadvantaged, defines pro bono legal service as legal work that is done without expectation of a fee for

> persons of limited means or to charitable, religious, civic, community, governmental and educational organizations in matters which are designed primarily to address the needs of persons of limited means; . . . individuals, groups, or organizations seeking to secure or protect civil rights, civil liberties or public rights; and . . . charitable, religious, civic, community, governmental or educational organizations in matters in furtherance of their organizational purposes, where the payment of standard legal fees would significantly deplete the organization's economic resources or would be otherwise inappropriate.[2]

Pro bono legal work takes many forms: volunteering at a legal advice desk, assisting a low-income entrepreneur in setting up a small business, representing an individual fleeing persecution in his home country in asylum proceedings, or helping a small nonprofit obtain 501(c)(3) status are all examples of common pro bono projects. Whatever type of project one chooses, the act of giving back to a cause or organization with which you have a connection can have a significant impact on a lawyer's overall level of happiness.

Numerous studies confirm that those who volunteer tend to have higher levels of self-esteem and happiness. United Health Group commissioned a national survey of 3,351 adults and found that the overwhelming majority of participants reported feeling mentally and physically better after a volunteer experience.[3] Ninety-six percent of people who volunteered in the last twelve months said that volunteering improved their mood. Similarly, researchers at the University of Exeter Medical School in England analyzed data from 40 published studies and found that volunteers had lower levels of depression, increased life satisfaction, and enhanced well-being.[4] This connection between volunteerism and satisfaction also bears out in the law firm context: in a 2015 survey of 651 associates in four large law firms, 60 percent of respondents said one of their primary reasons for doing pro bono work was that it made them feel

---

1. American Bar Association. MODEL RULES OF PROFESSIONAL CONDUCT r. 6.1. (2016), https://www.americanbar.org/groups/probono_public_service/policy/aba_model_rule_6_1.html (accessed June 12, 2017).

2. Pro Bono Institute. LAW FIRM PRO BONO PROJECT CHALLENGE® http://www.probonoinst.org/wpps/wp-content/uploads/Law-Firm-Challenge-2016-1.pdf (accessed June 12, 2017).

3. UnitedHealth Group, *Doing Good is Good for You: 2013 Health and Volunteering Study*, http://www.unitedhealthgroup.com/~/media/UHG/PDF/2013/UNH-Health-Volunteering-Study.ashx, (last visited June 12, 2017).

4. University of Exeter. 2013. "Go On, Volunteer—It Could Be Good For You!" SCIENCEDAILY, (22 August), www.sciencedaily.com/releases/2013/08/130822194451.htm (accessed June 12, 2017). Jenkinson, Caroline E., Andy P. Dickens, Kerry Jones, Jo Thompson-Coon, Rod S. Taylor, Morwenna Rogers, Clare L. Bambra, Iain Lang, and Suzanne H. Richards. 2013. *Is Volunteering a Public Health Intervention? A Systematic Review and Meta-Analysis of the Health and Survival of Volunteers.* BMC PUBLIC HEALTH 13, no. 1: 773. https://bmcpublichealth.biomedcentral.com/articles/10.1186/1471-2458-13-773 (accessed June 12, 2017).

good about being a lawyer.[5] When asked why they enjoy doing pro bono work, two associates at Kirkland & Ellis said, "We loved helping someone in need get through an extremely difficult phase of her life."

In addition to helping you feel good for giving back, pro bono work can provide valuable professional experiences early in one's career. As a junior lawyer, pro bono work can give you the chance to build new skills, establish relationships with clients, and take the lead on a project. It can also give you the opportunity to grow your professional network both within your firm and within your community, which may lead to more opportunities in the future. The following statements from younger associates are typical.

"Working on pro bono matters is professionally rewarding in that it has offered me an opportunity to take initiative, manage projects, and be a lead contact with clients as a junior associate. Further, I have met and enjoyed working with attorneys here at Kirkland through my pro bono efforts outside of the teams I typically work with on billable matters."

"My favorite thing about doing pro bono work is the opportunity to connect with and help improve my community. Unlike most of my corporate clients, my pro bono clients are local so I get to meet with them in person and see the impact of my work (and theirs) firsthand."

This last quote illustrates another way in which pro bono work can be satisfying: getting to see results and the impact of one's work. In a profession where one might work years on a case before seeing a resolution, or where a deal is completed for a project across the globe that one might never see, pro bono work can give an attorney the opportunity to see results and to have a tremendous impact on the lives of individuals and communities.

As the pro bono director at a large law firm, I've talked to many associates and partners over the years about their pro bono experiences. Their stories illustrate best the impact pro bono work can have on a lawyer's personal and professional fulfillment. The remainder of this chapter will be devoted to some of these great stories.

CHARLES JOHNSON[6]

In September 2016, after more than eight years of work, Kirkland attorneys secured the release of a pro bono client who had been wrongfully convicted of a 1995 double murder and had served 20 years of a mandatory life without parole sentence.

> Charles Johnson was a 19-year-old delivery driver at the time of his arrest. He had been sentenced to life in prison without parole for the murder of two employees at a used-car dealership in Chicago. He was convicted despite the absence of any physical or forensic evidence linking him to the crime. Johnson claims the Chicago Police Department tricked him into signing a confession to the crime, telling him that his alibi checked out, that he was signing routine release paperwork, and they would allow him to go home.

---

5. Shared with permission by Brenna DeVaney of Skadden, Arps and Jennifer Kroman of Cleary Gottlieb.

6. Special thanks to Ashley Post at Kirkland & Ellis for the descriptions of the cases of Charles Johnson and Leon Smallwood.

In 2008, professors at the Center on Wrongful Convictions at Northwestern University Pritzker School of Law (CWCY), which receives thousands of letters from inmates each year, selected Johnson's case. Two of the school's professors asked Kirkland to partner with them in representing Johnson.

After years of investigation and motion practice seeking additional fingerprint testing, the team uncovered numerous new matches from fingerprints left at the scene of the crime to previously unidentified convicted felons with no connection to Johnson. One of these individuals left multiple prints at the crime scene as well as on the adhesive side of a marketing sticker the perpetrators ripped from a car they stole to flee the scene. The cars were driven five miles from the scene of the crime and hidden in an alley less than a block away from where the newly discovered suspect lived.

Johnson's team also tracked down previously missing witnesses who revealed a motive for the crime that was far more consistent with the crime than the motive the state argued at trial.

Based on this new evidence, Kirkland and CWCY filed two post-conviction petitions on behalf of Johnson, including an innocence petition in 2010.

In 2013, the First District Appellate Court held that Johnson had "made a substantial showing of an actual innocence claim" based on the new fingerprint testing and ordered an evidentiary hearing.

On July 11, 2016, the Illinois Cook County State's Attorney's Office agreed to a new trial for Johnson and his co-defendants and vacated his conviction. Johnson was released from prison on September 26, 2016. In February 2017, the Cook County State's Attorney's Office dismissed all charges again all four men.

The litigation partner who led the work on Charles' case for nearly nine years was outside the Cook County Jail along with Johnson's family and friends to celebrate his release after serving more than 20 years in prison for a crime he did not commit. He shared his thoughts about what this case meant to him with me recently:

As a relatively young lawyer, I understood that there were many who simply did not have meaningful access to legal representation. But I did not and could not comprehend the enormity of the crisis. Nor did I fully understand the investment of time and resources that would be required to assure Charles received justice.

When I was first approached with Charles Johnson's case, I responded that I could not commit to represent him because he had signed a "confession." In my view, no person would sign a confession unless he was guilty. I had made a judgment based on very limited information that Charles must be guilty. The partner who asked me to take the case told me that he understood my initial impressions, but encouraged me to review the trial record before I made a final decision. I undertook an extensive review of the record. Over the course of this review, I quickly realized that whatever my initial impressions with respect to the "confession," the evidence did not seem to match the theory pursued by the state at Charles' trial. I agreed to represent Charles and over the course of a nearly 9-year battle we proved that Charles Johnson was innocent.

This experience was incredibly rewarding in countless ways. Here are just a few examples of the way Charles Johnson's case impacted my life:

1. I learned a valuable lesson about reserving judgment until I had considered all available facts.
2. I am a better lawyer for having stepped out of my comfort zone to practice a new area of law and in a setting very different from the state and federal civil courts.

3. I found tremendous satisfaction in giving a voice to Charles and his claims of innocence. As a convicted felon, no one would listen to him when he tried to point out the flaws in his wrongful conviction.
4. On a related note, I discovered that as amazing as our legal system is, it is less than perfect in that it does not serve all citizens with the same level of fairness. I learned first-hand that in practice the phrase "justice for all" does not actually equate to "equal justice for all." There is a tremendous imbalance in the way the legal system serves various groups of people.
5. I also caught a glimpse of how tragic this imbalance can be in the lives of those who are not afforded an equal measure of justice.
6. But I also discovered the significant power a lawyer has to counter that imbalance for his or her client.
7. Accordingly, I have a better understanding of the tremendous importance of pro bono work and how critical it is that I continue fulfilling my responsibility as a lawyer to serve those who would otherwise not have meaningful access to legal representation.
8. The often-grueling nature of high-stakes civil litigation can be physically, emotionally, and spiritually draining. Experiencing first-hand how I can positively impact the lives of Charles and his entire family has elevated my respect for the legal profession and recharged my satisfaction in the practice of law.
9. Finally, I feel incredibly fortunate to have developed a life-long friendship with Charles and his family.

LEON SMALLWOOD

Lest those transactional attorneys reading this believe that these types of cases are limited only to litigators, two corporate associates at Kirkland describe their thoughts about assisting Leon Smallwood with obtaining clemency after 19 years in prison.

For nearly two years, both attorneys worked on a clemency petition for Mr. Smallwood, an Illinois man who was sentenced to life in prison after being convicted of selling crack when he was 27 years old. In November 2016, after Smallwood had spent 19 years behind bars, the associates secured his clemency.

Smallwood's petition was part of the Clemency Project, a pro bono initiative in which attorneys directly assisted non-violent federal inmates who sought commutations of their lengthy prison sentences. The project began in 2014 when President Barack Obama and Attorney General Eric Holder launched a sweeping clemency initiative to address the large number of inmates serving sentences disproportionate to their crimes. Legal advocacy groups solicited the assistance of the nation's bar to help identify prisoners who met certain criteria and who, if sentenced today, would receive significantly lower sentences.

Smallwood, who was sentenced to life in prison in 1997 for a low-level drug offense, would likely face 171 months for the same crime under current sentencing standards. While incarcerated, he completed his GED and several college and specialist training courses, mentored his fellow prisoners and helped more than 150 of them obtain their GEDs. He also remained employed throughout his sentence, including in supervisory roles. His model behavior, as well as more than 20 letters of support from Smallwood's family members and others in his community, strengthened Smallwood's clemency petition.

Smallwood was officially released to reunite with his family on February 24, 2017, his birthday.

Mr. Smallwood's case has had a significant impact on both attorneys. "It's the best thing I've ever done. I still get choked up thinking about it," said one of the attorneys. She went on to describe how working on Leon's case has made her more empathetic to all of her clients.

Said her teammate, "When you are having rough times with your regular commercial practice, it's great to remind yourself that you've had an impact on someone's life."

This attorney also discussed the meaning she derives from participating in a Saturday legal clinic in her neighborhood: "It's nice to end the week on a positive note," she said. "It's also a chance to reconnect in your community. These are your neighbors. It's restorative."

Even when you have to tell someone you can't help them, because, for example, they don't qualify for the type of relief they are seeking, it is still an opportunity to be of service. "Sometimes people get value from you just by hearing their story and acknowledging what they've gone through."

CHAPTER 23
Bar Association Volunteerism

K. William Gibson, Esq.

Editor's Note: I am proud to call Bill a friend and a buddy. We have shared the ABA experience in many places around the US over the last 25 years. We have shared cigars in city and country settings. I was one of the delegates on his People to People tour of India exploring outsourcing of legal work when his ration of Jack Daniels saved us after a 20-mile, eight-hour bus ride during wedding season. Sometimes I wonder why he devotes the time he does to bar association activities. This chapter answers that question.

The author describes how he began a long career in bar association activities while still in law school and established relationships that have lasted throughout his nearly 40-year career. Attorney and arbitrator Bill Gibson decided to improve his ability to build and manage a small law office by getting involved in the ABA Law Practice Management Section. His efforts, he writes, paid off, and he encourages other lawyers to join and get involved in local, state, and national bar organizations.

Most of the lawyers I have known in the nearly 40 years I have been practicing law have never gotten involved in any bar association activities. Most practicing lawyers have their hands full running a practice, running the kids to practice, and trying to find a few precious minutes to go to the gym. I first got involved in bar activities

K. William Gibson is a longtime personal injury lawyer in Portland, Oregon. His practice now focuses on assisting other attorneys resolve their cases through arbitration and mediation. Bill is a 1979 graduate of Lewis & Clark Law School in Portland and holds a Master's Degree in Industrial & Labor Relations from the University of Oregon. He is a former Chair of the ABA Law Practice Division and former President of the College of Law Practice Management. Bill travels extensively, leading delegations of American lawyers to such places as China, India, and Cuba to meet with lawyers and judges in those countries.

when I was a law student. I have been involved ever since and, on balance, have found it to be a worthwhile use of my time.

My bar involvement started with the Law Student Division of the American Bar Association while I was in law school at Lewis & Clark Law School in Portland, Oregon. While there, I was selected as a regional representative for the ABA Law Student Division (LSD), representing Oregon and Washington. I got to know other law students and got my first look at some of the issues that practicing lawyers face.

After a year in law school, I decided that I wanted to become a trial lawyer. I had gotten a job as a law clerk for a state court trial judge in Portland and got to watch trials—civil and criminal—every day. Out of the blue, I was asked to become the law student liaison to the ABA Section of Litigation. I didn't know much about that group, but soon learned that some of the premier litigators in the country belonged. I served in that role for two years and got to attend Litigation Section meetings around the country. I was 25 years old and had never traveled before, so the trips were exciting, and getting to hobnob with a group of heavyweight lawyers, while a little intimidating, was an unbelievable honor.

If I hadn't been involved in ABA activities in law school, and had just kept my head down and focused only on my studies, my grades may well have been better, but I would have missed out on some great experiences.

After graduating from law school and starting my own practice with a friend, I ran for the board of my county bar association. I was also elected President of the Young Lawyers Division of that group. (To be fair, I ran unopposed.) I got to know the other new lawyers in that organization and organized events and wrote articles about the challenges facing younger lawyers. After a year or so of doing that, I was elected to the board of the county bar association. I got to know more people and sit at the "grown-up table." That experience gave me a chance to get to know local attorneys—many of whom worked in larger law firms. They were always generous with their time and advice. That alone made my efforts worthwhile.

As much as I enjoyed my county bar experience, I decided that the ABA Law Practice Management Section was where I would make my home. Law Practice Management focused on issues that I was facing every day in my two-lawyer practice—namely, how to be a good lawyer and be a good manager, marketer, technology guru, and human resources manager all at the same time. I joined and became a committee vice-chair. I read everything I could find and went to a lot of CLE programs. Eventually, when I had learned a little, I started writing articles about law practice management issues and eventually was asked to share my knowledge by speaking at ABA conferences. After a few years, I wrote my first book, called *How to Build and Manage a Personal Injury Practice*. I don't think I would have written a book—any book—if I hadn't spent a decade learning about law practice management issues. The experience, I like to think, made me a better manager.

In those days, advertising was still verboten and the conventional wisdom was that if you were a good lawyer, you didn't need to concern yourself with management issues—the money would take care of itself and you could hire consultants to handle issues that you didn't know much about. My view was that lawyers—whether in small firms or large—needed to know about such things as computers and technology, the Internet, hiring and keeping good employees, and marketing. It's strange to look back and see those things as being innovative—but they were.

After writing that book I was elected Secretary of the Law Practice Management Section and eventually became Chair of that group. Over the next decade I wrote two more editions of the personal injury book and edited two editions of a book called

Flying Solo: A Survival Guide for the Solo and Small Firm Lawyer. I also began writing a column for *Law Practice Magazine* and did that for about ten years.

In 1995, the ABA asked me to go to the former Soviet Republic of Belarus to teach Belarusian lawyers how to practice law in the post-communist era. I wouldn't have been given that opportunity if I hadn't gotten involved in bar activities. That was one of the best experiences of my career.

In 1997, I was inducted into the College of Law Practice Management and went on to serve as President of that group for two years. While in that position, I got to work with the best and brightest minds in the field of law practice management—people from all over the world. That position came about because of my years of service to the bar.

In 2007, I led a delegation of US lawyers to China to discuss areas of common concern in the area of law practice management. Later, I led delegations of American lawyers to India and Cuba.

In 2013, I was fortunate to be given the Samuel L. Smith Award—the highest award given by the ABA for commitment to law practice management. That award was the direct result of my time spent laboring in the vineyards of bar association activities.

One of the most satisfying bar activities I have participated in is the Oregon State Bar Mentor Program. I serve as a mentor for new lawyers in Oregon and regularly get calls and emails from young lawyers who have read my writings and want help starting a practice.

The thread that runs through my 40 years of bar service is the opportunity to learn about important issues, educate myself through the works of others, then use my knowledge to educate younger lawyers. I have a particular soft spot in my heart for solos—knowing from experience the isolation that comes with working on your own.

Had I not gotten involved in the ABA 40 years ago, I would not have gained the knowledge, experience, and expertise to put me in a position to offer advice to younger lawyers. I would not have met the people I have been fortunate to get to know.

In all honesty, I can say that I gained enormous personal benefit from my years of bar activities. I cannot count the times that I have called a bar colleague—in the US and abroad—to ask for advice about a matter of importance to my own practice. I have tried to repay all that I have gained by paying it forward to a younger generation that faces even more daunting challenges than my generation faced.

CHAPTER 24
You Can Too

Linda Alvarez, Esq.

Editor's Note: Linda is a champion—a champion and a warrior for the human spirit. She listened to her own voice, a voice that would rather suffer serious disability than do work that was out of the bounds of integrity for her. She used that creative leverage to push back, go against the grain, and create something new, something innovative, something that enabled her to stay true to her values and practice law. Her way. This path is challenging; having walked it myself, I know. It can be lonely, it can be frustrating, and it can make you wonder if you are compromising your identity as a lawyer because you can no longer practice the way everyone else is. Yet for many there is no choice, and following deeply held values leads to happiness of a deeper magnitude. I once heard the expression that practicing law is whatever a lawyer does. Each of us has the unique opportunity to embody our best personal self in practice, whatever that might mean. As you read about Linda's innovation, think about what you might do to innovate in your chosen area of specialty because you know it's the right thing to do.

The legal system is broken. Almost everyone who works within it concedes this. At the same time, most of us believe that the existing system is the best possible given the realities of human nature in the context of conflict. Linda Alvarez is one of a growing movement of change-makers calling themselves Integrative Lawyers who, in responding to the rapidly evolving needs of business, are shaking up the status quo. She adds her voice here to illuminate

Linda Alvarez, Esq., began her career in large firms—Wilson Sonsini Goodrich & Rosati (Palo Alto) and Vinson & Elkins (Houston)—where she represented multi-national corporations in matters concerning trademark rights, copyrights, advertising practices, and issues related to the conduct of online business. In 2005, Linda re-focused on transactional work and launched her solo practice. Her clients include best selling authors, filmmakers, and businesses from sole proprietorships to corporations with internationally recognized consumer brands. A pioneer in addressing the legal challenges faced by purpose-driven businesses, Linda developed an innovative approach to drafting and enforcing contracts, which she calls Discovering Agreement. In 2012, Linda was recognized by the American Bar Association as a "Legal Rebel" for her work bringing change to the legal system. Her book, *Discovering Agreement: Contracts That Turn Conflict into Creativity*—a Flagship publication of the ABA—was released in June 2016.

how even a lone attorney can catalyze system-wide change by shifting her/his perspective and expectations about the role of the lawyer and the meaning, purpose, and practice of managing conflict.

Not long ago, I was invited to give a keynote speech at a career-building conference for new lawyers. The organizers asked me to speak on the topic, "Building a Legal Career with Authenticity." It seemed to me, the questions implicit in the topic were:

- How do I live an authentic life in the context of my work as a lawyer?

and

- How do I create a legal career that doesn't generate dissonance between my nature and my work?

I find it fascinating that these are questions we need to ask. What about the practice of law is counter to our natural authenticity?

Our profession seems to dictate a certain Way of Being, and we assume that to deviate from that model is professionally irresponsible . . . perhaps impossible. There is the imperative to make no mistakes; rules and precedent are of primary importance; and we are taught that we must separate emotions from decision-making. Our culture, in general, imposes upon us an identity of champion and protector (at best) and hired gun and amoral shark (at worst), all of which plays out in a cultural context that frames everything we do as a zero-sum effort where winning requires a loser.

IN PRECEDENT WE TRUST

We are trained to look to the past, to preserve consistency in service of predictability. We believe we must conform to the "way things are done," even if our personal values (and common sense) are offended. Deviating from established practices is frowned upon. It is risky. And we know that lawyers are Not Allowed To Make Mistakes.

This loyalty to precedent makes sense in terms of *stare decisis*, but the primacy of convention and tradition tends to be applied to the whole of our legal life. Conformity becomes a value and non-conformity, a taboo. Idiosyncrasy and individuality are highly suspect.

NO EMOTIONS ALLOWED

Lawyers are asked to engage and be rational in life's most painful and paradoxical circumstances. We fear emotions, believing that they tend to run away with us and could easily lead to irrational behavior. "Feelings" are equated with vulnerability, and vulnerability with weakness and exposure to harm. Implicit in our training is the imperative to overcome our feelings, to set them aside when making decisions. So, we expect ourselves to partition our hearts from our work; but it is not possible to selectively numb emotion. If we make our emotions untrustworthy for one purpose, we lose the ability to access them when they are appropriate and most needed, such as in our intimate personal relationships.

POWER OF THE HEART

The reality is that the heart has power that will manifest even if we believe we've blocked its influence. Lawyers have disproportionately high rates of depression, substance abuse, burnout, divorce, and suicide. How can we engage the power of the heart and still be effective lawyers who are credible and successful (professionally, financially, and personally)? Can we "follow our hearts" and still pay off our student loans?

Anxiety, depression, and burnout are signals of a misalignment between the lawyer and her/his authentic self. These are evidence of the power of the heart manifesting in destructive ways—I believe due to lack of proper, healthy outlet. If we don't want the heart to take a subversive role in our lives, then we need to find a way to work with it, to harness its power for our own good, the good of those we love, and for the good of the world. Know your heart and align with it.

I'm not suggesting that we just start allowing unease or discomfort to call the shots or that we capriciously "follow our bliss" rather than making thoughtful and considered choices. I am suggesting, however, that we get really familiar with what *is* calling the shots and then decide if that's what we want governing our decisions.

For many of us, the expectations of family and culture have a strong influence on our decision-making. But we rarely take a clear-eyed look at just exactly what those expectations are, and whether those expectations make sense to us and lead to the life we want.

INTEGRITY: WHAT IS IT? AND WHY IS IT IMPORTANT?

The one thing over which you have complete control is your personal integrity. There will be times when others have the power to take away your money, your job, your freedom, even your life, but they can *never* take away your personal integrity. Personal integrity is yours. You can sell it. You can give it away. Or you can keep it. Integrity is the true seat of power in every life.

"Integrity," to my way of thinking, is actually a neutral term. It doesn't imply a particular set of moral principles and values so much as it indicates a fully integrated and consistent set of principles, values, and actions. Thus, my working definition of "integrity" is "*conscious alignment of action and values.*"

KNOW THYSELF AND TO THINE OWN SELF BE TRUE

To be in integrity, you need to know your core, deeply held values and the principles by which you want to live—the ones that generate unease within you if you go against them. You also need to know what it is that truly exerts on you a magnetic force—what are the stimulating ideas and concepts that pull your attention? What is the innate sense and vision within you that drives your interests and triggers your energy?

To be able to stand in your own power—your personal integrity—you must know your own, personal Truth and then consciously test your actions and decisions according to that truth.

LODESTAR

What do you stand for? Have you ever tried to capture that in writing? I find that many of us have a sense of what we believe is "right" and "true," what makes life and work meaningful, and what principles and values are worth standing up for, but it can be remarkably difficult to express these things in words, especially in writing. In my experience, having a clear articulation of my own personal lodestar for navigating decisions and crises is key to living whole-heartedly and in integrity.

When you know your unique vision of a better world—the world you wish could exist, the one you want to help bring into being—and when you can clearly state your core values and principles, you no longer have to wonder whether a decision is right or wrong. You don't have to wonder how to measure its virtue or faults. All you have to do is check to see whether it is in alignment with your deeply held values, whether it violates your core constraints and imperatives, whether it serves your vision of a better world and furthers your contribution to bringing that world into being.

The reason for putting these in writing is to create an easily accessible reminder that orients you to your core truths, your whole-hearted truth, so you can answer challenges with positive, creative exploration rather than triggered reactiveness. Having it in writing helps you shift out of "automatic drive" into "manual" even in the midst of heightened stress or emotion.

YOUR VISION

There is something you wish were different about the world. You have an idea of how things could be better. It might be that you just have a big complaint about something in "the way things are." It might be a big part of the reason you decided to become a lawyer. Healthy planet? A divorce process that truly honors and shelters the needs of children? A new model for having conflict that values and engenders common sense problem-solving? A political system that truly serves its constituents, creating harmony rather than polarization?

Try writing it down, a sentence or two describing a better world for everyone that you can imagine, or describing the brokenness you see that you wish could be fixed. You don't have to believe it is a realistic vision or a possible future. It is just something that you can imagine and wish could be true.

I envision a world where . . .

YOUR MISSION

What part do you want to play in fixing the brokenness? How can you contribute to bringing the better world into being? You may already be doing it. You may be taking first steps with an eye to gaining strength, capacity, abilities to do more in the future. Jot some notes.

My mission is to contribute to bringing this better world into being by . . .

VALUES AND PRINCIPLES / CONSTRAINTS AND IMPERATIVES

What are the "essential nutrients" for your own, personal well-being—physical, mental, emotional, spiritual? What are keys to your willingness to enter and remain in a relationship, a job, an endeavor? What are the keys to satisfaction in working together with others? Do you have a personal code of ethics? Do you have unwritten rules for what it means to "play well with others"? What *must never* and *must always* be present or a part of your relationships/work? Start a laundry list. (Don't forget "fun"!)

In everything I do, I value . . .

When I work with someone, it is important to me that . . .

In service of my Vision and Mission, I choose to practice law in accordance with the following principles and values . . .

This lodestar expresses the foundation of your personal power, your personal integrity. It is the star by which you chart your course, the touchstone you can use to assess the quality of every offer, decision, choice, and relationship. Even if you decide to accept a course of action that someone else has engineered for you through coercive means, or that does not fully align with your Vision, Mission, or Values, you can do it with consciousness, alert to the risk to your integrity, alert to the risk of emotional, mental, physical, and spiritual backlash.

OBLIQUITY

I promise you won't forget to think about the financial side of your career choices or about the expectations of your parents/friends/colleagues/etc., but if finances and the expectations of others govern your choices, you take a great risk—the risk that you will create a life you do not love, that does not match your true nature, and that demands of you a falseness and smallness that is unworthy of the potential you embody.

Obliquity shows us that if we are focused on meeting the highest level of needs (self-actualization), then the decisions we make and actions we take are far more likely to gather to us the resources to meet and satisfy lower-level needs (food, shelter, paying off student loans, etc.)

Don't aim at success. The more you aim at it and make it a target, the more you are going to miss it. For success, like happiness, cannot be pursued; it must ensue, and it only does so as the unintended side effect of one's personal dedication to a cause greater than oneself or as the by-product of one's surrender to a person other than oneself. Happiness must happen, and the same holds for success; you have to let it happen by not caring about it. I want you to listen to what your conscience commands you to do and go on to carry it out to the best of your knowledge. Then you will live to see that in the long run—in the long run, I say!—success will follow you precisely because you had forgotten to think about it.

—Viktor E. Frankl, *Man's Search for Meaning*

INTEGRITY AND INNOVATION

I began living and working from my own whole-hearted truth—an articulated Vision, Mission, Values statement—because I had to. I began my career working as an associate in big law firms and then joined a corporation as their in-house Senior Litigation Counsel. A highly effective advocate, I often joked with colleagues and clients that the opposition had no chance; we would "squish 'em like a bug." At the same time, anxiety had become a constant in my life, like a low-grade fever I could never really shake off. Then, one day, driving to the office, I caught myself wishing that I could be in an accident and be disabled "just enough" to never have to go into the office again. I was stunned by that thought, so stunned that for a moment my mind came to a complete halt. Happily, my next thought was, "I can wish for something better than that!"

A short time later, I quit my job and launched a solo practice. I began experimenting with how I could conduct my practice—and counsel my clients—without betraying my Truth. I began putting my Vision, Mission, and Values statement (VMV) in my engagement letters, and requiring my clients to include theirs. This brought a new level of transparency and clarity to the attorney/client relationship. My clients knew what to expect from me in terms of style and mindset; and if a potential client wanted a "hired gun" or "amoral shark," we discovered immediately that working with me would not be a good fit.

As I began working with clients—after calibrating the alignment of our respective values and visions—an unexpected and extremely useful side effect began to manifest. Having a clear expression, both broad and deep, of what was key to the client's satisfaction in their work, relationships, and endeavors, provided a valuable tool for assessing proposals and options that arose during the representation. It also helped both me and the client resist the temptation to respond in kind to emotional provocation. My clients and I were less susceptible to the trap of seeking fairness. We only needed to check for alignment with *what really mattered* to them.

Paradoxically, by paying attention to the whole-hearted, deeply felt truth—with all its emotional resonance—we created a more powerful, stable framework for meeting crises and disruption with calm creativity and effectiveness.

Out of this early exploration, I developed a practice for contract formation, drafting, and accountability that uses this same approach—investigating and calibrating the core values and vision of all parties, memorializing those in writing as the foundation for their ongoing relationship and endeavors—which I call "Discovering Agreement."

TRUSTWORTHINESS AND ACCOUNTABILITY

The question frequently arises about how it is possible to trust that someone will adhere to their VMV. Many a lofty aspiration is stated, but when conflicts arise and emotions are high, we can swiftly revert to our baser instincts and conditioned patterns without even noticing. For this reason, I find it is key to tie the content of the VMV to the parties' contractually agreed conflict resolution procedure.

In my engagement letter (and, whenever possible, in contracts that my clients enter) there is a provision titled, "Addressing Change and Engaging Conflict" (ACEC). The ACEC explicitly lays out steps for opening and conducting the conversation amongst ourselves if/when something happens and the relationship is no longer working as expected or in a way that works for one or both of us. In the ACEC, each party agrees to use the stated VMV as the criteria for deciding whether a proposed solution is acceptable. In short, we commit that our VMV is not just aspirational but embodies the *official and contractually agreed design specifications* for our ongoing relationship and work together. It is our lodestar and touchstone for evaluating options, proposals, decisions.

When faced with the contractual commitment *to hold themselves accountable to their VMV*, I find that parties are much more careful and realistic about its content. Once they understand that the VMV is not a public relations statement, but their real-life, rubber-meets-the-road guidelines for conducting the work and relationship, they get down to reality and honesty.

Gandhi coined the term "satyagraha." It is often defined as "Gandhi's campaign of passive resistance," but this is inaccurate. The word literally means "hold to truth," and that was the core of Gandhi's philosophy and *action* expressed in one word. He knew his truth and he held to it in the face of every challenge. In this way, he personally practiced his oft-quoted instruction, "You must be the change you want to see in the world." The practice of satyagraha is the power that led to the liberation of India from British rule. It is the same practice that Dr. Martin Luther King followed, and Nelson Mandela. Building a legal career with authenticity is a practice of satyagraha—holding to truth, your truth. By living and working from the heart, I have found a way to practice law in full authenticity without sacrificing power, effectiveness, or financial well-being.

YOU CAN TOO

I truly believe that we all, each of us, have a sense of purpose or vision (even if we haven't articulated it)—a sense that we have something to achieve, something unique and worthwhile to either contribute or contribute to. Some question, whether spoken or not, draws us forward towards actions and words, towards connections and jobs, and influences our decision-making whether or not we are consciously aware of it.

As a lawyer, do you practice your personal truth, your "vision of a better world," and your core values with integrity?

In other words:

- Are your vision and values fully integrated into the way you practice law and counsel clients?
- Do you secretly worry that it is not possible to conduct legal affairs in complete integrity?
- Are you actively watching for opportunities to conduct legal affairs in powerful alignment with your vision and values?
- Is it your belief that the existing legal-justice system is so pervasive and institutionalized that it would be foolhardy to operate in a collaborative, non-coercive way?
- Are you creating and strengthening the pathways for alternative, vision/values aligned practices and systems?
- Did you know you could?
- Do you think it would be difficult (complicated, tricky, hard to get permission or 'buy-in' from bosses/clients)?
- What if it only takes a shift in your own practice?

It has been my experience that to catalyze systemic transformation, I only need to shift how I practice law—how I engage the conversation with clients, and how, together, we engage conflict and approach problem-solving.

When we orient our decision-making and problem-solving to the vision and values that we have carefully considered and declared, we have begun not only to be the change, but to trigger the change we want to see in the world. We use those intentionally chosen navigational points as the powerful and resilient guides for conducting legal affairs, without losing strength, without losing effectiveness. In fact, we become more powerful—more effective—more likely to find innovative, agile, efficient, focused, and productive responses in times of crisis.

I dare you.

On September 11, 2001, the calls that were made from the Twin Towers were not about "why me?" or rage or revenge. Those people, who knew they were in their last moments, wanted only to reach out and express love.

What really matters is expressing love.

Bringing something of value and meaning into the world is an act of love. Your legal career is an expression of your true self. If you choose, it can be an expression of love.

> The consummation of work lies not only in what we have done,
> but who we have become while accomplishing the task.

—David Whyte, *Crossing the Unknown Sea: Work as a Pilgrimage of Identity*

CHAPTER 25
Integrative Law

J. Kim Wright, Esq.

Editor's Note: I have been active in the CA Holistic Law and Alternative Dispute Resolution movements since around 1991. I met Kim as part of the Network of Spiritual Progressives, a project of Tikkun. The focus on law was lead by Professor Peter Gabel, who was also the Dean of the San Francisco–based New College of Law. I've watched with awe as Kim trots around the globe educating and being educated by progressive movements in the field of law, which relieve some of the dissonance that traditional practice foists upon conscious lawyers. What's most interesting is that when we periodically get together and download what we've been up to, parallel tracks and learning horizons emerge. I'm grateful that Kim is able to share some of what she considers to be key areas of the emerging bodies of Integrative Law. A whole systems approach is useful. The one thing all troubled lawyers have in common is their participation in an adversarial system designed hundreds of years ago to solve problems. Some say it's a civilized version of jousting . . . that said, many would agree that there is little that is civil about a civil action.

It is hard to be well in a broken system. The predominant culture of the legal profession is dysfunctional and it encourages isolation and unhealthy competition. We can meditate and exercise and get sleep, but if we still get up and go to work in a dysfunctional system that doesn't align with our values, our well-being is going to suffer. If you could design law practice according to your values, what would it look like? Around the world, integrative lawyers are doing just that. They're finding tools for new ways of being and creating new models for practicing. This chapter is an overview of integrative law and some of those models.

J. Kim Wright is a graduate of the University of Florida Levin School of Law. She has been licensed as a lawyer since 1989 and since 1994 has been a member of the North Carolina bar. She's the author of two ABA best-sellers, *Lawyers as Peacemakers* (2010) and *Lawyers as Changemakers* (2016). In 2009, Kim was named one of the first ABA Legal Rebels (the visionaries of the profession). Since 2008, she has been a global nomad. Find her at @cuttingedgelaw.

By the time I graduated from law school in 1989, I had decided that I never wanted to be a lawyer. I'd gone to law school with high hopes for making social change and helping people. Interactions with my classmates and the legal system had dashed those hopes. I worked in the nonprofit world for a few years, running a domestic violence agency and working in an organization dedicated to ending hunger.

In November 1993, I was in a personal transformation course when a tall, distinguished man stood up to introduce himself. His presence got my attention. His words transformed my life. Forrest Bayard was a divorce lawyer and he shared his philosophy of practicing holistically, as a healer, granting dignity to everyone in the process. As a family lawyer, his goal was to help clients end their marriages and still be amicable co-parents. That brief introduction opened a new possibility for law and me. I wasted no time. By March 1994, I was a member of the North Carolina Bar.

I opened my office and soon found that a lot of what I had feared about being a lawyer was actually true. Many colleagues were argumentative and seemed to enjoy inflaming and escalating conflict. Litigation was often harmful to already precarious parenting relationships. I could see that the system was broken in many ways, but I was different. I had hope. I now knew that it was possible to practice law in a different way.

I began to design my law practice based on my own values and aspirations. As a self-identified holistic lawyer, I sought out the most innovative peacemaking and healing approaches to law. Over the course of the next 14 years, I became a mediator, a collaborative lawyer, a restorative justice practitioner, a lawyer-coach, and more. I learned plain language drafting and began to write relationship-focused contracts. I became involved in humanizing legal education, therapeutic jurisprudence, and creative problem-solving. I studied neuroscience, appreciative inquiry, systems change, and non-violent and powerful non-defensive communication. I worked on my personal transformation and looked for ways to integrate that in my law practice. My clients responded enthusiastically.

I began to meet other lawyers who were on similar paths. I was not alone! In 2007, I was involved in more than a dozen conferences as an organizer, speaker, and attendee: holistic law, humanizing legal education, collaborative law, Lawyers as Peacemakers, Association for Conflict Resolution, etc. The conferences were hosted by diverse groups, but the themes were similar; the content was holistic and innovative. My study of systems change had helped me to see that movements are created by innovators who connect with each other, share ideas, and gain courage from knowing they are not alone. I saw an opportunity to make a difference as a connector.

Early in 2008, I began an adventure of traveling around the world, finding, supporting, and connecting innovative lawyers, while chronicling this fledgling movement. I expected to be gone for a few months. Those months turned into years and, as I write this, I have spent a decade of living my nomadic lifestyle with no plans to settle in one place again.

INTRODUCTION TO INTEGRATIVE LAW

There is an ancient legend about six blind men who encounter an elephant for the first time. Each touches a part of the elephant: the man who touches the leg declares that the elephant is like a tree; the man who touches the tail is sure that an elephant is like a rope; the back calls to mind a wall; the tusks are spears; the trunk is a snake; and the ears are fans. The men are adamant about their viewpoints, each arguing for his own limited experience of an elephant.

When I am asked to explain Integrative Law, I usually start with that story of the blind men and the elephant. I even carry a stuffed elephant, designed and made by an artist friend. The fabric illustrates the allegory: brown wood-grained legs, a brick wall back, braided rope tail, etc. It is a good teaching tool and visual for talking about systems thinking, a complex concept.

Integrative Law is like that elephant. There are many angles and pieces to the movement. Many people have a clear view of one and know nothing of the others. Some have a vague idea about the other parts of the movement. Others have a sense of the whole elephant without distinguishing the various pieces. Some of the distinctions overlap the others. Mostly, we feel the shift and we express it in our own ways.

While I am arguably an expert in the topic of Integrative Law, I am still learning about this movement. Sometimes it seems that I can see a new angle in every conversation. I create models and frameworks to help myself understand it. I make presentations to a lot of different groups with different values and expertise, so that comes in handy. I can spend Monday talking about the integrative approach to contracts to commercial lawyers, then turn around on Tuesday and talk about restorative justice to defense lawyers, and then have a conversation with family lawyers on Wednesday. In each conversation, I am talking about the whole elephant, but starting from the specific piece that the group knows well. We start with something familiar, like the tree trunk legs (or need for clarity in contracts) and then we step back and discuss other aspects of the bigger context (like Values-based Contracts).

Integrative Law has emerged over the last 20 to 30 years. In criminal law, it showed up as restorative justice and problem-solving courts. In family law, collaborative practice and transformative approaches to mediation evolved. Academics studied and wrote about therapeutic jurisprudence. Corporate lawyers began to see their roles in multi-disciplinary teams.

In 2011, a summit of leaders in the evolution of law gathered in Colorado. It was a meeting without a preconceived agenda or structure, leaders coming together to talk about our work in the world. There were judges, professors, law students, a legislator, and representatives of collaborative law, restorative justice, sharing law, business, intellectual property, securities, and more. Because we were beginning on Sunday and flights into Colorado Springs were limited, we arranged to begin with a Conversation Café session. That way, people could join the conversations at any point. Questions were placed on tables and participants rotated from table to table every few minutes. They got to know each other by their passions, purposes, and values, not their titles or jobs. Camaraderie developed quickly.

The next morning, we sat in a circle. We talked about what we wanted to do. We recognized that, despite the ways we practiced, we all shared a perspective and values. From the floor came a suggestion that we needed a name to describe the movement that encompassed all our legal approaches. The name "Integrative Law" was suggested and quickly accepted by consensus.

INDIVIDUAL EVOLUTION LEADING TO SYSTEMIC EVOLUTION

In the past ten years, I have spoken with and to thousands of lawyers, law students, and others involved in law and conflict resolution. I've been to five continents and many countries, with plans to visit the last continent (South America) in the works. Just as I saw the seeds of a movement in the US in 2007, I've seen the same evolution among different practice areas, and across disciplines, in every country where I have visited.

What I've observed has been an evolution of law that reflects the evolution of society, although admittedly, our profession doesn't change as fast as others. That is partly by design: common law is based on precedent, so we are always looking back, moving forward in incremental change. It provides stability for society and keeps us from just jumping on fads. The existing system was built on the societal values of the past. New values are emerging and evolving. We're learning more about what works and inventing new approaches.

When lawyers change how they practice, collectively they have an impact on the system. Law is like the DNA of a society. It is the thread that winds through our lives and communities, providing a structure for our relationships. Law is how we design, maintain, repair, and heal our relationships. It sets the rules of how we live together. Law tells us who we can marry, when that marriage is over, that we should stop at the red light, that there are consequences when we break our agreements. It reflects the values of society and defines our rights and responsibilities to each other.

RESPONDING TO THE TRIPARTITE CRISIS: SOMETHING IS WRONG HERE!

The journey to integrative law often begins with a sense of "There is something *wrong*!" The "wrong" may show up in our personal well-being as high levels of stress or health problems. Statistics (and a lot of personal experience and observations) show that our profession has high levels of depression, addiction, relationship dysfunction, and suicide, as compared to the general public. The culture of law encourages cutthroat competition, even within the same firm. We push ourselves, too. Several law firms with sincere commitments to well-being have told me that their biggest challenge is making lawyers go home at a reasonable time.

Psychologist, author, and law professor Susan Daicoff describes a "tripartite crisis" in the legal profession: low levels of lawyer well-being, low public reputation, and incivility among professionals.

Prof. Daicoff's psychological research began with the well-being hazards of conventional law practice. Then she came across new models of practice, which included collaborative law, therapeutic jurisprudence, restorative justice, and others.[1] She called this "Comprehensive Law," and her research showed it was a healthier way to practice, that the lawyers did not report the high levels of dysfunction that she found in the adversarial models. Professor Larry Krieger's research[2] also shows that lawyers who practice with a sense of purpose are happier.

---

1. Daicoff identified several models and theories she called "Comprehensive Law" which overlaps Integrative Law. See Susan Swaim Daicoff, *Law as a Healing Profession: The Comprehensive Law Movement*, PEPPERDINE DISPUTE RESOLUTION LAW JOURNAL (2005) available at https://papers.ssrn.com/sol3/papers.cfm?abstract_id=875449.

2. *See*, for example, Krieger, Lawrence & Kennon, Sheldon, *What Makes Lawyers Happy?: A Data-Driven Prescription to Redefine Professional Success*, 83 GEORGE WASHINGTON LAW REVIEW 554 (2015) available at https://papers.ssrn.com/sol3/papers.cfm?abstract_id=2398989; and cuttingedgelaw, LARRY KRIEGER PART 1 YOUTUBE (2008), https://www.youtube.com/watch?v=J_vxHBgT7wI&list=PLD2C3B3D61E8D9B5A.

Comprehensive law evolved into what we now call the Integrative Law movement. Given the healthier approaches, meaningful engagement, and values-based approach, Integrative Law may actually be the answer to the crisis.

And, if that is not enough, some lawyers have told me that they actually make more money as Integrative Lawyers. Their clients are surprised and pleased to learn that lawyers can be problem-solvers, peacemakers, and healers of conflicts. They not only sing the praises of their lawyers, they pay their bills.

REFLECTING ON SELF, RELATIONSHIPS, THE PROFESSION

Integrative lawyers reflect on their motivations, their purposes, and the human condition. They bring those reflective skills to their work and to the world around them. They reflect as individuals and together, seeking a world that works for all. Integrative Lawyers tend to bring their whole selves (body, mind, soul, and emotions) to work together to create a better legal system. This is a group that likes personal growth and is spiritually curious.

Many of us engage in contemplative practices such as meditation. I know litigators who are yogis and bring principles of balance from yoga into their trial practices. There are Buddhists, Hindus, Catholics, Muslims, Jews, and Humanists in this movement. We walk different paths with authenticity.

Mindfulness meditation is a hot trend for lawyers. Stress may instigate a lawyer to meditate or practice yoga, as thousands of lawyers have. Most law schools now offer some form of contemplative practice. Law firms, bar associations, and independent groups offer opportunities for group meditation in many communities around the world. Conferences on contemplative practices and law now draw hundreds of attendees.

I think it is great that lawyers flock to mindfulness programs to handle stress. However, I have heard that ninja assassins learned to meditate so they could compartmentalize. They trained their minds to detach from their consciences and feelings about killing their victims. I can't confirm the story, but I can see the danger that lawyers might try to do the same. Are you viciously attacking someone in court and disconnecting from the damage to yourself and the others involved?

Reflection quiets the busy lawyer mind enough to allow in important questions about life. Music, art, and other forms of self-expression may also provide opportunities for reflection. The inner work of therapy or personal transformation work may also be part of the journey.

Of course, not all Integrative Lawyers meditate, but most Integrative Lawyers do critically reflect on the legal system. What is the purpose of law? What is my purpose as a lawyer? Is the legal process therapeutic? Does my role as lawyer express my values? Is the process aligned with my clients' values?

The ways that lawyers incorporate their inner work are as varied as the people. As an example, Kristin Scheel Downes was a Texas oil and gas lawyer in a stressful job. She took up yoga to relieve stress and soon became a yoga teacher. When she left the law firm a few years later, she opened her own combination of law firm and yoga studio. Later, she relocated and shifted to working as a lawyer, empowering values-based businesses, while continuing to practice yoga.

PURPOSE AND VALUES

Taking time to quiet the chaos of the lawyer-mind often leads a lawyer to inquire into her own purpose and values, to explore the purpose of law, and to ask the questions that lead to living aligned with those values.

In my early law practice, I was working with a coach when I identified myself as a Peacemaker . . . and then I wondered how in the world could I design a law practice based on that. The question led me to explore not only my own purpose and values, but those of my clients. I added questions to my intake forms, such as "What are your most cherished values?" Knowing this, I was much better able to represent what was important to my client—not just what he could get in a case, but what would reflect what he actually wanted.

Integrative Lawyers are inclined to believe that integrity is vital to the well-being of themselves and society. They encourage integrity in their clients' matters. We do have some values in common: listening, compassion, dignity, inclusivity, being relational, happiness, well-being, and love. We're inclined to focus on the future. Our values have influenced what we do and how we practice.

Our values tend to be intrinsic, not extrinsic. Research has shown that the law school ethos tends to sway students toward the prestige of a big law partnership with its corner office. Integrative lawyers seek to align with important intrinsic principles that guide their lives and how they practice law.

Estate-planning lawyer Sean Mason of California was doing some personal transformation work when he created his life purpose as Love. He began to tell people that the purpose of his law firm was to *help his clients show their love for those who are most important to them*. He even put his purpose on his website. Concerned about the potential impact of talking openly about love, he kept close financial records. He earned 70 percent more money the first year and greatly improved his quality of life and the lives of his clients.

Marque Lawyers in Sydney, Australia, was founded by lawyers who had reached the peak of their successful careers only to find that they were not happy. They left their traditional firms and created a new law firm with the purpose of happiness. One of the first things that was on their to-do list: doing away with the billable hour. They've been leaders in fixed fee services in Australia. The Happiness purpose has extended to even the design of their offices. There is no corner office. Rather, office spaces are assigned by lottery. They work in an open plan. The centerpiece of their office is a coffee bar and there are informal places to sit scattered around the office. They invite artists to be in residence, because they find it useful and entertaining to hang out with creative people. They are the only law firm to conduct an entire hiring campaign by Twitter. Applicants are instructed that they should not send resumes but instead show how their unique skills (like playing the saxophone or cooking Korean food) will make Marque a happier community.

THINKING SYSTEMICALLY

Integrative Lawyers often have an experience of the interconnectedness of all things. They believe they are part of a system where each person has the power to make a difference. They recognize that society is becoming more complex and that it is necessary to embrace the complexity while seeking to make the law understandable and workable.

We realize that there are many stakeholders in every conflict. We see that collaboration and cooperation are more workable than divisiveness and polarization. Integrative Lawyers default to collaborative approaches to problems, but are not afraid to take stands. We understand that full self-expression can lead to conflict, and that, when approached consciously, can be prevented or resolved in ways that are productive and preserve the relationships between all stakeholders.

We don't have to agree with one another to be kind to each other and grant dignity to Life. Often in systems change work, the quest is to find the pivot points where small change can lead to big shifts. One such example has become emblematic: the story of how wolves changed the rivers in Yellowstone National Park. Reintroducing the wolves catalyzed a cascade of changes that actually altered the course of the river.[3] (The four-minute video is well worth your time.)

HARBINGERS OF A NEW CULTURAL CONSCIOUSNESS AND LEADERS IN SOCIAL EVOLUTION

Integrative Law isn't just about legal procedures. It has to do with a fundamental shift in worldview and models that express the shift. Integrative Lawyers are leaders in an integral worldview that honors the wisdom and best parts of all previous worldviews while embracing emergent new ideas. Integrative lawyers bring this consciousness into the law and are partners with our colleagues in other disciplines. We are open to exploring and drawing upon many disciplines and wisdom traditions, such as philosophy, science, metaphysics, psychology, and spirituality.

INTEGRATIVE LAW IN ACTION: BECOMING THE CHANGEMAKERS

For most integrative lawyers, it is a natural progression to adopt or invent new models of practicing. As more than one lawyer told me, "I woke up one morning and I couldn't do it the old way; I had to find a new way to practice law that aligned with who I am." They are the lawyers whose purposes and values didn't fit the old paradigm. Rather than leave, they've created something new based on their own purpose and values.

I am always inspired and amazed at the creativity of lawyers. Often similar approaches will emerge simultaneously, without contact between the inventors. For example, the trend toward using images in legal documents seems to have independently originated on three continents at about the same time. In South Africa, lawyer Rob de Rooy created a Comic Contract, in the format of a comic book. He was inspired by the need to have clear agreements with domestic workers, many of whom had low levels of literacy in English. Across the ocean, Professor Camilla Andersen was incorporating visuals into contracts, too. About the same time, in India, lawyers and sisters Kanan and Keli Dhru created Lawtoons, a comic book to educate the public on legal issues. Using multisensory legal tools for educating clients arose synchronously, too. Rajesh Deoli uses music to teach legal principles to members of

---

3. *See* https://vimeo.com/86466357 or the Yellowstone site: http://www.yellowstonepark.com /wolf-reintroduction-changes-ecosystem/.

traditional legal communities in Northern India. In Spain, Javier Torán Zufía uses dance as a tool for creating harmony in relationships.

We really don't know how many Integrative Lawyers there are. The term is new enough and the group is emergent enough that many of the most "integrative" are not even aware of the label. I can tell you this: there are more than you think and we are not alone. I know that because I meet more of them than I ever imagined and I started out pretty optimistic. And we're a pretty diverse crowd, covering the globe, all practice areas, and a lot of personality types.

While we don't actually know how many of us there are, we do have some measures. Many of our approaches fall within the field of Alternative Dispute Resolution. The American Bar Association Section on Dispute Resolution website reports that they have 19,000 members. (The Litigation Section has about three times as many.) Jim Melamed of Mediate.com, the largest mediation site in the world, told me that he believes there are about 50,000 mediators in the world, and I'd say that the majority of mediators are lawyers. Tens of thousands of lawyers have now been trained in collaborative law around the world. Problem-solving courts now exist in more than 20 countries and there are thousands of them in the United States, with numbers growing steadily.

I've literally written books on the various models of Integrative Law. For sake of illustration in this chapter, I am including descriptions of some of the models that have emerged and taken hold. There are many others.

RESTORATIVE JUSTICE

Restorative justice (RJ) is not a particular program but an approach to justice. RJ takes a broader view of those affected by crime than the traditional judicial system provides. RJ helps victims, survivors, offenders, and communities to take a proactive approach to crime and engages all parties involved in the healing process after a crime has been committed. It can be utilized in crimes of severe violence or non-violent crimes as well as with juvenile offenders.

In most RJ programs, the victims or the victim's family are given an opportunity to fully share the harm caused by the offender. The process facilitates the offender taking full responsibility for his or her actions. This may be through a direct or indirect dialogue with the victim, the victim's family, and/or the community.

Unlike the traditional judicial system, restorative justice acknowledges that crime effects the persons directly involved as well as the community—in the traditional justice system, crime is treated as an offense against the state (i.e., Joe Smith vs. State of California). The victim becomes a witness in the government's case, not the owner of the process.

A restorative justice approach has traditionally been used by indigenous communities to maintain a unified community, while holding standards of conduct and addressing harms done to its community members and the community as a whole.

Some common restorative justice programs include:

- Restorative School Discipline and Anti-Bullying Programs
- Truth and Reconciliation Commissions
- Peace-making circles
- Community justice programs
- Family-group conferencing

- Sentencing circles
- Restorative Community Service
- Victim-Offender Conferencing
- Victim-Offender Mediation/Dialogue

COLLABORATIVE PRACTICE

Collaborative Law is a method of practicing law where the parties and the lawyers representing them sign a contract in which they agree to work towards settlement. If the parties are unable to settle and adversarial proceedings are to be filed, the lawyers are required to withdraw. New lawyers must be obtained for trial. In this method, the attorneys must focus on settlement and are free to use their creative problem-solving skills.

Communication is respectful and the process is future-focused. It works best if several lawyers in the community are trained in collaborative law so there are options for the clients and lawyers to work together.

Collaborative Law was created by Stu Webb, a Minnesota family lawyer. Stu was tired of the adversarial system and the damage it was doing—that *he* was doing. He was ready to leave the practice of law when he came up with an idea. In 1990, he wrote a letter to the Minnesota Supreme Court, which included this:

> . . . you and I have both experienced, I'm sure, those occasional times, occurring usually by accident, when in the course of attempting to negotiate a family law settlement, we find ourselves in a conference with the opposing counsel, and perhaps the respective clients, where the dynamics were such that in a climate of positive energy, creative alternatives were presented. In that context, everyone contributed to a final settlement that satisfied all concerned—and everyone left the conference feeling high energy, good feelings and satisfaction. More than likely, the possibility for a change in the way the parties related to each other in the future may have greatly increased. As a result, the lawyers may also develop a degree of trust between them that might make future dealings more productive.
>
> So my premise has been: why not create this settlement climate deliberately? I propose doing this by creating a context for settling family law matters by, where possible, removing the trial aspects from consideration initially. I would do this by creating a coterie of lawyers who would agree to take cases, on a case-by-case basis, for settlement only.[4]

Collaborative Law is suitable for many types of law, and lawyers are applying it to many civil contexts: probate, employment, medical error, and business. Still, it most often occurs in the domestic area.

PROBLEM-SOLVING COURTS

Integrative Law seeks best outcomes for clients and broader society. It often integrates elements of the old legal system with new ideas and perspectives. The judges who created the first drug courts saw that the old system of putting offenders in jail

---

4. *See* Adam B. Cordover, THE ORIGINS OF COLLABORATIVE DIVORCE: STU WEBB'S LETTER FAMILY DIPLOMACY | A COLLABORATIVE LAW FIRM (2016), http://familydiplomacy.com/the-origins-of-collaborative-divorce-stu-webbs-letter/.

for drug addiction didn't work. They modified the courts to focus on healing and resolving the underlying problem of addiction. They brought in the expertise of addiction specialists, social workers, and even neuroscientists to get to the underlying issues in addiction. The new models have saved millions in taxpayer dollars and have returned productive citizens to their families and communities.

Drug courts focus on addiction, but the model has extended to other societal problems. Other problem-solving courts focus on domestic violence, driving while intoxicated, homelessness, child support, veterans with PTSD, and many other recurring issues. They have broad-reaching impact.

To consider the difference in drug treatment court and the punitive courts, imagine that our client, Doris, is a drug addict. She is the single mother of two children. She used to have a job, but her addiction has taken over. In desperation, she steals her neighbor's checkbook and forges checks to get cash to buy drugs. When she is arrested, her children go to foster care. The punitive system is likely to send her to jail. If so, she may never get the children back and chances are she won't get off drugs in jail. When she comes out of jail with a record, no job, no place to go, and no children, she is likely to return to prison, a revolving door.

Instead, Doris is given the opportunity to participate in drug treatment court. She is helped to get into a rehab program. She comes to court often, being recognized for her successes and encouraged to stay clean. Caseworkers help her get a job and find a place to live. With their support, she kicks the drug habit. Her children are eventually returned to her. After 18 months in the program, she attends her graduation. Her family and friends come to celebrate with her . . . maybe even that neighbor whose checkbook she stole.

Drug courts have been so successful that recidivism rates are dropping and some states have closed prisons for lack of inmates.[5] Drug courts cost less than incarceration. The long-term impact on the children being raised by a functioning mother rather than in foster care is priceless.

SHARING LAW

Janelle Orsi is the author of *The Sharing Solution: How to Save Money, Simplify Your Life & Build Community* and *Practicing Law in the Sharing Economy: Helping People Build Cooperatives, Social Enterprise, and Local Sustainable Economies* (ABA). She is a sharing lawyer working in the sharing and collaborative economy. Sharing law is an area of law Janelle invented right after law school graduation. Sharing law supports legal approaches to living together in thriving, interactive communities. For example, imagine that your neighborhood wants to start a tool library. Everyone collects their ladders and carpet shampooers, those tools and equipment that are rarely used, and they consolidate all those items into a common shed. Now, what happens? Who is responsible if the ladder breaks due to poor maintenance?

---

5. *See,* for example, Ojmarrh Mitchell et al., *Assessing the Effectiveness of Drug Courts on Recidivism: A Meta-Analytic Review of Traditional and Non-Traditional Drug Courts,* 40 JOURNAL OF CRIMINAL JUSTICE 60–71 (2012); *As Inmate Population Continues to Fall, Florida Will Close 7 Prisons and 4 Work Camps,* FLAGLERLIVE (2012), https://flaglerlive.com/33002/florida-prison-population/. The closing of prisons was attributed to drug courts in a conversation between the author and a member of the governor's cabinet in 2012.

What if a neighbor fails to return an item? The sharing lawyer helps sort out those situations, along with more complex issues.

Janelle Orsi's first book, published by NOLO Press, includes legal advice and forms for those who wish to create neighborhoods where people share cars, live in intentional communities, start tool libraries and create cooperatively owned businesses. Her second book has been an ABA best-seller.

EARTH LAW

Many lawyers who explore what is most important to them find themselves with concerns for the Earth. They realize that climate change is related to the lack of connection and respect for the Earth. As Scottish barrister Polly Higgins says, "The Earth is in need of a good lawyer." Higgins advocates for a law of ecocide as a crime against peace, prohibiting extensive damage, destruction to or loss of human and non-human life.

South African Cormac Cullinan, an international environmental law attorney and consultant and the author of *Wild Law: A Manifesto for Earth Justice* (Green Books), is an advocate for recognizing the rights of nature. The idea has international support, and more than one country has included Nature's Rights in their constitutions and legislation.

Rights of Nature honors the Earth's rights. It is the recognition that our ecosystems—including trees, oceans, animals, mountains—have rights just as human beings have rights. Rights of Nature is about balancing what is good for human beings against what is good for other species, what is good for the planet as a world. It is the holistic recognition that all life, all ecosystems on our planet, are deeply intertwined. Rather than treating nature as property under the law, rights of nature acknowledges that nature in all its life forms has the right to exist, persist, maintain, and regenerate its vital cycles.[6]

The Whanganui River in New Zealand has become a legal entity with a legal voice. Two guardians, a member of the government and a member of an indigenous Iwi people, have been appointed with power to speak for the river. In India, two other rivers, the Ganges and Yamuna, have been declared to be legal persons and there are many pending actions for similar actions in other countries. If corporations can be people, why not rivers? (See also Christopher Stone's book, *Should Trees Have Standing?* published by Oxford University Press.)

VALUES-BASED CONTRACTS

Values-based contracts integrate values with legal provisions. They begin with a recitation of the meeting of the minds: values, shared goals, and a system for addressing change and engaging conflict to establish a sustainable relationship. (Or sometimes, the parties discover they're not on the same page after all and walk away before they're intertwined.)

Values-based contracts help provide clarity, safety, and predictability. The parties to the contract actually design a system for engaging conflict that aligns with their values. They can incorporate plain language drafting. They may include visuals

---

6. The Rights of Nature, http://therightsofnature.org/what-is-rights-of-nature/.

such as artwork that will help clarify the text. Many of these contracts look more like marketing documents, with colorful headings and relational language.

Unlike the typical contract that stays in a drawer until it is wielded as a weapon, they're living, breathing documents that focus on sustainable relationships. They recognize the reality of complex business environments, rapid change, and need for conscious communication.

ENGAGING CHALLENGES

There is a lot more to the transformation of the legal profession than just adopting another model. While I previously thought the key was peacemaking, I have met litigators who have clearly transformed their lives and practices in ways that felt integrative and evolutionary.

Being integrative is more of an issue of deportment and the unseen. A lot of what it takes to be an integrative lawyer isn't what you learn in a classroom; it isn't like the bar exam where analytical knowledge is measured. It isn't a certification or a list of books someone has read. How do you measure listening? How do you measure creativity or emotional maturity? What tools tell us about consciousness?

We can recognize when someone is connecting with us, but we don't necessarily have measures to gauge that. I have encountered many lawyers who had not made the paradigm shift, who took the integrative procedures into four-way meetings without also bringing the mindset.

The process of evolution feels slow to those who envision a better world, but with consistency and determination, momentum can be reached. I compare it to riding a bicycle up a steep hill. We undertake that hill in our personal lives and in our practices. We may put in a lot of effort in the beginning, but eventually we reach a point where something shifts and we can move faster. Soon, we're gliding down the hill, not sure why it took so much energy to get there.

CHAPTER 26
Heal the System, Heal Thyself

Marguerite Picard, Esq.

Editor's Note: I was connected to Marguerite by Kim Wright. The original title of this chapter was something to the effect of "What If It's Not About the Yoga," which unequivocally says it's the system that the lemmings are doing their best to adapt to—and not the individuals. It was refreshing to hear that because I quite agree in most cases. (That said, there are some situations for which battle is the best way. When the gorilla says let's fight, you don't have much of a choice, even though it's your least favored alternative.) Marguerite has lived in an alternative universe she has created. It stands as a model others can emulate.

Mainstream media tells us that depression and anxiety are the new normal for lawyers. Each one of us can contribute to healing the well-being issues for lawyers that have been brought about by systems that no longer serve us. We can all adopt new business practices, business models, billing practices, and alternative problem solving processes that avoid the emotional cost of a time-based adversarial system. There is now a large international discussion about changes to the legal system, rich with information and inspiration for the sharing.

I am a lawyer who exited the mainstream. I rescue couples and business partners in dispute from the belief they have a legal problem and need to see a lawyer first. I established MELCA with a financial advisor and psychologist in 2009. Our mission: changing the way families and businesses experience separation and conflict and setting them up for a positive future based on values of compassion, integrity, and excellence. We see whole families and business partnerships as our clients, and we view separation as an emotional crisis, not a legal problem. I am an accredited family law specialist, a collaborative practitioner, a mediator, and arbitrator.

VICTIM BLAMING? DON'T LET IT FEEL THAT WAY

There are countless reports of those who have considered giving up or actually given up the practice of law, suffering from work-related mental or physical ill health. In the reporting, the attraction of the intellectual challenge of law is seen as inevitably bound up with stress, pressure, anxiety, fears, doubts, and the fruitless search for "work-life balance."

By way of prevention, legal firms are urged not to eat their young, to "support" their lawyers, to provide "flexible workplaces" and family friendly practices. They are warned about the occupational health and safety risks of toxic, bullying, and stressful workplaces. They are told broadly and vaguely that there will be long-term savings to their bottom line if they take seriously the mental health of their lawyers.

Individual lawyers are urged by their membership groups, law societies, and employers to be aware of their well-being. They are advised to seek "support," to invest in mindfulness practices, to aim for work-life balance, to look for meaning in their lives outside of work. In other words, to find ways to stay within the system as it is. The implication is that it is the individual who is responsible, who is "not managing," or who is unable to appropriately respond to the stressors. Is this the language of personal responsibility or of victim blaming?

Not every lawyer experiences negative effects and unacceptable challenges in their working life, but there are enough who do to warrant an examination about whether it is the system or the lawyers who need to change. So far, the balance of the discourse puts that burden on the individual's response rather than on a systemic response, and many of us stand in solidarity with lawyers who are struggling with these challenges. You are the victim, not the architect!

PUSHING AGAINST THE STATUS QUO

What has not yet been fully developed is a discussion about changing the structural causes of the well-being deficits of lawyers, which makes for a more difficult conversation; one that needs to happen at policy and government level, and which is disempowering for individuals struggling to be okay with the status quo.

Today, the negative health challenges for lawyers focus on the twin harms of an adversarial system married to time costing. Much has been said about that by others.

There are heroic examples of change makers in the Appropriate Dispute Resolution world, modeling the possibility of alternative systems, and there are strong voices modeling alternatives to the billable hour and engaging with artificial intelligence to give both value and meaning in work. But it remains the case that the vast majority of legal firms are still asking their lawyers to sell time.

Governments and the legal profession as a whole have yet to embrace a discussion about how fundamentally new systems and work practices might deliver benefits for organizational and personal well-being.

ADVERSARIAL SYSTEMS AND PROBLEM SOLVING: INCOMPATIBLE BEDFELLOWS?

I came into law buying into the idea that lawyers and the legal system are problem solvers. I suppose I believed, all those years ago, that's what courts did in delivering adjudications. I don't subscribe to that any longer, and playing that game is incompatible with my mental health. I know I am not alone.

I now see it as not only dysfunctional, but supremely ironic that a system that is designed to solve problems starts by doing everything it can to polarize the disputants. The system puts both litigants in their own corners, defending their positions, from which they cannot afford to move or step down.

In what other system do we solve problems by polarization of arguments, other than as an exercise in analysis? Problem solving generally starts with root cause analysis, which is quite different from the data. As all lawyers know, data is the place where adversarial law starts to look at problems. It is the weapon by which one party will win, it is not the tool that will solve the actual problem. The law never does solve the actual problem, only the presenting problem, because the human behavior or drivers that create private law disputes are beyond the scope of law and lawyers' training and skills.

You may ask if it matters that the rules of litigation are different from the rules of other problem-solving methodologies. I think it does matter. Lawyers meet clients who have problems. Clients ask lawyers to solve their problems. The emotional and financial resources spent by litigants in data wars can be fruitless and disproportionate, are brutally affected by economic power imbalances, and the wars are often won by attrition. We know that, because we have the data about the low number of cases that make it to final hearing, and we know that it is not because litigants have actually resolved their conflict.

For many lawyers, the personal effects of conflict and a system that can't actually deliver create dissonance.

THE SEARCH FOR TRUTH: UNSTABLE BEDROCK

As a problem-solving method, litigation starts in the wrong place.

After not-so-many years in practice, I was more interested in looking for common ground and mutual and varied solutions in my cases. The system, though, is hung up on the impossible dream of empirical evidence and absolute truth. The futility and cost of that elusive search for truth via personal testimony stopped making sense to me a long time ago.

One of the few valuable lessons I can recall from my days at law school was an experiment conducted on us in which we had to give our recall of an intrusion into the lecture theatre by an unknown person, who spoke briefly to the lecturer and then left. (Thank you, Professor Richard Fox, Monash University.) Immediately, in the dissection of the event, it was beyond doubt that personal testimony is indeed personal! Was the sweater red or blue? What words were said? Were any words said? Did the intruder have a beard? Was he blonde or brunette? As I recall it, the only aspect agreed on by the group was the gender of the individual.

As a result of this experiment and further reading, I had stopped believing in the law of evidence as it related to personal recall and observation before I began practising. That made life uncomfortable! What I have since learned about memory—and observed in my own clients' tellings of their marriages and separations and business disputes—affirms that litigation is often founded on the most unreliable of bases. Litigation lawyers live this tension every day. It is no wonder trials that include competing personal testimony can be heart-stopping.

LITIGATING YOUR VALUES OUT OF EXISTENCE?

Maybe litigation is "healthy" stress for many lawyers? But what happens personally when the rules of the game conflict with a lawyer's own values?

For me, the hollowness of the promise that I could be a problem-solver in the traditional system, sitting alongside the knowledge that another game the client didn't sign up for was about to be played, was at odds with my values of honesty and helpfulness. By the time a matter gets to a court, there is the original problem and the one you have in the legal system. They are often not the same, and for me that felt like a fib.

The adversarial system has the potential to damage lawyers by placing them in conflict with other people and often their own values, as well as their sense of responsibility for what it does to their clients. This won't be true for all lawyers, or for all cases, but it was true for me.

COLLABORATION AND MEDIATION AS THE ANTIDOTE

My response to a lack of belief in adversarial law, time costing, and the challenge to my ethical and other values was initially to call it a day and work in something I enjoyed. The problem was, I actually enjoyed law as I understood it could be practiced.

So I found a way to remain a lawyer and to enjoy it.

With my financial planner and psychologist colleagues, Tricia Peters and Dr. Tina Sinclair, I founded MELCA in 2009 as a collaborative practice for separating families. We are a one-stop shop for all services families and people with business disputes need when they separate. Our primary commitment at MELCA is to keep them out of court by working in mediation and with collaborative teams.

The keys to my improved satisfaction and well-being are in having been able to create a sustainable business that has as its hallmarks:

- Collaborative practice and mediation
- Interdisciplinary teamwork
- Value pricing
- A practice that pays the same rate to lawyers as to all of the other valued team members
- Not being a law firm, but contracting in the professional services

My motivation for leaving traditional practice was multi-faceted, but essentially boils down to needing to find my own herd so that I could work constructively with separating families and people in conflict, look for common ground, and reduce the harms to all, by staying out of court.

I wanted to be able to deliver what I promised. To do that, I needed to be able to work with new rules, have my colleagues understand and agree to those same rules, and above all to mean what I said and say what I meant about the options I gave to clients.

For years before I left old law, I would wonder who my opposing lawyer would be, and based on that I would be able to gauge how difficult the case would be. Melbourne is not a small town. There are more than five million people in this state, and about 20,000 lawyers. So my concerns were not restricted to a clique of "difficult" practitioners. It was about the rules of court and the lack of rules for non-court negotiation. And what I found is that despite their self-belief, lawyers as a group have quite primitive negotiation skills.

It has been a great relief to me to work with collaborative lawyers who share my values, and whom I do not think of as "opposing." It has been an even greater relief not to have to field ongoing questions from clients about how much their case would cost—having to limit those discussions to one about an hourly rate and my promise to be efficient, but all the time knowing I had no control over how costs might escalate.

THE WELL-BEING BONUSES

The unexpected bonuses of creating MELCA have been:

- Developing a new awareness of just how crucial the role of the psychologists and financial planners are in separation, when those roles are allowed to play out to their best advantage
- The building of a collaborative community
- Representing the light on the hill in this town for other changemakers

THE DENOUNCED BILLABLE HOUR

We should not avoid talking to and about those who have a vested interest in the continuation of the billable hour, whatever the cost to lawyer's well-being. Partners in law firms have a huge investment in the billable hour as a costing method. It is simple in concept, measurable, and a ranking tool. And it delivers. How it delivers!

Like the greater issue of lawyers' well-being, this costing method has been thoroughly challenged, tested, and found wanting by Ron Baker, John Chisholm, Richard Susskind, Kim Wright, and others. Suffice to say I'm on their team. Litigation challenged my values, but nothing challenged my values like time costing did.

I much preferred the method of my first boss, who measured the thickness of a file and gave it a price per inch, or his friend who weighed his files on a bathroom scale and gave it a price per pound. I'm not sure there was any disclosure about these "methods," but nor were there any complaints, and both employers seemed to make a fair living.

Most non-lawyers can't imagine the daily horror of your PC blinking at you every hour telling you how your monthly time target is stacking up. Nor would they believe the confronting challenge of the "numbers person" suggesting that any deficits be made up by "sprinkling a few hours around" your files. For many lawyers, there is great and unwelcome pressure to bill unreasonably, without any eye for the value of the work, and to dabble with dishonesty, because the bankers are in charge.

THE HEALTH DOWNSIDES OF THE BILLABLE HOUR

I'm not the first or last to say that the billable hour is a personal tyranny. It is a challenge because of the lack of scrutiny, the lack of any measures about the worth of work done, and the implication in the model that it is to serve the firm and not the client. When I was a young lawyer, there was a firm that billed in 15-minute units, and it was legendary that many of them went home or to lunch at 11 am, because they had billed a day's work. Does this matter? It did to me, and I found it unethical. As a member of the profession, I choose not to be associated with the six-minute unit.

Stephanie West-Allen (Dean of Neuro-Science and Contemplative Practise) talks about the negative health effects of the billable hour. She argues that it affects all of your life, as an ingrained habit, right down to thinking of your personal life in units of time, whether that's your shower or your child's soccer game. She sees it as devastating to your personal life. She quotes Jeffrey M. Schwartz (PPI online seminar) as describing billable hours and time sheets as a form of self-inflicted OCD.

But there's more.

The billable hour encourages a feeding frenzy amongst lawyers in a firm, who are in competition with each other for promotion. They don't share, they don't problem solve together, they conceal their numbers, and they manifest other negative behaviors. The general public may see law firms as collective enterprises, but they are not; they are a series of silos, often housing lonely and stressed individuals.

OPTING FOR CHANGE?

There are increasing numbers of law firms that are moving away from time costing to some form of value or fixed pricing.

More and more practices and practitioners are finding new ways of practicing law that don't involve the adversarial system: collaboration, mediation, sharing law, conscious contracts, preventative law, problem-solving courts, and structured negotiation, to name a few. These practices confer individual benefits, and model possible change for others.

ARTIFICIAL INTELLIGENCE (AI) AND NEW LAW: A TOOL FOR GOOD

Australia has recently seen Adrian Cartland launch his law firm without lawyers, using a responsive Artificially Intelligent (AI) Legal Information Research Assistant. There are now numerous AI products on the market, which will free lawyers from less interesting work and allow billing based on value rather than time.

Ten years ago these stories belonged to a far distant future, and they were and are largely seen as a threat to the profession. I think AI is good news and highlights opportunities for lawyers to be creative, to focus on their client relationships, and to partner with their clients in developing systems and projects that are of mutual interest and benefit. There is liberation in not being the keeper of the knowledge, and being able to have the mundane tasks in legal practice done more quickly and accurately than we can do without technical help.

SYSTEMS, OLD AND NEW

It is my belief that the most likely way in which there will be systemic change to existing systems will be when people opt out of it into alternative processes. They are already doing that because access to regular "justice" is now well beyond the financial reach of the majority, and because the cost of access is even growing beyond the capacity of government. But it won't be only client-driven responses that change systems. Those of us on the inside have the chance to see threats as opportunities, to decide to live our values and to know that in doing so there are many lawyers who feel and are doing the same.

New systems are emerging and new practices are developing as lawyers look to heal themselves and the system. I look forward to the time when the shift to healthier systems is universal. Let's run towards that tipping point and control our own destiny rather than leaving that to fate.

CHAPTER 27
The Lawyer's Oath
Stewardship of Democracy

Cheryl L. Conner, MAE, JD

Editor's Note: I met Cheryl at a retreat for progressive lawyers around 1995. I have always appreciated her intelligence and creativity. Talking with her is like going on a multi-part journey. You never know where you'll end up, but the journey is rich, engaging, and fun. So it is with this chapter. I had no idea what she would write about, but I did want her to do a chapter. She did not disappoint. I knew about the Chorale she had produced based on the Declaration of Independence. I would not have predicted she would take us all back to the day we swore an oath. Likely we thought then it was a perfunctory necessity. She makes us all better by tying the real sanctity of that oath to both our personal and collective well-being within values of a governance structure some would say is currently under siege. Only Cheryl could evoke the duty of that oath as a reminder and call to action.

In this chapter, the author shares her reflections on the Lawyer's Oath and its call to lawyers to serve as stewards of democracy today. She suggests that its call to uphold the Constitution includes a broader call to support the constitutional democracy's values, principles, and practices in activities outside the lawyer–client relationship. Examples from her life and the life of two American Revolutionary patriots suggest myriad ways in which American democracy can be re-vitalized and for citizens to experience empowered and meaningful lives. She links to her musical composition based on the Declaration of Independence.

Cheryl L. Conner is a speaker, teacher, mediator, and consultant helping others activate highest competencies as individuals and in groups and organizations. She catalyzed numerous cutting-edge initiatives in health and business. Her traditional experience is in the private and public sectors and as a university professor, researcher, and administrator. Using experience as a musician, composer, and practitioner of wisdom traditions, she offers creative approaches to conflict and governance and inspires a call to living from ever-deeper values.

Essential to a well-lived life is operating from a sense of purpose, believing that one's life and actions as a human being and as a lawyer are significant to oneself and to others. The Lawyer's Oath offers both a personal and professional purpose and, perhaps, a duty. We declared aloud when we were sworn in to the Bar that we would uphold the Constitution and the laws of our nation and respective states. We did not vow to protect any arbitrary system of laws. We took an oath, before God, to protect the laws that are the foundational DNA of a constitutional democracy. They embody and reflect specific values, principles, and processes which were believed at the time to be the best guarantors to support each individual's rights and pursuit of life, liberty, and the pursuit of happiness.

If we fulfill the Lawyer's Oath by embodying, supporting, and defending this constitutional democratic system, we can find immense satisfaction and purpose. While I didn't always take its full meaning to heart, now I see it with fresh eyes. Our nation and world face stormy seas. I believe that if we renew our Lawyer's Oaths, taking the terms to heart, each with our unique gifts and situations, we will steer this nation to fulfill the democratic aspirations of our Founders.

FANEUIL HALL

On a cool autumn afternoon, 12 of us first-year associates in a large Boston law firm descended the elevators in our tall glass skyscraper. We walked together across the brick-paved sidewalks towards the Faneuil Hall Market. In the historic Faneuil Hall building, we ascended a winding wooden staircase lined with framed pictures of historical moments. We arrived with hundreds of others wearing dark jackets and serious faces, ready to be sworn in to the Bar of the Commonwealth of Massachusetts. On the platform before us were a member of the Supreme Judicial Court, the head of the Bar Association, and several other officials. Sitting in the hard wooden folding chairs, I remember references to the history of the room; it had served as the Colony's Legislature. The most vivid memory is of the moment when hundreds of us clamored to our feet to repeat the Oath. In a sea of people, we declared the Oath aloud, phrase by phrase, responding to the appointed official. "I promise to uphold the Constitution of the United States of America and of the Commonwealth of Massachusetts, so help me God."

Before the swearing in, I had not thought about the Lawyer's Oath. In the moment, it was a ritual culmination of law school and a threshold to my career. I had not reflected on the significance of stating the oath in public, before my peers, before members of the Bar and officials, with my hand raised "before God." After the swearing in, we re-traced our steps across those same brick-paved sidewalks, past the Old State House, and up to our gleaming corporate offices. I don't remember any conversations on the significance of the Lawyer's Oath. Aware of the significance of billing each hour in six-minute intervals, we got back to business. Each of us have our own memories of swearing-ins and conversations about the Lawyer's Oath; perhaps sharing these thoughts will engender more reflection.

THE LAWYER'S OATH

Some years later, I reflected in earnest on the Lawyer's Oath. As a law professor and administrator of a Clinical Internship Program, I relished fostering on-the-job reflection and student alignment with professional and personal values. While the Code of Professional Responsibility offered some guidance towards standards of conduct, the Lawyer's Oath invited something else. I led classes, programs, and workshops in which we reflected together on the Oath, and wrote our own personal oaths and shared them in community, with heart and inspiration.

I studied the history of professional oaths back to ancient times, when doctors and lawyers stood before the Gods. The Hippocratic Oath was made invoking Aesclepius, the God of healing. One promised to do more than simply "no harm." The doctors would promise to honor their teachers, refrain from abuse of the power arising from their positions, and refrain from recommending procedures that might be unnecessary.

Standing with the hand raised before the gods, or, in the lawyers' case, "before God" struck me as significant. The right hand, closely associated with the heart, was engaged, suggesting a heart-felt and authentic desire to be of service. As the hand was raised, the fingers were pointing to the sky. The gods were expressly invoked; the declarant acknowledged the world beyond the visible and called for both guidance and support. In addition, a request was made to the gods for swift retribution if the declarant violated the oath.

Despite the separation of Church and State, the phrase "under God" still remains in the Lawyer's Oath in most states. While the significance of its inclusion to each of us may vary, depending upon one's religious or spiritual perspective, it invites us to clarify how we see ourselves in relationship to the world. The Lawyer's Oath became an object of reflection for me, because I had become a Tibetan Buddhist during my adult life. In that tradition, promises, vows, and oaths had major significance, certainly more than in the liberal Protestant tradition of my family. Tibetan Buddhists emphasize that our words literally create reality and our expressed commitments define our lives in practical, spiritual, and energetic dimensions. There were different levels of commitments calling for the generation of particular intentions—that is, to benefit others or to clear one's own heart and mind of impurities. There were commitments to practices, prayers, liturgies, and conduct for relating to others, and to daily life.

I found the lessons on commitments to be enriching. Among them was that every day that we keep our promises, we gain in "virtue," personal energy and well-being. On days we don't keep them, our actions were forgivable because one would always return to re-commit to them, to assure ourselves of the strength and potential growth afforded from returning to our oaths and commitments.

I know that during much of my professional legal career, I did not treat my Lawyer's Oath with the active respect and attention that I gave my spiritual oaths. I did choose to attend law school to benefit the world; at the time, I was focused on women's rights and economic justice. Later, I did take more specific oaths, as Asst. Attorney General, Asst. U.S. Attorney, and as Senate Counsel to the Massachusetts legislature, and those additional oaths reiterated the commitment to defend the Constitution and state laws appropriately.

In other contexts, I didn't always maintain an awareness of the significance of the more general duty and fundamental Oath that I swore to back in historic Faneuil Hall. Now I see that Oath as an initiation and mandate to authentically and fiercely defend broader Democracy, as I defend the Constitution of the United States and of the Commonwealth of Massachusetts. This Oath is relevant in every aspect of our lives, in every setting in which democratic values, principles, or practices come into play. In the workplace, the neighborhood, the courtroom, or at home, do we always see others as equal beings, "endowed by their Creator with certain inalienable rights"? I invite you to consider maintaining a deeper awareness of how our profession's collective re-energizing of our Lawyers' Oaths may be necessary to preserve our democracy.

DUTY

The notion that lawyers have fiduciary duties to our clients is well established and the Code of Professional Responsibility addresses the topic in great detail. As fiduciaries, we are stewards of clients' interests and well-being and put their interests above our own in our interactions. The Code doesn't explicitly name a broader duty of lawyers as stewards to democracy per se. It does encourage lawyers to support access to justice and to improve the legal system. Certainly active engagement on these two fronts contributes to our nation.

The needs of our Constitutional democracy include, but are not limited to, the needs of individual clients and the legal system. Our Democracy is a system of values, principles as well as legal processes; at its best it is a culture of tolerance, free religion, and free speech. It is a way of life that values varieties of experience and growth and community. It is all that the Statue of Liberty represents. It points to all of the democratic goals which we seek to live up to as well as those we regularly fall short of.

It is difficult to claim that each of us has a legally defined fiduciary duty to our Democratic system with express requirements. The Oath calls us to look to our Constitution and its history and the goals and aspirations of the Founders. "I swear that I will uphold the Constitution of the United States of American and of the Commonwealth of Massachusetts, so help me God." The Founders' primary concerns were not about escrow accounts or fee-splitting. They outlined a system to support a new nation in which free and responsible citizens could pursue their god-given rights to life, liberty, and the pursuit of happiness. Free of Empire's controlling reach, a free people would create a new government, reflecting the people's consent, and fulfilling democratic ideals touted since the early days of ancient Greece. The government would reflect the consent of the people.

Our Oaths speak to a broader obligation, a broader duty, as public professionals with the privilege of learning and practicing the law. Like our ancient ancestors, we stood before our peers, our polity, invoking the Divine, in a profound formal oath, more serious than a promise or a commitment. What does such an Oath mean in today's world, in our nation in this moment?

THE OLD STATE HOUSE AND JAMES OTIS

Not far from Faneuil Hall in Boston, where I was sworn in, is the Old State House, the original home of the Superior Court in the colony of Massachusetts. It is here that one of the first great lawyer-stewards of democracy displayed professional acumen and patriotism for our nascent nation. James Otis Jr., a Harvard-trained Boston lawyer, considered himself a subject of the British Empire but ended up becoming one of the powerful Patriot orators. Otis served as pro bono counsel for the merchants after the King of England enacted the writs of assistance. These writs permitted British officials to enter colonist homes without notice, cause or reason. Otis gave a fiery and passionate five-hour oral argument against the writs at the Old State House.

John Adams claimed that this passionate powerful argument planted the seeds of the Revolution. While Otis didn't win the argument, he became one of the powerful orators and leaders in the decade 1760–1770. He subsequently wrote articles about how the writs violated the British constitution and the Magna Carta. He also suffered recrimination for his pronouncements; he was seriously injured by a group of British mercenaries in a pub near the Customs House downtown and was left mentally and physically disabled.

THE ARTS AND MERCY OTIS WARREN

James Otis Jr.'s injuries spurred the outrage of his classically educated sister, Mercy Otis Warren, who then amplified her own patriotic activities. Living in Plymouth with her husband, Patriot James Warren, she wrote political plays satirizing King George. These were distributed in chapters at local general stores around the Commonwealth and read aloud in people's homes. She wrote poetry and a history of the American Revolution, and she was instrumental in creating the Committees of Correspondence, which fortified both the community necessary to sustain a revolution and created the legacy of crimes committed by the King, subsequently outlined in the Declaration of Independence. After the Constitution was written, she was the only woman to publish an essay criticizing its omission of rights for women, blacks, and Indians. She was an artist and steward of democracy. I have read much of her work and can attest that she was as smart as any lawyer I have known.

Through oral argument, the arts, and community organizing, this family displayed stewardship for a nascent system emerging in the colonial consciousness. As Mercy would say, she engaged in the battle to assure that individual freedom would be victorious over political control, reason would win out over passion, and virtue would be victorious over excess.

THE LOS ANGELES COUNTY REGISTRY OF VOTING

Last June, as a new resident of California, I registered to vote in the June Presidential Primary. Two days before the primary, I responded to an appeal by local clean election groups for volunteer poll auditors. I replied that as a lawyer, licensed to practice only in Massachusetts, I was unfamiliar with California election law but could help as a "citizen." On the day before the primary, many of us addressed the fact that registrars were issuing inaccurate poll worker education materials. On the day of the primary, many of us were auditing and counting the number of voters who showed up at the polls to find their voter registration missing. The day after the race was called, many of us rolled up our sleeves because there were still 250,000 ballots uncounted in Los Angeles alone and several times that in the whole state. In the next 30 days, hundreds of volunteers came to oversee the ballot-counting process in counties around the state. Clean election NGOs reported many irregularities. Four lawsuits were filed to challenge procedures. Reports were distributed to media and politicians and they were unable to penetrate the allure of the media's new focus, not on California's significant unfinished vote count, but on whether the loser would concede. A newcomer to the strengths and weaknesses of our election system, I emerged wiser about it.

Lawyer stewardship of democracy can emerge a million ways. I have found meaning helping religious dissidents from the federal health care bill find their voice and explore their options. I have felt the exhilaration of consulting with those organizing 1000 volunteers to help monitor the ballot counting described above. I have felt the joy of helping a non-profit elder care facility bring democratic decision-making to the seniors living there. I have been proud when a class of graduating MBA students joyfully explored how to move beyond top-down leadership to systems-based sociocratic models.

Each day there are opportunities to educate people about their rights and assure that legal and political processes work properly. We can help neighbors learn how to challenge parking tickets or encourage corporations to adopt employee ownership. Current times may ask us to be even more committed and engaged.

STEWARDING DEMOCRACY

The Lawyer's Oath we declared aloud in public invokes the legacy of the profession as well as the foundational laws of our constitutional democracy. I believe that in community we share a fiduciary duty among lawyers to our democracy. Together we constitute a democracy stewardship collective. Just as stewards of property and homesteads maintain ongoing interests for current users, they also share a duty to future users. Environmentalists regularly invoke a call to stewardship of the earth and its constituent parts for now and forever. Churches talk about stewarding the life of the current church for future generations. And so it is. Lawyers possess understanding and skills about our political legal system that exceed those of many citizens. We serve our clients and our neighbors, no doubt. But, do we feel the call as a collective stewardship of our democracy? What would it look like if each one of us acted today as stewards of the whole democracy? What if we stewarded democracy as if our own lives depended on it? What if we stewarded democracy as if all of our lives, and all that we believed in, depended on it?

THE DECLARATION OF INDEPENDENCE, PHILADELPHIA, 1776

There have been times in recent years when my heart strings were pulled as I observed this great nation undertaking actions I believe were hurtful. When the human rights violations at Guantanamo Bay were revealed, I was despondent. I started meditating on the Declaration of Independence, hoping to find inspiration and understanding. I read it every day for a month and then began to hear music along with the text. The next thing I knew, I had composed a choral piece for communities to sing (https://www.youtube.com/watch?v=0du6qyjREVM).

As I write to you lawyers today about stewarding democracy, phrases of the Declaration of Independence and that Chorale come to mind. The Founders declared for posterity that all men are created equal with certain unalienable rights. Governments are instituted to "secure those rights of Life, Liberty and the pursuit of Happiness." "But whenever any Form of Government becomes destructive of these ends, it is the Right of the People to alter or to abolish it and to institute new Government." Is the government reflecting the will of the people? Is it acting for us, in accord with our consent?

The Founders listed in detail the injuries, usurpations, and abuses of the King, which they believed constituted his "Tyranny over the States." They let the "Facts be submitted to a candid world." What Facts would you submit today, to show your concern about whether our government is reflecting the "consent of the governed"?

Reading the Declaration and the Constitution reminds us of our Democracy's DNA. What else will I do to steward its integrity and vitality? Advocating election reform? Representing citizen plaintiffs in court in election cases, like James Otis? Getting more groups to sing my chorale based on the Declaration, using art to inspire community and action, like Mercy Otis Warren?

Life is full simply with work, family, and daily life. These times call us to stretch, as did the circumstances in the 1760s and 70s. After the Founders reflected on their "situation" and listed grievances against the Crown, they came together as a collective. "We . . . appeal to the Supreme Judge of the World for the rectitude of our intentions . . . and publish and declare that we are and ought to be free and independent States. All political connection between ourselves and the Crown is and ought to be totally dissolved." These words harbor strength and conviction. The Founders became rebels and visionaries, of necessity. "When in the course of human events, it becomes necessary for a people" to take action, they did.

The last sentence of the Declaration shows even more about the nature of the Founders' commitment to create and steward democracy; it continues to bring tears to my eyes. It reads: "And for the support of this Declaration, with a firm reliance on the protection of Divine Providence, **we mutually pledge to each other our Lives, our Fortunes and our sacred Honor.**"

What will we mutually pledge to each other? When we were sworn in, as a group, we raised our hands before God and pledged to support the Constitution of the United States and our home state. What does that Oath portend for this moment? What would the Founders do?

AFTERWORD
Risky Business
Staying Relational in a Transactional World

Louise Phipps Senft, Esq.

Editor's Note: I originally approached Louise for an endorsement. When she looked at the manuscript, she decided she belonged in the book. Even though it was way past deadline, I spoke with the publisher and they agreed to include her wonderful afterword. I so appreciate her clarity, courage, and commitment.

The chapter serves to bring full circle the first chapter in which Larry Krieger shares his empirical research revealing that what makes for happy lawyers are the personal and professional relationships that touch their lives. I'm so pleased we included Louise. She uses the opportunity to provoke lawyers to move from the transactional to the relational. It is a fundamental, foundational message for being a better lawyer. You must care for others!

Louise has given us a condensed version of her best-selling book (*Being Relational: The Seven Ways to Quality Interaction & Lasting Change*, Health Communications Inc. 2015) about being relational that captures all that is contributed in the previous chapters and more. In her book she synthesizes the best of self-help and mindfulness and science, something lawyers are not apt to seek as often as they could or perhaps should, and in this afterword, she challenges us to act in alignment naming the adversarial ethic in a transactional world that will push back. Louise invites us to be aware of the

Louise Phipps Senft, Founder and CEO of Baltimore Mediation, voted "Baltimore's Best" Mediator by *Baltimore Magazine* 2002 and named one of "Maryland's Top 100 Women" for 2004 and 2007 and 2009 by *The Daily Record*, and inducted into Maryland's "Circle of Excellence" for outstanding leadership in Maryland, and chosen for the Spirited Woman Award by the American Red Cross, MyCity4Her, and the *Baltimore Business Journal* in 2011, founded the Baltimore Mediation Center in 1993, the first mediation firm in Maryland with a focus on relational approaches to conflict resolution. In 2007, Ms. Senft, also an attorney, was honored with one of the *Baltimore Business Journal*'s "Most Enterprising Woman" awards, and in 2009, her firm was recognized as a "Top 100 MBE" minority-owned enterprise in the Mid-Atlantic region. In 2018, she was awarded by the Maryland State Bar Association the Chief Judge Robert M. Bell Award for Outstanding Contribution to the field of Alternative Dispute Resolution in the state, and she was inducted into the International Academy of Mediators as a Distinguished Fellow. She has written extensively, has been engaged in public service beyond the call, and has been adjunct faculty at the University of Maryland Law School and other noted institutions for more than 25 years.

personal wellness bypass and take a risk in our professional practices as well as in the intimacy of our personal lives, with our colleagues and families. And she goes one step further inspiring us with her provocative theory of Relational Reciprocity.

A final note for you, fellow counsellors-at-law, a relational note of love...

Having read the thoughtful ideas in this book, you are focused and energized to foster your own well-being. You have tools and renewed inspiration for your physical, mental, emotional, and spiritual wellness to do what is good for you. You have found yourself attracted to one or two of the authors' works that called to you. Wisdom imparted in these pages is an expression of a *Relational Mindset*. The act of taking the time to read, contemplate, and consider others' voices and discern how their expertise affects your thinking and moves you to act in ways that are good for you *and for others* is relational. And for others? What benefits are the insightful self-awareness, self-management, and new forms of practice management if the new you doesn't show up differently for others? For lawyers, that means being different in our lawyering, everyday interactions, and advising clients. Lawyer wellness and well-being hinges on whether you can translate your commitment to personal wellness into a commitment to client and others' wellness as well: how you advise and advocate on behalf of and with clients and how you interact and advocate with the other side. There is more to this wellness journey and you have the capacity to do the more.

PERSONAL WELL-BEING ALIGNMENT OR PERSONAL WELLNESS BYPASS?

Every lawyer has to make choices. Imagine a practice that was aligned with your personal physical, mental, emotional, and spiritual wellness. It would be revolutionary. Benefits to you? Absolutely. Benefits to your clients? Absolutely. Expected by your clients? Requested by your clients? Not likely. That takes your courage.

Because you practice in a transactional world, your thinking is shaped by that context. Decision-making, advising, and actions are in reaction to a transactional world. Your clients come to you for legal expertise, they abdicate responsibility to you for their messes and broken lives, and you accept the role, often finding yourself as gladiator and henchman, puffing and inflating, driving wedges as the threatening force, lying in wait like a wolf litigator, squeeze-the-last-dollar negotiator, and get-all-you-can-to-win advocate. They expect you to do that day and night and weekends. They reward you for it in an insidious interaction. They become more and more dependent on you as you become more and more enslaved by them and their expectations. You thrive on each other's weaknesses. The irony is that lawyers have disempowered clients by perpetuating their experience of weakness and self-absorption and failing to see them as full human beings. Clients in turn have viewed and used their lawyers as tools, failing to see them as full human beings. This has led to a great deal of lawyer suffering over the decades and a more adversarial and transactional world. It's now imperative to renew focus on well-being for ourselves and for our clients. That's the invitation.

Turning inward to explore the true Self is an essential component of restoring and sustaining personal well-being. When we turn inward regularly, we develop an inner resource that provides inner alignment and peace that can help soothe, cope with, and escape from a transactional world. Taking the time for inner exploration and nurturing is a worthwhile endeavor. Unfortunately, inner contemplation and work toward personal wellness often remain in the private sphere, unconnected to what we do as practicing lawyers. It doesn't have to be this way. You hold the power to ensure you don't get hijacked into what I'll call a *personal wellness bypass*.

In a highly transactional world, imagine yourself with the new tools and insights about yourself:

- mindfulness
- reflective practice
- connecting with and finding value in my colleagues and team
- tapping into and regulating my emotions
- finding new ways to self-manage
- reducing and harnessing stress
- minimizing self-sabotage and replacing it with positive self-talk
- engaging in smart collaborations
- thinking outside the box about the billable hour slave driver
- ensuring financial good housekeeping
- taking care of my body with nutrition and exercise
- volunteering
- writing a personal vision statement guided by heart and authentic self
- considering integrative and creative ways of practice
- seeing myself as part of a system and staying true to stewarding the democratic process

While healing myself, do I foster the same quality of well-being for clients as I choose for myself? Or do I work on my authentic self to relieve some of my own suffering and continue to contribute to my clients' suffering? How in alignment are you? The potential payoff for alignment is huge. Can you avoid the personal wellness bypass?

When you turn inward on a regular basis, it strengthens your capacity to act outwardly *with others* in ways that align with the self you nurtured when you went inward and found peace. When you act in alignment you experience resonance with the happier contented person you have the capacity to be. Unfortunately, all the inner work doesn't produce different responses with others, the personal wellness bypass, when we keep it a private affair.

THE CHOICE: TO BE TRANSACTIONAL OR RELATIONAL AND THE ADVERSARIAL ETHIC PUSHBACK

Choosing to live in alignment with your *Relational Mindset* requires taking a risk.

In the real world, we interact with others all the time. In the transactional world of legal practice, each interaction presents a moral choice about well-being for humankind. Will you be Transactional or will you choose to be Relational? As a lawyer you are faced with this choice every time you meet with, prepare, or advise a client. You are capable of connecting the inner private authentic relational self to this choice. If it's relational alignment you are committed to for your practice, that can be a risky choice in a transactional world. If you reject the personal wellness bypass and take the risk to practice with a *Relational Mindset*, you can expect pushback, not only from the others who are operating in a highly transactional world, but also from your own fine-tuned years of practice in what I will call the *Adversarial Ethic*, which you have honed to cope with the transactional world.

Let's look a little closer at what a *Relational Mindset* might look like in your practice, and you decide if you are willing to take the risk of living in alignment to be the Best Lawyer You Can Be.

A *Relational Mindset* is a Self *and Other* approach, rooted in the belief that all humans have great capacity and need for connection with others. That includes your capacity, your clients' capacity, and the capacity of the opposing counsel and clients on the other side. A *Relational Mindset* recognizes that human capacity has the potential for good and evil, and the human preference is for good. A *Relational Mindset* believes that one thing that sets humans apart from the animal kingdom is our ability for moral thinking. A *Relational Mindset* believes that the moral impulse is one that doesn't want to be a victim or a victimizer. Believing we are a victim or that we have the license or entitlement to be a victimizer and acting from either of those stances is what fuels the Adversarial Ethic, our transactional thinking and rationalizing transactional behavior. It is at the root of much of our suffering as humans and lawyers. You know what this looks like because you have been on the receiving end of transactional behavior and likely participated in and perpetuated such behavior.

The opposite of a *Relational Mindset,* a Transactional Mindset is usually knee-jerk in its reaction: they did something you think is wrong, you blame them. They broke the law, you punish them. They hurt you, you hurt them back. They cheat you, you get your pound of flesh later. They fail to do something to protect themselves, their loss. They leave themselves exposed, you move in for the kill. You'll never see them again, you do whatever you want. They have more resources than you, you take from them. They have fewer resources than you, you kick them to the curb. These are dramatic transactional examples but they are everyday examples for both litigators and transactional lawyers. A Transactional Mindset maximizes self-interests over others' interests, competing at all costs in a winner-takes-all mentality, losing sight of the humanity of the participants in the deal. In its most base manifestation, it's a dog-eat-dog world, where you are the hunter or you are the hunted, on the run to get, on the run to hide, and the more they get, the less you get, so you squeeze the last penny out of every deal, you bully to get your way, which often includes outright lying, and you stonewall when you are in the weaker position. All the commitment to inner work and self-awareness and self-management and creative thinking gets hijacked if you are not deeply grounded in understanding the difference in *Relational Mindset* choices and Transactional Mindset choices.

For us as lawyers, here are a few daily Transactional examples in client interactions.

- A client comes and complains they have been wronged, you agree, and you whip off a threatening letter or make preparations to draft documents for a lawsuit.

- You tell your client not to expect much in the amount of settlement even though they have a very legitimate claim to protect yourself from inflated expectations and so you'll look good in their eyes with the settlement you expect to get.
- A client has a legitimate claim for $275,000, yet you file a complaint and ask for $1 million.
- A divorce client comes to you and you file a Petition for Absolute Divorce and include requests related to cruelty and domestic violence even if the client never mentioned such facts, but you want to gain every edge.
- You reduce your legal bill automatically because you know your client expects a discount and you want to keep the client happy even though you worked very hard for every billable hour and then some.
- You begin to respond to interrogatories and you answer as minimally as possible and add a number of "protected client attorney privilege communication" statements so you don't have to divulge anything of substance.
- A filing mistake was made and your client complained; you fire your paralegal and let the client know you fired him or her.

The examples are plentiful and that was all in a day or two.

THE RELATIONAL MINDSET IN LAW PRACTICE: THE RELATIONAL PAUSE AND THE SEVEN RELATIONAL WAYS

Yes, the Transactional world is all around us and lawyers contribute to and perpetuate it as much as feel victimized by it. As I have said, acting and advising clients in purely transactional ways causes suffering for clients as well as the other side and society. *Relational Mindset* choices are more in alignment with your own wellness, restore well-being, and can bring lasting meaningful change. The choice is yours. The potential is in every interaction. I will focus on client interactions, but the potential is all around us. As human beings, we have the ability to think and act in ways that are both good for ourselves and good for others. Relational choices are both strong and vulnerable. The legal profession admires strength, so that makes sense. The choice to be vulnerable, open, and more authentic and practice in alignment with your own well-being—that is the risky part.

Will you take the risk? Will you make room for a pause before placing yourself *over* other, room for a pause to consider a different choice rather than the well-trodden route, the knee-jerk response, the self-interested narrow course? Let's look at what is possible when we choose instead to practice relationally.

Here's how to consider a *Relational Mindset* in law practice with clients.

Go easy on yourself. But be bold and courageous. Small incremental steps can be gigantic in the path of well-being. Here are seven things you can try. You'll need to pause to allow them full expression as there is so much more than what meets the eye. But that is the work you've been cultivating with your personal wellness plan, so you are ready and have capacity to pause.

1. Be Engaged.
2. Be Centered.
3. Be Grounded.

4. Be Clear.
5. Be Generous.
6. Be Humble.
7. Be Kind.

Sure, it makes sense with your friends and family (most of the time!) but what about with clients and the other side? What about with clients you don't like?

Let's look harder at those Transactional choices and reimagine them as *Relational* choices in your practice.

- When a client comes and complains they have been wrongfully injured and you agree, before you send a threatening letter or make preparations to draft documents for a lawsuit, a *Relational Mindset* pauses and might say: It sounds like you've been hurt, I'm wondering what led up to this and what if anything I need to know about the history and how the interaction between the two of you went before this happened. (Centered, Grounded)
- When you meet with a client and form a quick analysis and are about to tell the client the causes of action they have, a *Relational Mindset* pauses and thinks this out more fully from perspectives that are not solely legal. (Centered, Grounded, Humble)
- To protect yourself from inflated expectations and so you'll look good with the settlement you expect to get, you are about to tell your client not to expect much even though you know they have a very legitimate claim. A *Relational Mindset* pauses and might say: I think you have a very good claim and I will work with you to get what I hope for you is a fair settlement. There is always a range in these matters and it can be x to y (not inflated). I think we should start our negotiations with reasoned numbers and then reassess to see where we are in that range. I want you to be happy with the result and I want the other side to feel they can pay. What are your thoughts? (Engaged, Centered, Grounded, Clear, Generous)
- A client has a legitimate claim for $275,000, and you would normally file a complaint and ask for $1 million. A *Relational Mindset* pauses and realizes doing so creates a false sense of expectation in the eyes of the client and diminishes your integrity. Instead you might say to the client: we will name the $275,000 and request that. If it looks as if the claim is for more, I will amend but that will be another filing. I do not want to just say $1 million because that is not what this case is and I think it cheapens our integrity. Your thoughts about that? (Engaged, Centered, Grounded, Clear, Generous)
- A divorce client comes to you and you would normally file a Petition for Absolute Divorce and include requests related to cruelty and domestic violence even though the client never mentioned that since you want to protect yourself and the client just in case. A *Relational Mindset* pauses and might say: I could file a petition and add cruelty and domestic violence but it's likely to make your spouse more hostile. It's cruel and unkind to impute things that are not true. (Engaged, Centered, Grounded, Clear, Generous)
- You are reducing your legal bill automatically because you know your client expects a discount and you want to keep the client happy even though you worked very hard for every billable hour and then some. A *Relational Mindset* pauses and might call the client and ask to set aside a few minutes to talk about the bill they are about to receive and how you normally discount your

bill, that you value them as clients and that this matter took a lot of time and care and you were not putting in the discount you had in the past and didn't want that to strain relations and wanted to discuss that with them. (Engaged, Centered, Clear, Generous, Humble)

- If a client complains or asks for a reduced invoice, a *Relational Mindset* pauses and realizes the many relational choices and acts on them: You engage in that conversation, preferably face-to-face, and you listen, reflect, and then explain how you keep time and round down, such that the bill sent is already shy of serious time spent. You engage by phone with clients before the monthly bill goes out to let them know it's large and that you worked hard and hope they found value in your representation and your work and that upon payment you hope they would consider calling upon you again. Or you can see that a bill here and there seems out of proportion with the value the client actually received. You pick up the phone to have that conversation or you appropriately cut your bill with an explanation and a personal phone call. Or you meet with the client and let the client know you might do things differently next time and rather than litigating the claim through multiple motions and hearings, look instead to alternative forms of dispute resolution that more directly involve the client. You would more often call the lawyer for the opposing side with the goal of talking and the end goal of swift resolution via listening and frank and forthright discussions, including what you see are the strengths of his case and the weaknesses of yours and asking him or her to do the same for your case, perhaps shaping the discovery together and coming back together again, noting the cost to the clients for prolonged unresolved matters and offering a few options for resolution that are reasonable and could be accepted by everyone with the goal of creating well-being for all. (Engaged, Centered, Grounded, Clear, Generous, Humble, Kind) Imagine a practice like that, small or large, simple or complex.
- You are responding to interrogatories sent to your client and about to answer as minimally as possible by adding a number of "protected client attorney privilege communication" statements so you don't have to divulge anything of substance, but instead, a *Relational Mindset* pauses and calls opposing counsel to see if he or she would like to get together to discuss the case, with clients. Then you set up a face-to-face meeting with your client to go through all the questions, asking the client how he or she would like to respond with your input in preparation for the meeting and to be responsive if the other side still requests that the discovery is completed. (Engaged, Clear)
- A filing mistake was made and your client complained. When this happened before, you fired your paralegal and let the client know. This time, a *Relational Mindset* pauses and you ask yourself: what part of this mistake can I own? Supervision? Training? Communication? Then you set up a meeting to calmly speak with the paralegal, letting him or her know you are containing your upset but that you are open to understanding the full reason of why it happened. If he or she admits the error, you thank him or her and together decide the appropriate next steps. You talk with him or her about what you will tell the client so everyone knows and no more angst is spent on the what if's and uncertainty. (Humble, Generous, Engaged, Centered, Grounded, Clear, Kind)

Imagine your opportunities to live a *Relational Mindset* in regular everyday law practice.

Relational choices:

- Responding to client calls within a day.
- Responding to client and opposing counsel emails and letting them know you will respond, are working on a response, or need time to consider so as not to leave anyone stonewalled or dangling.
- Calling difficult counsel back and suggesting face-to-face meetings.
- No longer sending stern or threatening letters on your legal letterhead without first meeting the other side, or calling to suggest a meeting.
- Not looking the other way when groups of people are slighted.
- Taking time to give authentic direct constructive feedback face-to-face to new hires and associates.
- Speaking up with "maybe, maybe not" when someone is disparaging another.
- Taking what you hear at face value and saying that it might be true but not yet complete.
- If sucked into participating in putting others down, having the courage to say there might be more that the other doesn't realize or know.
- Apologizing for being an oaf if you speak too soon and acknowledge whatever is legitimate stated by the other person.
- Being direct about your opinions and also open to others'.
- Being gracious by asking if what you say rings true to others or if there is something they think you don't see or understand.
- Apologizing when you screw up or hurt someone.
- Giving your client permission and even encouragement to apologize from his or her heart for the part he or she was responsible for.

The opportunities are endless.

A law practice lived with a *Relational Mindset* is a practice from the inside out. It's a way of practicing in alignment with your own well-being and the well-being of your clients. Your choosing *just one* of the Relational Seven Ways can revolutionize your practice. The enticing part is that a Relational practice is the way to sustain your wellness and well-being journey. And you will discover that when you choose one of the Relational Seven Ways in your practice, your thinking will expand and your behavior will naturally encompass *all* the seven relational ways as they are interconnected. The more often you choose one of the ways, the more you will be choosing other ways as well. The more time you choose to be relational, the stronger and more open you will be. And that brings me to one last piece: Relational Reciprocity.

RELATIONAL RECIPROCITY

A *Relational Mindset* knows that the more relational you are with others, the more relational they will be with you. Imagine that. Please pause and take that in.

Think about the above sampling of examples. Your client whom you called about the large bill and had the difficult conversation with is grateful for your forthrightness letting him know you value his choosing you as his lawyer. Your divorce client is more thoughtful and confident in you after you explained why you did not add inflammatory clauses and gave her a chance to walk in her husband's shoes. Your commercial client respects you more when you explained you would first call the other side and try to meet, and if you filed an action that you would not be inflating the claim.

When you practice, negotiate, and advise from a *Relational* engaged, authentic, grounded, clear, generous, humble, and kind *Mindset,* clients and opponents will be more empowered, open, and responsive *to you.* This is what I call *Relational Reciprocity.* Energy follows attention. Where you place your attention matters. When you embrace a *Relational Mindset,* and place your attention on Self *and* Other, your attention is broader and the energy for change and possibility expands. You've been cultivating placing your attention internally on you. Now place your attention on your interactions with others. *Relational Reciprocity* brings many tangible and intangible emotional and material rewards for ourselves, clients, and assumed adversaries. *Relational Reciprocity* is real and it happens when you practice with a *Relational Mindset.* That is good for you and also for society.

Of course the inverse is true, but you know about that since that is why the Transactional Mindset has become so pervasive and invasive and has wormed its way into a lawyer's ethos. We have done that to ourselves, narrowing how we place our attention. It started with law school education spawning the Adversarial Ethic. It is pervasive. Practicing with a *Relational Mindset* you have the capacity to change that, one interaction, one client advising, one negotiation with other counsel, one moment at a time. Yes it is risky in a transactional world. It's also hopeful and it's very real. It's what will allow you to live in more alignment. Maybe you'll take the risk.

Making a Relational choice is not just a part or piece, not just a glimpse, not just what you do sometimes or once or twice. A *Relational Mindset* is a way of being. A *Relational Mindset* is a way of practicing. It's a whole approach that encompasses all of what you have read in these pages for your personal wellness, and it encompasses what you have the potential to do for your clients' wellness and the well-being of your profession.

When you are more in touch with that which resonates internally, you are more plugged into your internal moral compass, which is always there to guide you if you tune in. That moral compass points to a *Relational Mindset,* a true North. We can all become not only more aware of our choices to do good for ourselves and others, but we can also tap our strength to act on those impulses and act relationally in our practices. Greater well-being. More personally and professionally aligned. Rather than a personal wellness bypass, take the moment for a relational pause. The wisdom is there. You've been nurturing it within. Then give that Self and Other wisdom expression in your law practice.

Sending love to you, and your well-being and your capacity to practice relationally.

Index